Snitching on Sinners according to Islamic Shariah

I0092687

Gregory Heary

This book is intended to clarify a misconception and taboo regarding the topic of snitching on sinners and what the ruling on that is according to the Islamic Shariah. Currently Islam is the fastest growing religion in the world, including America and particularly in American prisons. For example, 1% of America's general population claims to be Muslim while 18% of America's prison population claims to be Muslim. Astonishingly 80% of religious conversions in America's prisons are to Islam. This statistic is likely due to the sincerity of prisoners when it comes to religion along with their time to study, since in prison there is a high motivation to research the best way to not be imprisoned eternally in hell and intellectually Islam is the exclusive truth when compared with other religions. Therefore it is natural that Islam would prosper amongst people who are confined in a hyper-religious environment without the distractions of normal life. Many Muslim prisoners and Muslim non-prisoners have strong feelings and preconceived notions about snitching and snitches as do people who are non-Muslim, prisoner and non-prisoner alike. Popular culture tends to frown on the practice and criminal gangster culture outright prohibits and punishes it with brutish violence. Sadly many Muslims fall into the trap of basing their opinions of the practice on other than Islamic sources, while others may misinterpret the Islamic evidences related to the topic and come to incorrect conclusions. This book will look at snitching on sinners from the perspective of the Quran with accompanying Tafsir, the hadith and some instances of the Sahabah where snitching occurred and what the ruling on such occurrences were. Other commentary by scholars on enjoining the good and forbidding the evil is included as well as my personal commentary throughout attempting to explain some of the evidences as they are mentioned. You may be surprised to learn that snitching on sinners, when done according to Shariah law, is actually a virtuous practice that in some circumstances is even obligatory for a Muslim to do. I write this book in the hopes that snitching on sinners according to Shariah law will increase and lose the stigma it has, for surely in a civilized society governed by Islamic Shariah the sinful are snitched on due to their sins and the honest snitch, also known as a witness, is not harmed in any way whatsoever as a result. This practice of the Sahabah must be commended and practiced by Muslims rather than condemned or shied away from. Hopefully non-Muslims may appreciate the Prophetic Islamic Shariah more when they learn its position on sin and how snitching on sinners is just one of the many consequences of sins and a means to rectify society. As a result of snitching perhaps a less sinful society will develop amongst us. To soundly defeat the Satanic soldiery, snitching on sinners must take place. Thus we must learn from the Salaf, our pious predecessors, and follow their example step by step into paradise as the prophets have taught us as they were commanded. Whether you like it or not snitching on sinners is a sunnah of Allah, of Muhammad, other prophets, the angels, the Sahabah and the Salaf and even animals such as the hoopoe bird of prophet Solomon.

The only ones with a problem with snitching on sinners is Satan, his sinful soldiers and those who wish for sin to increase amongst our species. Snitching is a sacred spiritual type of warfare against the multitudes of devils amongst humans and jinn that if abandoned will be no less calamitous than if an aspect of military warfare were abandoned by a nation's military. The spiritual security of society is cultivated by the seeds and fruits of snitching on sinners. I ask that after you finish reading this book, please properly prepare to snitch on sinners when appropriate; all the way to paradise.

Prior to examining the data I must say that fundamentally Gangster activities are contrary to how Islam teaches a human being to live. Linguistically a Muslim is one who submits and surrenders themselves entirely to Allah. The phrase "Muslim gangster" is an oxymoron that has been invented by morons. It is impossible for a Muslim who submits to Allah to be a gangster. It's like saying someone is a vegetarian carnivore, a virgin adulterer or a elderly youth. Someone simply cannot simultaneously be both things, such a person would be a walking contradiction. This relates to the principle of loving what Allah loves and hating what Allah hates. Allah hates the sins gangsters participate in, if you don't hate those as well then you are not a complete Muslim. This principle of hating what and who Allah hates also means that Muslims must hate all gangsters too to the extent their sins merit. So how could a practicing Muslim choose to be someone who they and Allah hates? It is hypocritical and difficult to be both good and bad at the same time. A theoretical "Muslim gangster" at the best would have one foot going toward heaven and one foot going towards hell, having each foot on a different road would only result in wasted time, energy and groin pain. Allah did not create time for us to waste. There are 3 types of people: one who does more good deeds today than they did yesterday, one who does more bad deeds today than they did yesterday and the one who does the same amount of good and bad deeds today as they did yesterday. The one who does more good has learned from the prior day and improved. The one who does the same hasn't learned anything from the day before and is wasting their days by not reflecting and improving. The one who does more bad today than yesterday is only digging themselves into a deeper hole and erasing their good deeds, which if they continue down that path will end up having all their good deeds erased. May Allah make us one of those who do less bad deeds and more good deeds with each day that passes. An important factor to remember regarding this Gangster vs. Muslim controversy is that Gangsterism is a religion. Yes indeed, gangsters follow the faith of Gangsterism. In the religion of Gangsterism their man-made laws are referred to as the "G-code". The "G-code" does not mean "God's code" it stands for the Gangster code of conduct and it involves such gangster themed laws of "No snitching.", "Bros before Hoes, Gangsters over Girls, Get Riches **** *******" and "Life for Life"(in perpetuity with Killers of Killers Getting Killed For Killing Killers (KKGKFKK)). I actually just made up that KKGKFKK acronym code for the killing cycle, but that's how the G-code goes; every gangster has their own unique unwritten code. Yet they all pretend it's the same for all and all the "true G's" really know what it really is. In reality the "G-code" is a myth of gangster folklore. Just as there is no honor amongst thieves there is no code amongst G's. Whereas then there is always the ignorant idiot who says, "*You may have book smarts, but you don't have street smarts. I got street smarts, you wouldn't survive out there on the streets like I do/would. Because you only got book smarts.*" While those people don't even know english because "smarts" is not a word and more importantly they don't have street smarts either. If they had some "book smarts" (intelligence from reading non-fiction books like this) they would learn that there is no such thing as "street smarts". This is because the G-code is a fantasy and the rules of the streets aren't written down nor agreed upon. Every single literal street has its own rules because the people on those streets have their own customized G-codes. Nobody writes their G-code down because that's a violation of most G-codes. So if by some miracle you learned one person's G-code who ruled one street, as soon as you go to another street or across the street, you got different people with different rules. Sometimes even 1 street has multiple unwritten unknown rules. Plus even if you learn the imaginary rules then they change according to circumstances and over time as different people take charge who got their own special codes too. So, anyone who ever claims they got valuable "street smarts" is certifiably street stupid and book stupid and are the most likely candidate to get harmed on the streets because their confidence makes them think they know something when they don't know nothing. In comparison the "book smart" person knows what they know and has a slight grasp on what they don't know and are smart enough to know they don't know the many different G-codes the various thugs follow. Thereby because they know they are ignorant they are cautious and safer because of their caution, while the "street smart" sass mouth becomes a victim really quick because gangsters love targeting "street smart" people and have respect for "book smart" people and so they leave the "book smart" people alone unless they present themselves as unrespectable wannabe book smart people. Whereas if any gangster breaks a tenant of the "G-code" they get punished accordingly depending on the infraction they commit and the interpretation of "G-code" by the gangsters who are to enforce it. All too frequently the punishments for a gangster who breaks the "G-code" of the religion of Gangsterism can be fatal. Yet the "G-code" is NOT Shariah nor is it compliant with Allah's code of conduct which he ordained for mankind and Muslims alike. This "G-code" is in direct opposition and conflict with the code of conduct Muhammad taught Muslims to believe in, live by and preach to others. So any gangster or wannabe gangster who believes in, lives by, preaches and dies by the mythical "G-code" is going to be in the hellfire forever because they would have died upon the false man-made (or rather Gangster made, because gangsters aren't even men) religion of Gangsterism. On top of that the religion of Gangsterism ain't even fun or enjoyable. Everyone involved with the religion of Gangsterism knows this fact, but the rules of most mythical "G-codes" of Gangsterism dictates members never show it. Or at least the "real gangsters" never show or tell it, unless they are a musician then it's allowed to admit the pain. The only "real gangster" is the devil, everyone else is faking. "Gangsters" are the greatest actors in the world and they know it. Then when/if you call them out, most G-codes dictate that they have to do a violent action in retaliation to keep up the performance for the public and themselves. Thus most gangster violence is actually religious violence so that the gangster is not seen as tolerant of blasphemers, since most G-codes say that controlling one's anger when insulted is "not gangster" unless it's only done momentarily as part of a gangsterish revenge plot. Most of the G-codes do not permit the gangster to ever forgive another for any offense, real or imagined, or perceived as such by the public. Obviously all the G-codes have commandments that the prophets of God would not approve of. Why then are most "gangsters" religious? For the same reason most of the religious people are religious. All the false religions have commandments and teach things which the prophets of God hate which they would refute and denounce. So why do people think the gangsters of Gangsterism shouldn't be religious when other members of false faiths are? Is it because it's less popular and less easy to refute and denounce the other false faiths? Fundamentally the man-made religion of Gangsterism is exactly the same as all false religions in that they have man-made beliefs and rules. The main difference is that adherents of Gangsterism admit that their religion and G-code doesn't come from God, they are frequently unashamed to be sinful and they do many things which governments may decree to be illegal. So essentially the special feature of Gangsterism is that it admits it's a false faith that has a negative impact on its practitioners and society at large. Now if only the rest of the false religions would honestly admit the same then the world would be a better place. The redeeming quality of Gangsterism is its honesty. Gangsters are basically an evolved more glorified version of pirates. In plain terms, Islam is a religion and Gangsterism is a different religion, and Muslims and Gangsters are enemies to each other who vehemently hate each other. There has never been a truce between the two groups and there never will be, though due to proximity and cultural diffusion there are relationships between the members of both faiths and conversions from one faith to the other and vice versa. Snitching is not the only tool to use to defeat gangsterism or crime it is just one of the tools used against the devil which the devils recently de-popularized with devastating results. Snitching is not a relationship ender nor the final measure taken against a gangster, even if a gangster were unjustly imprisoned for a life sentence that doesn't mean they were not created to worship Allah. So religious dialogue should still continue until the individuals correctly repent because repentance and sincere pure monotheistic worship is the goal for our entire species. The war against crime isn't a game like chess where once someone snitches then an opposing player/piece is taken off the board out of the equation forever or for however long they are imprisoned. Rather sometimes that is the beginning of a person's journey to the truth and snitching on someone can actually transform their life if they are properly treated as Islam commands us to do. Everyone sins and commits crimes the Creator decreed forbidden and we all should repent and improve, so never think an incident of snitching is the end of the interaction. It may not always be best for the snitch to maintain communication if the one snitched on is averse or dangerous but someway the message of Islam must reach everyone so all are given the opportunity to fulfill their true life-purpose. Some of the worst gangsters ended up becoming the best Muslims and achieving ranks in paradise due to being snitched on despite disliking the incident when it first occurred. However this is when snitching is accompanied with sincerity, goodwill, supplication and knowledge with proper systems in place to genuinely rehabilitate sinners into Salafi believers.

Snitching is also a much broader topic than one would guess as it involves many sins which are not considered criminal offences meriting legal punishments. For example, the innovators and people of desires or hypocrites are also targets for sound snitching but to snitch on ahl-bida can be more difficult than doing so on hardened violent gangsters with sometimes greater danger as well. Yet it is perhaps more virtuous to snitch on ahl-bida than ordinary criminals because the threat innovators pose to the religion is greater than the damage done by mere criminals of gangster culture. Though since most ahl-bida are peaceful and pose as law-abiding they are the devils in disguise who are harder to convict without the aid of Allah. So as a disclaimer don't think snitching only applies to gangsters it can apply to people who are seen as saints by society as well. It can take much more courage to snitch on a societal saint than one seen as a street criminal though the Muslim snitches equally. Those are the cases that determine who are the truthful and who are the liars especially if snitching is done without immediate justice following it and people must deal with the risk of snitching without achieving the desired result. Such is similar to waging Jihad and losing a battle, does that mean one doesn't fight the forces of the faithless because one may have lost? Or does one regret the past or stop forbidding the evil in the future? Nay to do such is to stop snitching as Satan desires and proves one was insincere in snitching or perhaps impatient or sinful themselves in some way that prevented victory.

Lastly this book is about snitching on non-rulers, the crimes or inadequacies of rulers are addressed according to Shariah in a different manner as compared to snitching. This is because one snitches to the rulers to implement justice so snitching is a method of informing rulers about crime, it is not the method of reforming rulers themselves. Yet it is a deterrent itself to corruption amongst rulers for a people who snitch on themselves send a message to rulers that crime is not tolerable and thus set the standard by which the rulers will rule if Allah wills. So know that rulers are generally an exception to the snitching rules in that you don't snitch on a head of state to the head of state himself or to lesser than that as to snitch on a ruler to someone less than the ruler would be foolish revolutionary gossip. Most in our era though snitch on the rulers to everyone else, while they ignore all the opportunities they have to snitch on all the people who are the non-rulers who are criminals. So most today are mere rebel peasants indulging in gossip and backbiting giving their good deeds to the ruler who is likely innocent of the evils they attribute to them. In fact, most peasants who are ruled over have no business ever saying anything about a ruler and those who do so are committing a crime that may be snitch-worthy in itself. Thus know the topic of snitching is broad encompassing many types of criminals and in this book it is restricted to non-rulers unless you count complaining to Allah alone about the rulers as snitching. However as the hoopoe snitch of Solomon teaches even with this apparent exception rulers still can be snitched on in some circumstances, but they are snitched on to other rulers. But this is not what happens today. People don't go to other rulers to complain about rulers, they are modern peasants complaining to peasants in the worst of ways without etiquette or morals fomenting rebellions and bloodshed ignorantly in the manners of the disbelievers who many imitate and give allegiance to and even love contrary to Islamic Shariah. Snitching on rulers is an intricate political topic beyond the scope of this book. This book is about snitching on sinners generally, not politically, though politics is an integral part of religion and whoever separates their politics from the faith has opposed the prophetic practice. Woefully snitching on those who gossip about Muslim rulers is one of the most taboo of topics amongst Muslims even moreso than snitching on gangsters because many don't even view treasonous revolutionary gossip as a crime or sin; let alone snitch-worthy.

Ibn Abbas reported:

The Messenger of Allah said, "Whoever sees something from his ruler that he hates, let him be patient. Whoever secedes from the community by as much as a handspan and dies will have died a death of ignorance."

Source: Ṣaḥīḥ al-Bukhārī 7054, Ṣaḥīḥ Muslim 1849

Abdullah ibn Umar reported:

The Messenger of Allah said, "Whoever pulls his hand away from lawful obedience to the ruler, he will meet Allah on the Day of Resurrection without any argument in his favor. Whoever dies without any ties of allegiance, he will have died a death of ignorance."

Source: Ṣaḥīḥ Muslim 1851

Ubadah ibn al-Samit reported:

The Messenger of Allah, said: "Listen and obey authorities in hardship, in ease, and in what you dislike, even if they give undue preference over you, even if they consume your property and they strike your back, unless they order flagrant disobedience to Allah."

Source: Ṣaḥīḥ Ibn Ḥibbān 4566 Grade: Hasan

Wa'il al-Hadrami reported:

Salamah ibn Yazid asked the Messenger of Allah saying, "O Prophet of Allah, what do you think if rulers are charged over us who demand their rights and prevent us from our rights? What do you command us to do?" The Prophet turned away from him, then he asked a second or third time, so Al-Ash'ath ibn Qays pulled him to the side.

The Prophet said, "Listen and obey, for their burdens are upon them and your burdens are upon you."

Source: Ṣaḥīḥ Muslim 1846

Abu Sa'id al-Khudri reported:

The Prophet said, "There will be rulers after me whose malevolence will deceive the people. Whoever affirms their lies and helps their wrongdoing, I disavow myself from him and he is disavowed from me. Whoever does not affirm their lies, nor helps their wrongdoing, I am part of him and he is part of me."

Source: Ṣaḥīḥ Ibn Ḥibbān 286 Grade: Sahih

Umm Salamah reported:

The Messenger of Allah said, "There will be rulers from whom you will see both goodness and corruption. One who recognizes their evil and hates it will maintain his innocence, but one who is pleased with it and follows them will be sinful." It was said,

"Shall we not fight them?" The Prophet said, "No, as long as they pray."

Source: Ṣaḥīḥ Muslim 1854

Imam al-Tahawi commented, "*We do not rebel against our leaders or those in charge of our affairs, even if they are tyrannical. We do not supplicate against them, nor withdraw from obedience to them. We view obedience to them as obedience to Allah Almighty, an obligation, as long as they do not order disobedience to Allah. We supplicate on their behalf for righteousness and wellness.*"

Source: al-ʿAqīdah al-Ṭaḥāwīyah 1/68

Anas ibn Maalik said:

"*The senior amongst the Companions of Allaah's Messenger forbade us (saying), 'Do not revile your Rulers (Umaraa), not act dishonestly with them, nor hate them and have taqwaa of Allaah and be patient — for verily the matter is close (at hand).*" [As-Sunnah of Ibn Abee 'Aasim, 2/488]

Abu-Dardaa said, "*Beware of cursing the Rulers (Wullaat), for verily, cursing them is clipping (i.e., of the religion) and hating them is barrenness.*" It was said, 'O Abu Dardaa, then how should we behave when we see in them that which we do not like?' He said, "*Have patience, for verily, when Allaah sees that from you He will take them away from you with death.*"

[As-Sunnah, 2/488]

Ibn Saʻad related that a group of Muslims came to al Hasan al Basri seeking a verdict to rebel against al Hajjaaj.

So they said, "*O Abu Sa'eed! What do you say about fighting this oppressor who has unlawfully spilt blood and unlawfully taken wealth and did this and that?*"

Hasan said: "*I hold that he should not be fought. If this is the punishment from Allah, then you will not be able to remove it with your swords. If this is a trial from Allah, then be patient until Allah's Judgement comes, and He is the best of Judges.*"

So they left Al Hasan, disagreed with him and rebelled against al Hajjaaj - so al Hajjaaj killed them all. [Tabaqaatul Kubraa (7/163-165)]

Umar Ibn Yazeed said, "*I heard al-Hasan al-Basri during the days of Yazeed Ibnul-Mahlab, and there came to him a group of people. So he commanded them to stay in their houses and to close their doors. Then he said: "By Allaah! If the people had patience when they were being tested by their unjust ruler, it will not be long before Allaah will make a way out for them. However, they always rush for their swords, so they are left to their swords. By Allaah! Not even for a single day did they bring about any good."*

 [It is related by Ibn Sa'd in at-Tabaqaat (8/164), and by IbnAbee Haatim in his Tafseer (3/178)]

Abdullah Ibn Idrees said:

'*I will never ever help in the blood of a Khaleefah after Uthmaan.*' It was said to him, '*O Abu Ma'bad, did you help in (bringing about the shedding of his blood)?*' So he said, '*Verily, I consider the mentioning of his faults and Shortcomings to have been of help in (the shedding of blood).*"

[At-Tabaqaat 6/115]

Ibn Rajab reported:

Hasan al-Basri, said regarding the rulers, "They take charge of five matters: the Friday prayer, the congregational prayers, the Eid celebration, guarding the frontiers, and the legal punishments. By Allah, the religion will not be upheld without them, even if they are tyrannical and oppressive. By Allah, what Allah sets right by them is greater than their corruption. By Allah, obedience to them is difficult, but seceding from them is unbelief."

Source: Jāmi' al-'Ulūm wal-Ḥikam 2/117

Anas ibn Malik reported: *The eminent among the companions of the Messenger of Allah, peace and blessings be upon him, prohibited us, saying, "Do not curse your leaders, do not deceive them, and do not hate them. Fear Allah and be patient, for the matter is close at hand."*

Source: al-Sunnah li-Ibn Abī 'Āṣim 1015

Imam al-Barbahari said: *"If you see a man supplicating against the ruler, then know he is a follower of his whims. If you hear a man supplicating for the ruler's improvement, then know he is a follower of the Sunnah, if Allah wills."*

Source: Sharḥ al-Sunnah lil-Barbahārī 1/113

Al-Fudayl ibn 'Iyad said: *"If I had one supplication to be answered, I would make it for no one but the ruler. If the ruler is righteous, it will lead to the righteousness of the country and the people."*

Source: Siyar A'lām al-Nubalā 8/434

Quranic Ayat regarding Snitching on Sinners

Quran 2:11-15

وَإِذَا قِيلَ لَهُمْ لَا تُفْسِدُواْ فِى ٱلْأَرْضِ قَالُوٓاْ إِنَّمَا نَحْنُ مُصْلِحُونَ (١١) أَلَآ إِنَّهُمْ هُمُ ٱلْمُفْسِدُونَ وَلَـٰكِن لَّا يَشْعُرُونَ (١٢) وَإِذَا قِيلَ لَهُمْ ءَامِنُواْ كَمَآ ءَامَنَ ٱلنَّاسُ قَالُوٓاْ أَنُؤْمِنُ كَمَآ ءَامَنَ ٱلسُّفَهَآءُ أَلَآ إِنَّهُمْ هُمُ ٱلسُّفَهَآءُ وَلَـٰكِن لَّا يَعْلَمُونَ (١٣) وَإِذَا لَقُواْ ٱلَّذِينَ ءَامَنُواْ قَالُوٓاْ ءَامَنَّا وَإِذَا خَلَوْاْ إِلَىٰ شَيَـٰطِينِهِمْ قَالُوٓاْ إِنَّا مَعَكُمْ إِنَّمَا نَحْنُ مُسْتَهْزِءُونَ (١٤) ٱللَّهُ يَسْتَهْزِئُ بِهِمْ وَيَمُدُّهُمْ فِى طُغْيَـٰنِهِمْ يَعْمَهُونَ (١٥)

And when it is said to them: "Make not mischief on the earth,"
they say: "We are only peacemakers." (11) Verily! They are the
ones who make mischief, but they perceive not. (12) And when
it is said to them (hypocrites): "Believe as the people (followers
of Muhammad, Al-Ansâr and Al-Muhajirûn) have believed,"
they say: "Shall we believe as the fools have believed?" Verily,
they are the fools, but they know not (13) And when they meet
those who believe, they say: "We believe," but when they are
alone with their Shayâtin (devils - polytheists, hypocrites), they
say: "Truly, we are with you; verily, we were but mocking."
(14) Allâh mocks at them and gives them increase in their
wrong-doings to wander blindly. (15)

In his Tafsir, As-Suddi said that Ibn `Abbas and Ibn
Mas`ud commented,

﴿وَإِذَا قِيلَ لَهُمْ لاَ تُفْسِدُواْ فِى الأَرْضِ قَالُواْ إِنَّمَا نَحْنُ مُصْلِحُونَ﴾

(And when it is said to them: "Do not make mischief on
the earth," they say: "We are only peacemakers.") "They
are the hypocrites. As for,

$$\{لاَ تُفْسِدُواْ فِى الأَرْضِ\}$$

("Do not make mischief on the earth"), that is disbelief and acts of disobedience." Abu Ja`far said that Ar-Rabi` bin Anas said that Abu Al-`Aliyah said that Allah's statement,

$$\{وَإِذَا قِيلَ لَهُمْ لاَ تُفْسِدُواْ فِى الأَرْضِ\}$$

(And when it is said to them: "Do not make mischief on the earth,"), means, "Do not commit acts of disobedience on the earth. Their mischief is disobeying Allah, because whoever disobeys Allah on the earth, or commands that Allah be disobeyed, he has committed mischief on the earth. Peace on both the earth and in the heavens is ensured (and earned) through obedience (to Allah)." Ar-Rabi` bin Anas and Qatadah said similarly.

Ibn Jarir said, "The hypocrites commit mischief on earth by disobeying their Lord on it and continuing in the prohibited acts. They also abandon what Allah made obligatory and doubt His religion, even though He does not accept a deed from anyone except with faith in His religion and certainty of its truth. The hypocrites also lie to the believers by saying contrary to the doubt and hesitation their hearts harbor. They give as much aid as they can, against Allah's loyal friends, and support those who deny Allah, His Books and His Messengers. This is how the hypocrites commit mischief on earth, while thinking that they are doing righteous work on earth."

The statement by Ibn Jarir is true, taking the disbelievers as friends is one of the categories of mischief on the earth. Allah said,

﴿وَالَّذِينَ كَفَرُواْ بَعْضُهُمْ أَوْلِيَآءُ بَعْضٍ إِلاَّ تَفْعَلُوهُ تَكُنْ فِتْنَةٌ فِى الأُرْضِ وَفَسَادٌ كَبِيرٌ﴾

(And those who disbelieve are allies of one another, if you do not do this (help each other), there will be turmoil and oppression on the earth, and great mischief.) (8:73), In this way Allah severed the loyalty between the believers and the disbelievers. Similarly, Allah said,

﴿يَـٰأَيُّهَا الَّذِينَ ءَامَنُواْ لاَ تَتَّخِذُواْ الْكَـٰفِرِينَ أَوْلِيَآءَ مِن دُونِ الْمُؤْمِنِينَ أَتُرِيدُونَ أَن تَجْعَلُواْ لِلَّهِ عَلَيْكُمْ سُلْطَاناً مُّبِيناً﴾

(O you who believe! Do not take disbelievers as Awliya' (protectors or helpers or friends) instead of believers. Do you wish to offer Allah a manifest proof against yourselves) (4: 144).

Allah then said,

﴿إِنَّ الْمُنَـٰفِقِينَ فِى الدَّرْكِ الأَسْفَلِ مِنَ النَّارِ وَلَن تَجِدَ لَهُمْ نَصِيراً﴾

(Verily, the hyprocrites will be in the lowest depth of the Fire; no helper will you find for them) (4:145).

Since the outward appearance of the hypocrite displays belief, he confuses the true believers. Hence, the deceitful behavior of the hypocrites is an act of mischief, because they deceive the believers by claiming what they do not believe in, and because they give support and loyalty to the disbelievers against the believers.

If the hypocrite remains a disbeliever (rather than pretending to be Muslim), the evil that results from him would be less. Even better, if the hypocrite becomes sincere with Allah and makes the statements that he utters conform to his deeds, he will gain success. Allah said,

﴿وَإِذَا قِيلَ لَهُمْ لاَ تُفْسِدُواْ فِى الأَرْضِ قَالُواْ إِنَّمَا نَحْنُ مُصْلِحُونَ ﴾

(And when it is said to them: "Do not make mischief on the earth," they say: "We are only peacemakers.") meaning, "We seek to be friends with both parties, the believers and the disbelievers, and to have peace with both parties." Similarly, Muhammad bin Ishaq reported that Ibn `Abbas said,

﴿وَإِذَا قِيلَ لَهُمْ لاَ تُفْسِدُواْ فِى الأَرْضِ قَالُواْ إِنَّمَا نَحْنُ مُصْلِحُونَ ﴾

(And when it is said to them: "Do not make mischief on the earth," they say: "We are only peacemakers.") means, "We seek to make amends between the believers and the People of the Book. " Allah said,

﴿أَلا إِنَّهُمْ هُمُ الْمُفْسِدُونَ وَلَـكِن لاَّ يَشْعُرُونَ ﴾

(Verily, they are the ones who make mischief, but they perceive not.). This Ayah means that the hypocrites' behavior, and their claim that it is for peace, is itself mischief, although in their ignorance, they do not see it to be mischief.

Allah said that if the hypocrites are told,

﴿ءَامِنُواْ كَمَآ ءَامَنَ النَّاسُ﴾

("Believe as the people believe,"), meaning, `Believe just as the believers believe in Allah, His angels, His Books, His Messengers, Resurrection after death, Paradise and Hellfire, etc. And obey Allah and His Messenger by heeding the commandments and avoiding the prohibitions.' Yet the hypocrites answer by saying,

﴿قَالُواْ أَنُوْمِنُ كَمَا آمَنَ السُّفَهَآءُ﴾

("Shall we believe as the fools have believed") they meant (may Allah curse the hypocrites) the Companions of the Messenger of Allah . This is the same Tafsir given by Abu Al-`Aliyah and As-Suddi in his Tafsir, with a chain of narration to Ibn `Abbas, Ibn Mas`ud and other Companions. This is also the Tafsir of Ar-Rabi` bin Anas and `Abdur-Rahman bin Zayd bin Aslam. The hypocrites said, "Us and them having the same status, following the same path, while they are fools!" `The fool' is the ignorant, simple-minded person who has little knowledge in areas of benefit and harm. This is why, according to the majority of the scholars, Allah used the term foolish to include children, when He said,

﴿وَلاَ تُؤْتُواْ السُّفَهَآءَ أَمْوَلَكُمُ الَّتِى جَعَلَ اللّهُ لَكُمْ قِيَـماً﴾

(And do not give your property, which Allah has made a means of support for you, to the foolish) (4:5).

Allah answered the hypocrites in all of these instances. For instance, Allah said here,

﴿أَلاَ إِنَّهُمْ هُمُ السُّفَهَآءُ﴾

(Verily, they are the fools). Allah thus affirmed that the hypocrites are indeed the fools, yet,

$$﴿وَلَـكِن لاَّ يَعْلَمُونَ﴾$$

(But they know not). Since they are so thoroughly ignorant, the hypocrites are unaware of their degree of deviation and ignorance, and such situation is more dangerous, a severer case of blindness, and further from the truth than one who is aware.

Allah said that when the hypocrites meet the believers, they proclaim their faith and pretend to be believers, loyalists and friends. They do this to misdirect, mislead and deceive the believers. The hypocrites also want to have a share of the benefits and gains that the believers might possibly acquire. Yet,

$$﴿وَإِذَا خَلَوْاْ إِلَى شَيَـطِينِهِمْ﴾$$

(But when they are alone with their Shayatin), meaning, if they are alone with their devils, such as their leaders and masters among the rabbis of the Jews, hypocrites and idolators.

Ibn Jarir said, "The devils of every creation are the mischievous among them. There are both human devils and Jinn devils. Allah said,

$$﴿وَكَذَلِكَ جَعَلْنَا لِكُلِّ نَبِيٍّ عَدُوًّا شَيَـطِينَ الإِنسِ وَالْجِنِّ يُوحِى بَعْضُهُمْ إِلَىٰ بَعْضٍ زُخْرُفَ ٱلْقَوْلِ غُرُورًا﴾$$

(And so We have appointed for every Prophet enemies - Shayatin (devils) among mankind and Jinn, inspiring one another with adorned speech as a delusion (or by way of deception)) (6:112).

Allah said,

﴿قَالُواْ إِنَّا مَعَكُمْ﴾

(They say: "Truly, we are with you"). Muhammad bin Ishaq reported that Ibn `Abbas said that the Ayah means, "We are with you,

﴿إِنَّمَا نَحْنُ مُسْتَهْزِءُونَ﴾

(Verily, we were but mocking), meaning, we only mock people (the believers) and deceive them." Ad-Dahhak said that Ibn `Abbas said that the Ayah,

﴿إِنَّمَا نَحْنُ مُسْتَهْزِءُونَ﴾

(Verily, we were but mocking), means, "We (meaning the hypocrites) were mocking the Companions of Muhammad." Also, Ar-Rabi` bin Anas and Qatadah said similarly. Allah's statement,

﴿اللَّهُ يَسْتَهْزِىءُ بِهِمْ وَيَمُدُّهُمْ فِي طُغْيَـٰنِهِمْ يَعْمَهُونَ﴾

(Allah mocks at them and leaves them increasing in their deviation to wander blindly) answers the hypocrites and punishes them for their behavior. Ibn Jarir commented, "Allah mentioned what He will do to them on the Day of Resurrection, when He said,

﴿يَوْمَ يَقُولُ الْمُنَـٰفِقُونَ وَالْمُنَـٰفِقَتُ لِلَّذِينَ ءَامَنُواْ انظُرُونَا نَقْتَبِسْ مِن نُّورِكُمْ قِيلَ ارْجِعُواْ وَرَآءَكُمْ فَالْتَمِسُواْ نُوراً فَضُرِبَ بَيْنَهُم بِسُورٍ لَّهُ بَابٌ بَاطِنُهُ فِيهِ الرَّحْمَةُ وَظَـٰهِرُهُ مِن قِبَلِهِ الْعَذَابُ﴾

(On the Day when the hypocrites - men and women - will say to the believers: "Wait for us! Let us get something from your light!" It will be said: "Go back to your rear! Then seek a light!" So a wall will be put up between them, with a gate therein. Inside it will be mercy, and outside it will be torment.) (57:13), and,

$$﴿وَلاَ يَحْسَبَنَّ الَّذِينَ كَفَرُواْ أَنَّمَا نُمْلِى لَهُمْ خَيْرٌ لأَنفُسِهِمْ إِنَّمَا نُمْلِى لَهُمْ لِيَزْدَادُواْ إِثْمَاً﴾$$

(And let not the disbelievers think that Our postponing of their punishment is good for them. We postpone the punishment only so that they may increase in sinfulness.) (3:178)."

He then said, "This, and its like, is Allah's mockery of the hypocrites and the people of Shirk."

Allah stated that He will punish the hypocrites for their mockery, using the same terms to describe both the deed and its punishment, although the meaning is different. Similarly, Allah said,

$$﴿وَجَزَآءُ سَيِّئَةٍ سَيِّئَةٌ مِّثْلُهَا فَمَنْ عَفَا وَأَصْلَحَ فَأَجْرُهُ عَلَى اللَّهِ﴾$$

(The recompense for an offense is an offense equal to it; but whoever forgives and makes reconciliation, his reward is with Allah) (42:40), and,

$$﴿فَمَنِ اعْتَدَى عَلَيْكُمْ فَاعْتَدُواْ عَلَيْهِ﴾$$

(Then whoever transgresses (the prohibition) against you, transgress likewise against him) (2:194).

The first act is an act of injustice, while the second act is an act of justice. So both actions carry the same name, while being different in reality. This is how the scholars explain deceit, cunning and mocking when attributed to Allah in the Qur'an. Surely, Allah exacts revenge for certain evil acts with a punishment that is similar in nature to the act itself. We should affirm here that Allah does not do these things out of joyful play, according to the consensus of the scholars, but as a just form of punishment for certain evil acts.

Allah said,

﴿وَيَمُدُّهُمْ فِي طُغْيَـنِهِمْ يَعْمَهُونَ﴾

(Allah mocks at them and leaves them increasing in their deviation to wander blindly). As-Suddi reported that Ibn `Abbas, Ibn Mas`ud and several other Companions of the Messenger of Allah said that,

﴿وَيَمُدُّهُمْ﴾

(and leaves them increasing) means, He gives them respite. Also, Mujahid said, "He (causes their deviation) to increase." Allah said;

﴿أَيَحْسَبُونَ أَنَّمَا نُمِدُّهُم بِهِ مِن مَّالٍ وَبَنِينَ - نُسَارِعُ لَهُمْ فِى الْخَيْرَتِ بَل لاَّ يَشْعُرُونَ ﴾

(Do they think that by the wealth and the children with which We augment them. (That) We hasten to give them with good things. Nay, but they perceive not.) (23:55-56).

Ibn Jarir commented, "The correct meaning of this Ayah is `We give them increase from the view of giving them respite and leaving them in their deviation and rebellion.' Similarly, Allah said,

$$\{وَنُقَلِّبُ أَفْئِدَتَهُمْ وَأَبْصَـٰرَهُمْ كَمَا لَمْ يُؤْمِنُواْ بِهِ أَوَّلَ مَرَّةٍ وَنَذَرُهُمْ فِى طُغْيَـٰنِهِمْ يَعْمَهُونَ\}$$

(And We shall turn their hearts and their eyes away (from guidance), as they refused to believe in it the first time, and We shall leave them in their trespass to wander blindly). " (6:110).

Tughyan used in this Ayah means to transgress the limits, just as Allah said in another Ayah,

$$\{إِنَّا لَمَّا طَغَا الْمَآءُ حَمَلْنَـٰكُمْ فِى الْجَارِيَةِ\}$$

(Verily, when the water Tagha (rose) beyond its limits, We carried you in the ship) (69:11).

Also, Ibn Jarir said that the term `Amah, in the Ayah means, `deviation'. He also said about Allah's statement,

$$\{فِي طُغْيَـٰنِهِمْ يَعْمَهُونَ\}$$

(in their deviation to wander), "In the misguidance and disbelief that has encompassed them, causing them to be confused and unable to find a way out of it. This is because Allah has stamped their hearts, sealed them, and blinded their vision. Therefore, they do not recognize guidance or find the way out of their deviation."

As it pertains to snitching when the mischief makers make their mischief, Allah informs us, "*it is said to them: "Make not mischief on the earth,"* and *it is said to them (hypocrites): "Believe as the people (followers of Muhammad, Al-Ansâr and Al-Muhajirûn) have believed. "* Meaning responsible Muslims don't just witness mischief as silent bystanders without advising and critiquing the mischief doers for the error of mischief of whatever type which contradicts the Shariah. Rather they advise them to believe as the companions of Muhammad believed so the mischievous don't fall into the hellfire for any amount of time whether permanently or temporarily as the hadith about the 72 sects entitled to the hellfire states.

Abdullah bin 'Amr narrated that the Messenger of Allah (ﷺ) said: *"What befell the children of Isra'il will befall my Ummah, step by step, such that if there was one who had intercourse with his mother in the open, then there would be someone from my Ummah who would do that. Indeed the children of Isra'il split into seventy-two sects, and my Ummah will split into seventy-three sects. All of them are in the Fire Except one sect."* He said: *"And which is it O Messenger of Allah?"* He said: *"What I am upon and my Companions."*

These initially analyzed ayat also essentially mean that if you aren't upon the way of Islam as practiced by Muhammad's companions then you are most surely a mischief maker even if you claim to be a peacemaker amongst creatures. The only valid way to practice Islam is the way Muhammad taught as was practiced by the sahabah, any other version is a distortion of the devils.

Quran 2:30

وَإِذْ قَالَ رَبُّكَ لِلْمَلَٰٓئِكَةِ إِنِّى جَاعِلٌ فِى ٱلْأَرْضِ خَلِيفَةًۖ قَالُوٓاْ أَتَجْعَلُ فِيهَا مَن يُفْسِدُ فِيهَا وَيَسْفِكُ ٱلدِّمَآءَ وَنَحْنُ نُسَبِّحُ بِحَمْدِكَ وَنُقَدِّسُ لَكَۖ قَالَ إِنِّىٓ أَعْلَمُ مَا لَا تَعْلَمُونَ (٣٠)

And (remember) when your Lord said to the angels: "Verily, I am going to place (mankind) generations after generations on earth." They said: "Will You place therein those who will make mischief therein and shed blood, - while we glorify You with praises and thanks and sanctify You." He (Allâh) said: "I know that which you do not know." (30)

The angels meant that this type of creature usually commits the atrocities they mentioned. The angels knew of this fact, according to their understanding of human nature, for Allah stated that He would create man from clay. Or, the angels understood this fact from the word Khalifah, which also means the person who judges disputes that occur between people, forbidding them from injustice and sin, as Al-Qurtubi said.

The statement the angels uttered was not a form of disputing with Allah's, nor out of envy for the Children of Adam, as some mistakenly thought. Allah has described them as those who do not precede Him in speaking, meaning that they do not ask Allah anything without His permission. When Allah informed them that He was going to create a creation on the earth, and they had knowledge that this creation would commit mischief on it, as Qatadah mentioned, they said,

﴿أَتَجْعَلُ فِيهَا مَن يُفْسِدُ فِيهَا وَيَسْفِكُ الدِّمَآءَ﴾

(Will You place therein those who will make mischief therein and shed blood)

This is only a question for the sake of learning about the wisdom of that, as if they said, Our Lord! What is the wisdom of creating such creatures since they will cause trouble in the earth and spill blood "If the wisdom behind this action is that You be worshipped, we praise and glorify You (meaning we pray to You) we never indulge in mischief, so why create other creatures?"

Allah said to the angels in answer to their inquiry,

$$﴿إِنِّي أَعْلَمُ مَا لاَ تَعْلَمُونَ﴾$$

(I know that which you do not know.) meaning, "I know that the benefit of creating this type of creature outweighs the harm that you mentioned, that which you have no knowledge of. I will create among them Prophets and send Messengers. I will also create among them truthful, martyrs, righteous believers, worshippers, the modest, the pious, the scholars who implement their knowledge, humble people and those who love Allah and follow His Messengers."

The Sahih recorded that when the angels ascend to Allah with the records of the servant's deeds, Allah asks them, while having better knowledge, "How did you leave My servants" They will say, "We came to them while they were praying and left them while they were praying." This is because the angels work in shifts with mankind, and they change shifts during the Fajr and `Asr prayers. The angels who descended will remain with us, while the angels who have remained with us ascend with our deeds. The Messenger of Allah said,

$$«يُرْفَعُ إِلَيْهِ عَمَلُ اللَّيْلِ قَبْلَ النَّهَارِ وَعَمَلُ النَّهَارِ قَبْلَ اللَّيْلِ»$$

(The deeds of the night are elevated to Allah before the morning, and the deeds of the morning before the night falls.)

Hence, the angels' statement, "We came to them while they were praying and left them while they were praying," explains Allah's statement,

﴿إِنِّي أَعْلَمُ مَا لاَ تَعْلَمُونَ﴾

(I know that which you do not know.)

It was said that the meaning of Allah's statement,

﴿إِنِّي أَعْلَمُ مَا لاَ تَعْلَمُونَ﴾

(I know that which you do not know.) is, "I have a specific wisdom in creating them, which you do not have knowledge of." It was also said that it is in answer to,

﴿وَنَحْنُ نُسَبِّحُ بِحَمْدِكَ وَنُقَدِّسُ لَكَ﴾

(While we glorify You with praises and thanks and sanctify You) after which Allah said,

﴿إِنِّي أَعْلَمُ مَا لاَ تَعْلَمُونَ﴾

(I know that which you do not know). Meaning, "I know that Iblis is not as you are, although he is among you." Others said,

﴿أَتَجْعَلُ فِيهَا مَن يُفْسِدُ فِيهَا وَيَسْفِكُ الدِّمَآءَ وَنَحْنُ نُسَبِّحُ بِحَمْدِكَ وَنُقَدِّسُ لَكَ﴾

"(Will You place therein those who will make mischief therein and shed blood, - while we glorify you with praises and thanks and sanctify You.) is their request that they should be allowed to inhabit the earth, instead of the Children of Adam. So Allah said to them,

﴿إِنِّي أَعْلَمُ مَا لاَ تَعْلَمُونَ﴾

(I know that which you do not know) if your inhabiting the heavens is better, or worse for you." Ar-Razi as well as others said this.

The point is that the angels, who cannot sin, collectively snitched on the humans before they were even created or even sinned their first sin. So snitching on sinners by default and by virtue of the sinless angels cannot be a sin unless one calls the angels sinful for snitching on humanities crimes to Allah. Rather snitching is a practice of the angelic proving it is honorable to report sins to the Creator with specific angels explicitly created just for this purpose alone. Some angels are created solely to snitch on humans so if a human snitches on a sinful human he is imitating the angels and it is virtuous because of the difficulty in snitching on oneself or one's species. As long as the prophetic etiquettes regarding snitching are followed regarding intentions and actions every time and place one snitches, then it is a good deed to do so and sinful to abstain from.

Quran 2:34

وَإِذْ قُلْنَا لِلْمَلَـٰئِكَةِ ٱسْجُدُوا۟ لِـَٔادَمَ فَسَجَدُوٓا۟ إِلَّآ إِبْلِيسَ أَبَىٰ وَٱسْتَكْبَرَ وَكَانَ مِنَ ٱلْكَـٰفِرِينَ (٣٤)

And (remember) when We said to the angels: "Prostrate yourselves before Adam.". And they prostrated except Iblîs

(Satan), he refused and was proud and was one of the disbelievers (disobedient to Allâh) (34)

Muhammad bin Ishaq reported that Ibn `Abbas said, "Before he undertook the path of sin, Iblis was with the angels and was called `Azazil.' He was among the residents of the earth and was one of the most active worshippers and knowledgeable persons among the angels. This fact caused him to be arrogant. Iblis was from a genus called Jinn."

The point being Allah snitched on Iblis to expose his error and enmity for our species as a warning to us and deterrent. So snitching can also serve as a warning to others to prevent imitation of crimes or allying/befriending criminals. This happened before Adam was conscious so no human would've known had Allah not told us by revealing the sin of Iblis that turned him into Shaitan. Snitching can serve as lessons for future generations while remaining silent to sin is to aid in covering up crimes, which is a category of crime in itself.

Quran 2:36

فَأَزَلَّهُمَا ٱلشَّيْطَـٰنُ عَنْهَا فَأَخْرَجَهُمَا مِمَّا كَانَا فِيهِ ۖ وَقُلْنَا ٱهْبِطُوا۟ بَعْضُكُمْ لِبَعْضٍ عَدُوٌّ ۖ وَلَكُمْ فِى ٱلْأَرْضِ مُسْتَقَرٌّ وَمَتَـٰعٌ إِلَىٰ حِينٍ (٣٦)

Then the Shaitân (Satan) made them slip therefrom (the Paradise), and got them out from that in which they were. We said: "Get you down, all, with enmity between yourselves. On earth will be a dwelling place for you and an enjoyment for a time." (36)

This ayat is another example of snitching on the devil by Allah in that our species was ejected from paradise due to plots of Shaitan and then we are commanded to have enmity for the Shaitan which extends to the followers of Shaitan or anyone following other than the Islamic path of all the prophets. Though we don't snitch on shayalteen due to enmity, it is due to adherence to the prophetic code of conduct and the angelic code of conduct and the divinely legislated code of conduct to ensure justice and in opposition to the Satanic code of conduct that wishes for crimes to spread without prosecution or justified consequences.

Quran 2:53-54

وَإِذْ ءَاتَيْنَا مُوسَى ٱلْكِتَٰبَ وَٱلْفُرْقَانَ لَعَلَّكُمْ تَهْتَدُونَ (٥٣) وَإِذْ قَالَ مُوسَىٰ لِقَوْمِهِۦ يَٰقَوْمِ إِنَّكُمْ ظَلَمْتُمْ أَنفُسَكُم بِٱتِّخَاذِكُمُ ٱلْعِجْلَ فَتُوبُوٓاْ إِلَىٰ بَارِئِكُمْ فَٱقْتُلُوٓاْ أَنفُسَكُمْ ذَٰلِكُمْ خَيْرٌ لَّكُمْ عِندَ بَارِئِكُمْ فَتَابَ عَلَيْكُمْ إِنَّهُۥ هُوَ ٱلتَّوَّابُ ٱلرَّحِيمُ (٥٤)

And (remember) when We gave Mûsa (Moses) the Scripture [the Taurât (Torah)] and the criterion (of right and wrong) so that you may be guided aright. (53) And (remember) when Mûsa (Moses) said to his people: "O my people! Verily, you have wronged yourselves by worshipping the calf. So turn in repentance to your Creator and kill yourselves (the innocent kill the wrongdoers among you), that will be better for you with your Creator." Then He accepted your repentance. Truly, He is the One Who accepts repentance, the Most Merciful. (54)

This was the repentance required from the Children of Israel for worshipping the calf. Commenting on Allah's statement;

﴿وَإِذْ قَالَ مُوسَى لِقَوْمِهِ يَقَوْمِ إِنَّكُمْ ظَلَمْتُمْ أَنفُسَكُم بِاتِّخَاذِكُمُ الْعِجْلَ﴾

(And (remember) when Musa said to his people: "O my people! Verily, you have wronged yourselves by worshipping the calf..."), Al-Hasan Al-Basri said, "When their hearts thought of worshipping the calf,

﴿وَلَمَّا سُقِطَ فَى أَيْدِيهِمْ وَرَأَوْاْ أَنَّهُمْ قَدْ ضَلُّواْ قَالُواْ لَئِن لَّمْ يَرْحَمْنَا رَبُّنَا وَيَغْفِرْ لَنَا﴾

(And when they regretted and saw that they had gone astray, they (repented and) said: "If our Lord does not have mercy upon us and forgive us") (7:149). This is when Musa said to them,

﴿يَقَوْمِ إِنَّكُمْ ظَلَمْتُمْ أَنفُسَكُم بِاتِّخَاذِكُمُ الْعِجْلَ﴾

(O my people! Verily, you have wronged yourselves by worshipping the calf...)." Abu `Al-`Aliyah, Sa`id bin Jubayr and Ar-Rabi` bin Anas commented on,

﴿فَتُوبُواْ إِلَى بَارِئِكُمْ﴾

(So turn in repentance to your Bari') that it means, "To your Creator." Allah's statement,

﴿إِلَى بَارِئِكُمْ﴾

(to your Bari' (Creator)) alerts the Children of Israel to the enormity of their error and means, "Repent to He Who created you after you associated others with Him in worship."

An-Nasa'i, Ibn Jarir and Ibn Abi Hatim recorded Ibn `Abbas saying, "Allah told the Children of Israel that their repentance would be to slay by the sword every person they meet, be he father or son. They should not care whom they kill. Those were guilty whom Musa and Harun were not aware of their guilt, they admitted their sin and did as they were ordered. So Allah forgave both the killer and the one killed."

Ibn Jarir narrated that Ibn `Abbas said, "Musa said to his people,

﴿فَتُوبُواْ إِلَى بَارِئِكُمْ فَاقْتُلُواْ أَنفُسَكُمْ ذَلِكُمْ خَيْرٌ لَّكُمْ عِندَ بَارِئِكُمْ فَتَابَ عَلَيْكُمْ إِنَّهُ هُوَ التَّوَّابُ الرَّحِيمُ﴾

("So turn in repentance to your Creator and kill each other (the innocent kill the wrongdoers among you), that will be better for you with your Creator." Then He accepted your repentance. Truly, He is the One Who accepts repentance, the Most Merciful.)

Allah ordered Musa to command his people to kill each other. He ordered those who worshipped the calf to sit down and those who did not worship the calf to stand holding knives in their hands. When they started killing them, a great darkness suddenly overcame them. After the darkness lifted, they had killed seventy thousand of them. Those who were killed among them were forgiven, and those who remained alive were also forgiven."

The point being that they had to snitch on the guilty in order to find out who was guilty and deserving of execution. Had even one person gotten away with the crime then none would've been forgiven at all and the execution of the command of Allah's law would've been incomplete and thus their repentance would be void. Thus in order for Moses' people to repent they had to utilize snitching so in this case snitching was a key to repentance and the forgiveness and healing of the nation. Also it should be noted that the proper killing or execution of criminals can only be accomplished via a legitimate Islamic government not just anybody and certainly not vigilantes, thugs or other criminals in the name of restoring justice and balance. Sometimes crimes get punished via further crimes and criminals are punished by criminals due to them getting snitched on or not but this ayat proves proper snitching to a proper Islamic government results in true justice and restoration of the society at large and the potential forgiveness for all involved both the snitching and those snitched on. So snitching on someone can result in their forgiveness by the Creator and expiation for huge sins can be attained if the prophetic protocols legislated for repentance and crime prevention and prosecution are followed.

Quran 2:67-73

وَإِذْ قَالَ مُوسَىٰ لِقَوْمِهِ إِنَّ ٱللَّهَ يَأْمُرُكُمْ أَن تَذْبَحُواْ بَقَرَةً قَالُواْ أَتَتَّخِذُنَا هُزُوًا قَالَ أَعُوذُ بِٱللَّهِ أَنْ أَكُونَ مِنَ ٱلْجَٰهِلِينَ (٦٧) قَالُواْ ٱدْعُ لَنَا رَبَّكَ يُبَيِّن لَّنَا مَا هِىَ قَالَ إِنَّهُ يَقُولُ إِنَّهَا بَقَرَةٌ لَّا فَارِضٌ وَلَا بِكْرٌ عَوَانٌ بَيْنَ ذَٰلِكَ فَٱفْعَلُواْ مَا تُؤْمَرُونَ (٦٨) قَالُواْ ٱدْعُ لَنَا رَبَّكَ يُبَيِّن لَّنَا مَا لَوْنُهَا قَالَ إِنَّهُ يَقُولُ إِنَّهَا بَقَرَةٌ صَفْرَآءُ فَاقِعٌ لَّوْنُهَا تَسُرُّ ٱلنَّٰظِرِينَ (٦٩) قَالُواْ ٱدْعُ لَنَا رَبَّكَ يُبَيِّن لَّنَا مَا هِىَ إِنَّ ٱلْبَقَرَ تَشَٰبَهَ عَلَيْنَا وَإِنَّآ إِن شَآءَ ٱللَّهُ لَمُهْتَدُونَ (٧٠) قَالَ إِنَّهُ يَقُولُ إِنَّهَا بَقَرَةٌ لَّا ذَلُولٌ تُثِيرُ ٱلْأَرْضَ وَلَا تَسْقِى ٱلْحَرْثَ مُسَلَّمَةٌ لَّا شِيَةَ فِيهَا قَالُواْ ٱلْـَٰٔنَ جِئْتَ بِٱلْحَقِّ فَذَبَحُوهَا وَمَا كَادُواْ يَفْعَلُونَ (٧١) وَإِذْ قَتَلْتُمْ نَفْسًا فَٱدَّٰرَٰٔتُمْ فِيهَا وَٱللَّهُ مُخْرِجٌ مَّا كُنتُمْ تَكْتُمُونَ (٧٢) فَقُلْنَا ٱضْرِبُوهُ بِبَعْضِهَا كَذَٰلِكَ يُحْىِ ٱللَّهُ ٱلْمَوْتَىٰ وَيُرِيكُمْ ءَايَٰتِهِ لَعَلَّكُمْ تَعْقِلُونَ (٧٣)

And (remember) when Mûsa (Moses) said to his people:
"Verily, Allâh commands you that you slaughter a cow." They

said, "Do you make fun of us?" He said, "I take Allâh's Refuge from being among Al-Jâhilûn (the ignorants or the foolish)." (67) They said, "Call upon your Lord for us that He may make plain to us what it is!" He said, "He says, 'Verily, it is a cow neither too old nor too young, but (it is) between the two conditions', so do what you are commanded." (68) They said, "Call upon your Lord for us to make plain to us its color." He said, "He says, 'It is a yellow cow, bright in its color, pleasing to the beholders.' " (69) They said, "Call upon your Lord for us to make plain to us what it is. Verily to us all cows are alike, And surely, if Allâh wills, we will be guided." (70) He [Mûsa (Moses)] said, "He says, 'It is a cow neither trained to till the soil nor water the fields, sound, having no other color except bright yellow.' " They said, "Now you have brought the truth." So they slaughtered it though they were near to not doing it. (71) And (remember) when you killed a man and fell into dispute among yourselves as to the crime. But Allâh brought forth that which you were hiding. (72) So We said: "Strike him (the dead man) with a piece of it (the cow)." Thus Allâh brings the dead to life and shows you His Ayât (proofs, evidences, verses, lessons, signs, revelations, etc.) so that you may understand. (73)

Ibn Abi Hatim recorded `Ubaydah As-Salmani saying, "There was a man from among the Children of Israel who was impotent. He had substantial wealth, and only a nephew who would inherit from him. So his nephew killed him and moved his body at night, placing it at the doorstep of a certain man. The next morning, the nephew cried out for revenge, and the people took up their weapons and almost fought each other. The wise men among them said, `Why would you kill each other, while the Messenger of Allah is still among you' So they went to Musa and mentioned the matter to him and Musa said,

$$\{إِنَّ اللَّهَ يَأْمُرُكُمْ أَن تَذْبَحُواْ بَقَرَةً قَالُواْ أَتَتَّخِذُنَا هُزُوَا قَالَ أَعُوذُ بِاللَّهِ أَنْ أَكُونَ مِنَ الْجَـٰهِلِينَ\}$$

("Verily, Allah commands you that you slaughter a cow." They said, "Do you make fun of us" He said, "I take Allah's refuge from being among Al-Jahilin (the ignorant or the foolish))." "Had they not disputed, it would have been sufficient for them to slaughter any cow. However, they disputed, and the matter was made more difficult for them, until they ended up looking for the specific cow that they were later ordered to slaughter. They found the designated cow with a man, who only owned that cow. He said, `By Allah! I will only sell it for its skin's fill of gold.' So they paid the cow's fill of its skin in gold, slaughtered it and touched the dead man with a part of it. He stood up, and they asked him, `Who killed you' He said, `That man,' and pointed to his nephew. He died again, and his nephew was not allowed to inherit him. Thereafter, whoever committed murder for the purpose of gaining inheritance was not allowed to inherit." Ibn Jarir reported something similar to that.

Allah mentioned the stubbornness of the Children of Israel and the many unnecessary questions they asked their Messengers. This is why when they were stubborn, Allah made the decisions difficult for them. Had they slaughtered a cow, any cow, it would have been sufficient for them, as Ibn `Abbas and `Ubaydah have said. Instead, they made the matter difficult, and this is why Allah made it even more difficult for them. They said,

﴿ادْعُ لَنَا رَبَّكَ يُبَيِّنَ لَّنَا مَا هِىَ﴾

(Call upon your Lord for us that He may make plain to us what it is!), meaning, "What is this cow and what is its description" Musa said,

﴿إِنَّهُ يَقُولُ إِنَّهَا بَقَرَةٌ لاَّ فَارِضٌ وَلاَ بِكْرٌ﴾

(He says, `Verily, it is a cow neither too old nor too young'), meaning, that it is neither old nor below the age of breeding. This is the opinion of Abu Al-`Aliyah, As-Suddi, Mujahid, `Ikrimah, `Atiyah Al-`Awfi, `Ata', Al-Khurasani, Wahb bin Munabbih, Ad-Dahhak, Al-Hasan, Qatadah and Ibn `Abbas. Ad-Dahhak reported that Ibn `Abbas said that,

﴿عَوَانٌ بَيْنَ ذلِكَ﴾

(But (it is) between the two conditions) means, "Neither old nor young. Rather, she was at the age when the cow is strongest and fittest." In his Tafsir Al-`Awfi reported from Ibn `Abbas that,

﴿فَاقِعٌ لَّوْنُهَا﴾

(bright in its colour) "A deep yellowish white."

As-Suddi said,

﴿تَسُرُّ النَّـظِرِينَ﴾

(pleasing the beholder) meaning, that it pleases those who see it. This is also the opinion of Abu Al-`Aliyah, Qatadah and Ar-Rabi` bin Anas. Furthermore, Wahb bin Munabbih said, "If you look at the cow's skin, you will think that the sun's rays radiate through its skin." The modern version of the Tawrah mentions that the cow in the Ayah was red, but this is an error. Or, it might be that the cow was so yellow that it appeared blackish or reddish in color. Allah's knows best.

﴿إِنَّ الْبَقَرَ تَشَـبَهَ عَلَيْنَا﴾

(Verily, to us all cows are alike) this means, that since cows are plentiful, then describe this cow for us further,

﴿وَإِنَّآ إِن شَآءَ اللَّهُ﴾

(And surely, if Allah wills) and if you further describe it to us,

﴿لَمُهْتَدُونَ﴾

(we will be guided.)

﴿قَالَ إِنَّهُ يَقُولُ إِنَّهَا بَقَرَةٌ لاَّ ذَلُولٌ تُثِيرُ الأَرْضَ وَلاَ تَسْقِى الْحَرْثَ﴾

(He says, `It is a cow neither trained to till the soil nor water the fields') meaning, it is not used in farming, or for watering purposes. Rather, it is honorable and fair looking. `Abdur-Razzaq said that Ma`mar said that Qatadah said that,

﴿مُسَلَّمَةٌ﴾

(sound) means, "The cow does not suffer from any defects." This is also the opinion of Abu Al-`Aliyah and

Ar-Rabi`. Mujahid also said that the Ayah means the cow is free from defects. Further, `Ata' Al-Khurasani said that the Ayah means that its legs and body are free of physical defects.

Also, Ad-Dahhak said that Ibn `Abbas said that the Ayah,

﴿فَذَبَحُوهَا وَمَا كَادُواْ يَفْعَلُونَ﴾

(So they slaughtered it though they were near to not doing it) means, "They did not want to slaughter it."

This means that even after all the questions and answers about the cow's description, the Jews were still reluctant to slaughter the cow. This part of the Qur'an criticized the Jews for their behavior, because their only goal was to be stubborn, and this is why they nearly did not slaughter the cow. Also, `Ubaydah, Mujahid, Wahb bin Munabbih, Abu Al-`Aliyah and `Abdur-Rahman bin Zayd bin Aslam said, "The Jews bought the cow with a large amount of money." There is a difference of opinion over this.

Al-Bukhari said that,

﴿فَادَّارَأْتُمْ فِيهَا﴾

(And disagreed among yourselves as to the crime) means, "Disputed."

This is also the Tafsir of Mujahid. `Ata' Al-Khurasani and Ad-Dahhak said, "Disputed about this matter." Also, Ibn Jurayj said that,

﴿وَإِذْ قَتَلْتُمْ نَفْسًا فَادَّارَأْتُمْ فِيهَا﴾

(And (remember) when you killed a man and disagreed among yourselves as to the crime) means, some of them said, "You killed him," while the others said, "No you killed him." This is also the Tafsir of `Abdur-Rahman bin Zayd bin Aslam. Mujahid said that,

$$﴿وَاللَّهُ مُخْرِجٌ مَّا كُنتُمْ تَكْتُمُونَ﴾$$

(But Allah brought forth that which you were Taktumun) means, "what you were hiding."

Allah said,

$$﴿فَقُلْنَا اضْرِبُوهُ بِبَعْضِهَا﴾$$

(So We said: "Strike him (the dead man) with a piece of it (the cow)") meaning, "any part of the cow will produce the miracle (if they struck the dead man with it)." We were not told which part of the cow they used, as this matter does not benefit us either in matters of life or religion. Otherwise, Allah would have made it clear for us. Instead, Allah made this matter vague, so this is why we should leave it vague. Allah's statement,

$$﴿كَذَلِكَ يُحْيِ اللَّهُ الْمَوْتَى﴾$$

(Thus Allah brings the dead to life) means, "They struck him with it, and he came back to life." This Ayah demonstrates Allah's ability in bringing the dead back to life. Allah made this incident proof against the Jews that the Resurrection shall occur, and ended their disputing and stubbornness over the dead person.

Yet how did this incident occur in the first place? By snitching to the prophet that somebody was killed. Even though nobody knew who did the murder, aside from the murderer, it was reported to the authority of Moses and by virtue of snitching a miracle occurred with the dead being resurrected to solve the dispute that arose due to the snitching and subsequent blame game. Even regarding anonymous murder, snitching was resorted to prior to any other method of resolving the incident. Had they listened to the murdering nephew injustice would've been done with false prosecution, blood money and inheritance. So while snitching didn't prevent the murder it did prevent the crimes that motivated the murder from occurring and served as a severe deterrent to future murderers who blamed to murder for inheritance or otherwise. Snitching or reporting crime to authorities is always the best option in a bad situation of an occurred crime so justice may be pursued in a courtly ordered matter derived from Islamic Shariah and not the unjust Christianesque jury system derived from the pagan 12-star zodiac where allegedly unbiased peers determine criminality. There is never a need for a 12 person jury in a case of criminal or civil law, the law is clear as is the evidence so the cases need no input from "peers of the people". If there is a divine law the interpretation stems from the prophetic teachings that have been preserved, it is only disbelieving non-Muslims who invent such jury scams of injustice to cope with their other man-made courts of injustice that were never founded on the justice of prophetic religion to begin with. But rather than accept

Islamic Shariah they choose to make it up as they go along with arbitrary legal gibberish based on nonsense philosophy like the standard 12 person jury system based on Christ allegedly having 12 disciples based on the pagan zodiac worshippers belief that the number 12 was sacred while Jesus' true disciples numbered much more than 12. They held the number 12 so holy as to make 1 foot divisible by 12 inches, the clock divisible by 12 hours and even applied it to cooking making a dozen (12) a standard unit of measurement due to their numerical superstitions inherited from pagan zodiacal maniacs. Truly pagans believed 12 was sacred so when Christians invented their nonsensical aberration in the name of Jesus they sanctified the number 12 to appease pagan convert sensitivities then the Christian legal systems adopted this junk jury number and determine a human court of 12 is sacrosanct and immune to committing corrupt rulings. Then when they force the masses to participate, who don't utilize religious exemptions as they should, the fools who serve the jury are told to become unprejudiced and unbiased judging according to the ever-changing corrupted man-made laws that are currently on the books. Of which the law books are merely based on philosophical precedents passed off as "justice" by previous judges who typically made up law as situations arose without even considering what Muhammad or other prophets taught from God. Whereas if the judge versed in law needs a jury because of the judge's inability to be biased then it is pure religious placebo to believe 12 unqualified non-legally learned idiots can judge a case of any violation of any law. Basically the jury system is sin incorporated into law with Christian/Pagan ceremonialism to justify oppression without guilt of the judge, jury and executors of the evil man-made legal systems. To top it all off the Judges wear the Islamic thobes to fool the people into thinking they studied in Islamic Spain as priests would do in the past because Islamic Spain was where the elite most just most learned Christians would go to learn anything and everything to enlighten the medieval Europe out of the dark ages. Even until today the Islamic thobe is adopted by graduation students as gowns worldwide to seem smart, learned and just. Yet it makes sense for students, but why the pomp and ceremony in a court of law? If the courts built by kufr oppose Islamic Shariah why do their judges continue to dress like ancient Muslims when judging people? Because Islamic justice is so well known from ancient times that even today judges fear appearing in unislamic garb since appearing to give the justice of Islamic judgeship became a cultural societal staple the crusaders imported and kept from Islamic Spain despite the criminal Christians exterminating Islam and Muslims during the Inquisition. Even though Christians banned the laws of Shariah and the true prophetic Islamic religion they still could not get away with injustice without looking like the Muslim purveyors of Justice. Yet sadly one cannot merely garb oneself in the clothes of justice and achieve justice that way, the Islamic Shariah is a total package that must be applied in total for justice to be served and that includes civilians snitching on sinners.

Even if you are a sinner it doesn't discount your duty to snitch on sinners either because nobody is sinless and if the sinners stopped snitching due to sins no snitch would ever exist and crime would spread even more rapidly.

Quran 2:75-79

﴿ أَفَتَطْمَعُونَ أَن يُؤْمِنُواْ لَكُمْ وَقَدْ كَانَ فَرِيقٌ مِّنْهُمْ يَسْمَعُونَ كَلَـٰمَ ٱللَّهِ ثُمَّ يُحَرِّفُونَهُۥ مِنۢ بَعْدِ مَا عَقَلُوهُ وَهُمْ يَعْلَمُونَ (٧٥) وَإِذَا لَقُواْ ٱلَّذِينَ ءَامَنُواْ قَالُوٓاْ ءَامَنَّا وَإِذَا خَلَا بَعْضُهُمْ إِلَىٰ بَعْضٍ قَالُوٓاْ أَتُحَدِّثُونَهُم بِمَا فَتَحَ ٱللَّهُ عَلَيْكُمْ لِيُحَآجُّوكُم بِهِۦ عِندَ رَبِّكُمْ أَفَلَا تَعْقِلُونَ (٧٦) أَوَلَا يَعْلَمُونَ أَنَّ ٱللَّهَ يَعْلَمُ مَا يُسِرُّونَ وَمَا يُعْلِنُونَ (٧٧) وَمِنْهُمْ أُمِّيُّونَ لَا يَعْلَمُونَ ٱلْكِتَـٰبَ إِلَّآ أَمَانِىَّ وَإِنْ هُمْ إِلَّا يَظُنُّونَ (٧٨) فَوَيْلٌ لِّلَّذِينَ يَكْتُبُونَ ٱلْكِتَـٰبَ بِأَيْدِيهِمْ ثُمَّ يَقُولُونَ هَـٰذَا مِنْ عِندِ ٱللَّهِ لِيَشْتَرُواْ بِهِۦ ثَمَنًا قَلِيلًا فَوَيْلٌ لَّهُم مِّمَّا كَتَبَتْ أَيْدِيهِمْ وَوَيْلٌ لَّهُم مِّمَّا يَكْسِبُونَ (٧٩)

Do you (faithful believers) covet that they will believe in your religion inspite of the fact that a party of them (Jewish rabbis) used to hear the Word of Allâh [the Taurât (Torah)], then they used to change it knowingly after they understood it? (75) And when they (Jews) meet those who believe (Muslims), they say, "We believe", but when they meet one another in private, they say, "Shall you (Jews) tell them (Muslims) what Allâh has revealed to you [Jews, about the description and the qualities of Prophet Muhammad Peace be upon him , that which are written in the Taurât (Torah)], that they (Muslims) may argue with you (Jews) about it before your Lord?" Have you (Jews) then no understanding? (76) Know they (Jews) not that Allâh knows what they conceal and what they reveal? (77) And there are among them (Jews) unlettered people, who know not the Book, but they trust upon false desires and they but guess. (78) Then woe to those who write the Book with their own hands and then say, "This is from Allâh," to purchase with it a little price! Woe to them for what their hands have written and woe to them for that they earn thereby. (79)

Qatadah commented that Allah's statement;

﴿ثُمَّ يُحَرِّفُونَهُ مِن بَعْدِ مَا عَقَلُوهُ وَهُمْ يَعْلَمُونَ﴾

(Then they used to change it knowingly after they understood it) "They are the Jews who used to hear Allah's Words and then alter them after they understood and comprehended them." Also, Mujahid said, "Those who used to alter it and conceal its truths; they were their scholars." Also, Ibn Wahb said that Ibn Zayd commented,

﴿يَسْمَعُونَ كَلَمَ اللَّهِ ثُمَّ يُحَرِّفُونَهُ﴾

(used to hear the Word of Allah (the Tawrah), then they used to change it) "They altered the Tawrah that Allah revealed to them, making it say that the lawful is unlawful and the prohibited is allowed, and that what is right is false and that what is false is right. So when a person seeking the truth comes to them with a bribe, they judge his case by the Book of Allah, but when a person comes to them seeking to do evil with a bribe, they take out the other (distorted) book, in which it is stated that he is in the right. When someone comes to them who is not seeking what is right, nor offering them bribe, then they enjoin righteousness on him. This is why Allah said to them,

﴿أَتَأْمُرُونَ النَّاسَ بِالْبِرِّ وَتَنسَوْنَ أَنفُسَكُمْ وَأَنتُمْ تَتْلُونَ الْكِتَـبَ أَفَلاَ تَعْقِلُونَ﴾

(Enjoin you Al-Birr (piety and righteousness and every act of obedience to Allah) on the people and you forget (to practise it) yourselves, while you recite the Scripture (the Tawrah)! Have you then no sense) (2:44)"

Allah said next,

﴿وَإِذَا لَقُواْ الَّذِينَ ءَامَنُواْ قَالُواْ ءَامَنَّا وَإِذَا خَلاَ بَعْضُهُمْ إِلَى بَعْضٍ﴾

(And when they (Jews) meet those who believe (Muslims), they say, "We believe", but when they meet one another in private..). Muhammad bin Ishaq reported that Ibn `Abbas commented,

﴿وَإِذَا لَقُواْ الَّذِينَ ءَامَنُواْ قَالُوا ءَامَنَّا﴾

(And when they (Jews) meet those who believe (Muslims), they say, "We believe") "They believe that Muhammad is the Messenger of Allah, `But he was only sent for you (Arabs)'" However, when they meet each other they say, "Do not convey the news about this Prophet to the Arabs, because you used to ask Allah to grant you victory over them when he came, but he was sent to them (not to you)." Allah then revealed,

﴿وَإِذَا لَقُواْ الَّذِينَ ءَامَنُواْ قَالُواْ ءَامَنَّا وَإِذَا خَلاَ بَعْضُهُمْ إِلَى بَعْضٍ قَالُواْ أَتُحَدِّثُونَهُم بِمَا فَتَحَ اللَّهُ عَلَيْكُمْ لِيُحَاجُّوكُم بِهِ عِندَ رَبِّكُمْ﴾

(And when they (Jews) meet those who believe (Muslims), they say, "We believe," but when they meet one another in private, they say, "Shall you (Jews) tell them (Muslims) what Allah has revealed to you, that they (Muslims) may argue with you (Jews) about it before your Lord") meaning, "If you admit to them that he is a Prophet, knowing that Allah took the covenant from you to follow him, they will know that Muhammad is the

Prophet that we were waiting for and whose coming we find foretold of in our Book. Therefore, do not believe in him and deny him." Allah said,

﴿أَوَلاَ يَعْلَمُونَ أَنَّ اللَّهَ يَعْلَمُ مَا يُسِرُّونَ وَمَا يُعْلِنُونَ﴾

(Know they (Jews) not that Allah knows what they conceal and what they reveal).

Al-Hasan Al-Basri said, "When the Jews met the believers they used to say, `We believe.' When they met each other, some of them would say, `Do not talk to the companions of Muhammad about what Allah has foretold in your Book, so that the news (that Muhammad is the Final Messenger) does not become a proof for them against you with your Lord, and, thus, you will win the dispute.'" Further, Abu Al-`Aliyah said about Allah's statement,

﴿أَوَلاَ يَعْلَمُونَ أَنَّ اللَّهَ يَعْلَمُ مَا يُسِرُّونَ وَمَا يُعْلِنُونَ﴾

(Know they (Jews) not that Allah knows what they conceal and what they reveal), "Meaning their secret denial and rejection of Muhammad, although they find his coming recorded in their Book." This is also the Tafsir of Qatadah. Al-Hasan commented on,

﴿أَنَّ اللَّهَ يَعْلَمُ مَا يُسِرُّونَ﴾

(That Allah knows what they conceal), "What they concealed refers to when they were alone with each other away from the Companions of Muhammad . Then they would forbid each other from conveying the news that Allah revealed to them in their Book to the Companions of Muhammad , fearing that the Companions would use this news (about the truth of Muhammad) against them before their Lord."

Allah said,

﴿وَمِنْهُمْ أُمِّيُّونَ﴾

(And there are among them Ummyyun people) meaning, among the People of the Book, as Mujahid stated. Ummyyun, is plural for Ummi, that is, a person who does not write, as Abu Al-`Aliyah, Ar-Rabi`, Qatadah, Ibrahim An-Nakha`i and others said. This meaning is clarified by Allah's statement,

﴿لاَ يَعْلَمُونَ الْكِتَـبَ﴾

(Who know not the Book) meaning, are they not aware of what is in it.

Ummi was one of the descriptions of the Prophet because he was unlettered. For instance, Allah said,

﴿وَمَا كُنتَ تَتْلُو مِن قَبْلِهِ مِن كِتَـبٍ وَلاَ تَخُطُّهُ بِيَمِينِكَ إِذاً لاَّرْتَـبَ الْمُبْطِلُونَ﴾

(Neither did you (O Muhammad) read any book before it (this Qur'an) nor did you write any book (whatsoever) with your right hand. In that case, indeed, the followers of falsehood might have doubted) (29:48).

Allah also said,

﴿هُوَ الَّذِى بَعَثَ فِى الأُمِّيِّينَ رَسُولاً مِّنْهُمْ﴾

(He it is Who sent among the Ummiyyin ones a Messenger (Muhammad) from among themselves) (62:2).

Ad-Dahhak said that Ibn `Abbas said that Allah's statement,

$$﴿إِلاَّ أَمَانِىَّ﴾$$

(But they trust upon Amani) means, "It is just a false statement that they utter with their tongues." It was also said that Amani means `wishes and hopes'. Mujahid commented, "Allah described the Ummiyyin as not understanding any of the Book that Allah sent down to Musa, yet they create lies and falsehood." Therefore, the word Amani mentioned here refers to lying and falsehood. Mujahid said that Allah's statement,

$$﴿وَإِنْ هُمْ إِلاَّ يَظُنُّونَ﴾$$

(And they but guess) means, "They lie." Qatadah, Abu Al-`Aliyah and Ar-Rabi` said that it means, "They have evil false ideas about Allah."

Allah said,

$$﴿فَوَيْلٌ لِّلَّذِينَ يَكْتُبُونَ الْكِتَـبَ بِأَيْدِيهِمْ ثُمَّ يَقُولُونَ هَـذَا مِنْ عِندِ اللَّهِ لِيَشْتَرُواْ بِهِ ثَمَنًا قَلِيلاً﴾$$

(Then Waylun (woe) to those who write the book with their own hands and then say, "This is from Allah," to purchase with it a little price!).

This is another category of people among the Jews who called to misguidance with falsehood and lies about Allah, thriving on unjustly amassing people's property. `Waylun (woe)' carries meanings of destruction and perishing, and it is a well-known word in the Arabic language. Az-Zuhri said that `Ubadydullah bin `Abdullah narrated that Ibn `Abbas said, "O Muslims! How could you ask the People of the Book about anything, while the Book of Allah (Qur'an) that He revealed to His Prophet is the most recent Book from Him and you still read it fresh and young Allah told you that the People of the Book altered the Book of Allah, changed it and wrote another book with their own hands. They then said, `This book is from Allah,' so that they acquired a small profit by it. Hasn't the knowledge that came to you prohibited you from asking them? By Allah! We have not seen any of them asking you about what was revealed to you." This Hadith was also collected by Al-Bukhari. Al-Hasan Al-Basri said, "The little amount here means this life and all that it contains."

Allah's statement,

﴿فَوَيْلٌ لَّهُمْ مِّمَّا كَتَبَتْ أَيْدِيهِمْ وَوَيْلٌ لَّهُمْ مِّمَّا يَكْسِبُونَ﴾

(Woe to them for what their hands have written and woe to them for that they earn thereby) means, "Woe to them because of what they have written with their own hands, the lies, falsehood and alterations. Woe to them because of the property that they unjustly acquired." Ad-Dahhak said that Ibn `Abbas commented,

﴿فَوَيْلٌ لَّهُمْ﴾

(Woe to them), "Means the torment will be theirs because of the lies that they wrote with their own hands,

﴿وَوَيْلٌ لَّهُمْ مِّمَّا يَكْسِبُونَ﴾

(And woe to them for that they earn thereby), which they unjustly acquired from people, be they commoners or otherwise."

This section condemns the fabricating Jews who would fabricate scripture via commentaries, translations and flat out forgery in rewriting along with mistranslating and miscopying and misinterpreting intentionally creating their own books claiming they were from the divine Creator. For example, it is known the physical Torah revealed by God to Moses no longer remains accessible to man today because the Jews misplaced it. Its actually reported that the original Torah was either written on pearl tablets by God or on emerald tablets with gold as ink. Yet the Jews so thoroughly changed the Torah that we don't even get told the material of the original document to be able to ask where they put them or search for them because everybody knows the Jews have no emerald or pearl tablets today. Hence they coverup the composition of the composite texts to avoid condemnation. This condemnation also applies to the Christians who copied this horrendous innovative practice of the Jews of mislabeling human writings as sacred scriptures. Today they know full well that their writings are written by men, by authors other than those they claim them to be in actuality and attested to by biblical scholars, but even at face value they know their bibles and torahs were not authored by God. Yet they claim they have divine revelation or they'll say "inspired" by God as if God merely dictated the words these anonymous unknown contradicting authors blasphemously penned, at times also unidentifiable by any historically sound method. Yet the importance as it pertains to this topic isn't that the Jews and Christians committed forgery in God's name, evil as that is, it's that they weren't stopped due to the failure of their scholars and laypeople to snitch and that is the lesson. When people change divine laws or violate them if it is not reported and exposed then the crimes perpetually reoccur and worsen in degree devastating societies. This directly applies to bida in that religious innovations are exactly the same as writing fake scriptures, because false religious practices are false teachings via example while the false texts only harm those who read them. Bida however can infect all both the literate and illiterate. So there must be a zero tolerance policy towards people making stuff up religiously regardless of what it is or who does it or how positive it may seem to be. The prophet's religion is perfect as is the one who adds to it in anyway is equal to the one that subtracts from it in any way and both are on the road to disbelief and hellfire for a temporary time if not eternally depending on the severity of their error and their knowledge and intentions. It's too risky to tolerate and is the sole reason that new prophets and Messengers had to be sent. Due to the failure to snitch and get results in line with God's laws as a result of snitching on innovators God had to send new prophets to people. But it's not that simple because Jews and Christians still exist, yet they don't follow the revisions to the innovations and disbelieve in the God-sent prophets' religion as a result of the fake filling their heart up to such a complete darkness that they can't even sort themselves out anymore. Therefore God sending new prophets didn't even solve the problem that snitching could've solved, if done correctly by Jews in the beginning when bida first spread amongst them. Since some people respected religious leaders who made stuff up and failed to snitch on them when they did it they got away with it in this life and we have had worldwide warfare ever since due to religious differences due to the invented doctrines and writings and the failure to nip the problem in the bud before these man-made faiths developed doctrines, dogmas and devilish adherents grew. So I beg you don't take these verses as "O those cursed jews of old really were fools to do that May God damn them!" Instead you should wait for the opportunity to snitch on someone you know who falls into the error of bida whether in doctrine or practice and prepare to correct them regardless of the consequences because chances are they won't listen to you. Then what do you do? If you know somebody is making something up in the prophetic religion you must do all you legally can to stand against it to protect the religion and society from this human devil who might've once been a close companion prior to exposing themselves or being exposed to you. Don't test people looking for errors or ignorance but be prepared because in this era it's almost impossible not to come across someone doing something somebody invented. Typically they are just doing what they learned themselves but that doesn't justify it in anyway. It does merit gentleness and considerations in technique but the principle remains that snitching must be done or else God will curse them and possibly those who failed to snitch on the accursed too since to fail to snitch amounts to siding with the religion inventors against the prophetic teachers. If you really love God and the prophets you will defend their religion against the corruptors in the prophetic manner even if you have to do it all alone against many.

Quran 2:102

وَٱتَّبَعُواْ مَا تَتْلُواْ ٱلشَّيَـٰطِينُ عَلَىٰ مُلْكِ سُلَيْمَـٰنَ وَمَا كَفَرَ سُلَيْمَـٰنُ وَلَـٰكِنَّ ٱلشَّيَـٰطِينَ كَفَرُواْ يُعَلِّمُونَ ٱلنَّاسَ ٱلسِّحْرَ وَمَآ أُنزِلَ عَلَى ٱلْمَلَكَيْنِ بِبَابِلَ هَـٰرُوتَ وَمَـٰرُوتَ وَمَا يُعَلِّمَانِ مِنْ أَحَدٍ حَتَّىٰ يَقُولَآ إِنَّمَا نَحْنُ فِتْنَةٌ فَلَا تَكْفُرْ فَيَتَعَلَّمُونَ مِنْهُمَا مَا يُفَرِّقُونَ بِهِ بَيْنَ ٱلْمَرْءِ وَزَوْجِهِ وَمَا هُم بِضَآرِّينَ بِهِ مِنْ أَحَدٍ إِلَّا بِإِذْنِ ٱللَّهِ وَيَتَعَلَّمُونَ مَا يَضُرُّهُمْ وَلَا يَنفَعُهُمْ وَلَقَدْ عَلِمُواْ لَمَنِ ٱشْتَرَىٰهُ مَا لَهُ فِى ٱلْآخِرَةِ مِنْ خَلَـٰقٍ وَلَبِئْسَ مَا شَرَوْاْ بِهِ أَنفُسَهُمْ لَوْ كَانُواْ يَعْلَمُونَ (١٠٢)

They followed what the Shayâtin (devils) gave out (falsely of the magic) in the lifetime of Sulaimân (Solomon). Sulaimân did not disbelieve, but the Shayâtin (devils) disbelieved, teaching men magic and such things that came down at Babylon to the two (angels,) Hârût and Mârût, but neither of these two angels taught anyone (such things) till they had said, "We are only for trial, so disbelieve not (by learning this magic from us)." And from these (angels) people learn that by which they cause separation between man and his wife, but they could not thus harm anyone except by Allâh's Leave. And they learn that which harms them and profits them not. And indeed they knew that the buyers of it (magic) would have no share in the

Hereafter. And how bad indeed was that for which they sold their ownselves, if they but knew. (102)

These verses are a prime example of Allah snitching on magician liars or Kabbalists centuries after the fact, showing it is never too late to snitch to set the story straight and give victory to the truth exonerating the innocent from criminal slander. The nuance and disclaimer of magic is also exposed in that every true magician knows what they are doing is disbelief and criminal activity because such an acknowledgement of guilt is a prerequisite to get magical abilities.

As-Suddi said that Allah's statement,

﴿وَاتَّبَعُواْ مَا تَتْلُواْ الشَّيَـٰطِينُ عَلَى مُلْكِ سُلَيْمَـٰنَ﴾

(They followed what the Shayatin (devils) gave out (falsely of the magic) in the lifetime of Sulayman) means, "'During the time of Prophet Solomon.' Beforehand, the devils used to ascend to heaven and eavesdrop on the conversations of the angels about what will occur on the earth regarding death, other incidents or unseen matters. They would convey this news to the soothsayers, and the soothsayers would in turn convey the news to the people. The people would believe what the soothsayers told them as being true. When the soothsayers trusted the devils, the devils started to lie to them and added other words to the true news that they heard, to the extent of adding seventy false words to each true word. The people recorded these words in some books. Soon after, the Children of Israel said that the Jinns know matters of the

Unseen. When Solomon was sent as a Prophet, he collected these books in a box and buried it under his throne; any devil that dared get near the box was burned. Solomon said, `I will not hear of anyone who says that the devils know the Unseen, but I will cut off his head.' When Solomon died and the scholars who knew the truth about Solomon perished, there came another generation. To them, the devil materialized in the shape of a human and said to some of the Children of Israel, `Should I lead you to a treasure that you will never be able to use up' They said. `Yes.' He said, `Dig under this throne,' and he went with them and showed them Solomon's throne. They said to him, `Come closer.' He said, `No. I will wait for you here, and if you do not find the treasure then kill me. ' They dug and found the buried books, and Satan said to them, `Solomon only controlled the humans, devils and birds with this magic.' Thereafter, the news that Solomon was a sorcerer spread among the people, and the Children of Israel adopted these books. When Muhammad came, they disputed with him relying on these books. Hence Allah's statement,

﴿وَمَا كَفَرَ سُلَيْمَـنُ وَلَـكِنَّ الشَّيْاطِينَ كَفَرُواْ﴾

(Sulayman did not disbelieve, but the Shayatin (devils) disbelieved).

Allah said,

﴿وَمَآ أُنزِلَ عَلَى الْمَلَكَيْنِ بِبَابِلَ هَـرُوتَ وَمَـرُوتَ وَمَا يُعَلِّمَانِ مِنْ أَحَدٍ حَتَّى يَقُولاَ إِنَّمَا نَحْنُ فِتْنَةٌ فَلاَ تَكْفُرْ فَيَتَعَلَّمُونَ مِنْهُمَا مَا يُفَرِّقُونَ بِهِ بَيْنَ الْمَرْءِ وَزَوْجِهِ﴾

(And such things that came down at Babylon to the two angels, Harut and Marut, but neither of these two (angels) taught anyone (such things) till they had said, "We are for trial, so disbelieve not (by learning this magic from us)." And from these (angels) people learn that by which they cause separation between man and his wife).

There is a difference of opinion regarding this story. It was said that this Ayah denies that anything was sent down to the two angels, as Al-Qurtubi stated and then referred to the Ayah,

$$﴿وَمَا كَفَرَ سُلَيْمَـنُ﴾$$

(Sulayman did not disbelieve) saying, "The negation applies in both cases. Allah then said,

$$﴿وَلَـكِنَّ الشَّيْاطِينَ كَفَرُواْ يُعَلِّمُونَ النَّاسَ السِّحْرَ وَمَآ أُنزِلَ عَلَى الْمَلَكَيْنِ﴾$$

(But the Shayatin (devils) disbelieved, teaching men magic and such things that came down at Babylon to the two angels).

The Jews claimed that Gabriel and Michael brought magic down to the two angels, but Allah refuted this false claim."

Also, Ibn Jarir reported, that Al-`Awfi said that Ibn `Abbas said about Allah's statement,

$$﴿وَمَآ أُنزِلَ عَلَى الْمَلَكَيْنِ بِبَابِلَ﴾$$

(And such things that came down at Babylon to the two angels)

"Allah did not send magic down."

Also, Ibn Jarir narrated that Ar-Rabi` bin Anas said about,

﴿وَمَآ أُنزِلَ عَلَى الْمَلَكَيْنِ﴾

(And such things that came down to the two angels), "Allah did not send magic down to the them." Ibn Jarir commented, "This is the correct explanation for this Ayah.

﴿وَاتَّبَعُواْ مَا تَتْلُواْ الشَّيَـطِينُ عَلَى مُلْكِ سُلَيْمَـنَ﴾

(They followed what the Shayatin (devils) gave out (falsely) in the lifetime of Sulayman.) meaning, magic. However, neither did Solomon disbelieve nor did Allah send magic with the two angels. The devils, on the other hand, disbelieved and taught magic to the people of the Babylon of Harut and Marut."

Ibn Jarir continued; "If someone asks about explaining this Ayah in this manner, we say that,

﴿وَاتَّبَعُواْ مَا تَتْلُواْ الشَّيَـطِينُ عَلَى مُلْكِ سُلَيْمَـنَ﴾

(They followed what the Shayatin (devils) gave out (falsely) in the lifetime of Sulayman.) means, magic. Solomon neither disbelieved nor did Allah send magic with the two angels. However, the devils disbelieved and taught magic to the people in the Babylon of Harut and Marut, meaning Gabriel and Michael, for Jewish sorcerers claimed that Allah sent magic by the words of Gabriel and Michael to Solomon, son of David. Allah denied this false claim and stated to His Prophet Muhammad that Gabriel and Michael were not sent with magic. Allah also exonerated Solomon from practicing magic, which the devils taught to the people of Babylon by the hands of two men, Harut and Marut. Hence, Harut and Marut were two ordinary men (not angels or Gabriel or Michael)." These were the words of At-Tabari, and this explanation is not plausible.

Many among the Salaf, said that Harut and Marut were angels who came down from heaven to earth and did what they did as the Ayah stated. To conform this opinion with the fact that the angels are immune from error, we say that Allah had eternal knowledge what these angels would do, just as He had eternal knowledge that Iblis would do as he did, while Allah referred to him being among the angels,

﴿وَإِذْ قُلْنَا لِلْمَلَـئِكَةِ اسْجُدُواْ لأَدَمَ فَسَجَدُواْ إِلاَّ إِبْلِيسَ أَبَى﴾

(And (remember) when We said to the angels: "Prostrate yourselves before Adam." And they prostrated except Iblis (Satan), he refused) (20:116) and so forth. However, what Harut and Marut did was less evil than what Iblis, may Allah curse him, did. Al-Qurtubi reported this opinion from `Ali, Ibn Mas`ud, Ibn `Abbas, Ibn `Umar, Ka`b Al-Ahbar, As-Suddi and Al-Kalbi.

Allah said,

﴿وَمَا يُعَلِّمَانِ مِنْ أَحَدٍ حَتَّى يَقُولاَ إِنَّمَا نَحْنُ فِتْنَةٌ فَلاَ تَكْفُرْ﴾

(But neither of these two (angels) taught anyone (such things) till they had said, "We are for trial, so disbelieve not (by learning this magic from us).)

Abu Ja`far Ar-Razi said that Ar-Rabi' bin Anas said that Qays bin `Abbad said that Ibn `Abbas said, "When someone came to the angels to learn magic, they would discourage him and say to him, `We are only a test, so do not fall into disbelief.' They had knowledge of what is good and evil and what constitutes belief or disbelief, and they thus knew that magic is a form of disbelief. When the person who came to learn magic still insisted on learning it, they commanded him to go to such and such place, where if he went, Satan would meet him and teach him magic. When this man would learn magic, the light (of faith) would depart him, and he would see it shining (and flying away) in the sky. He would then proclaim, `O my sorrow! Woe unto me! What should I do." Al-Hasan Al-Basri said that this Ayah means, "The angels were sent with magic, so that the people whom Allah willed would be tried and tested. Allah made them promise that they would not teach anyone until first proclaiming, `We are a test for you, do not fall into disbelief.'" It was recorded by Ibn Abi Hatim. Also, Qatadah said, "Allah took their covenant to not teach anyone magic until they said, `We are a test. Therefore, do not fall in disbelief.'"

Also, As-Suddi said, "When a man would come to the two angels they would advise him, `Do not fall into disbelief. We are a test. ' When the man would ignore their advice, they would say, `Go to that pile of ashes and urinate on it.' When he would urinate on the ashes, a light, meaning the light of faith, would depart from him and would shine until it entered heaven. Then something black that appeared to be smoke would descend and enter his ears and the rest of his body, and this is Allah's anger. When he told the angels what happened, they would teach him magic. So Allah's statement,

$$﴿وَمَا يُعَلِّمَانِ مِنْ أَحَدٍ حَتَّى يَقُولاَ إِنَّمَا نَحْنُ فِتْنَةٌ فَلاَ تَكْفُرْ﴾$$

(But neither of these two (angels) taught anyone (such things) till they had said, "We are for trial, so disbelieve not (by learning this magic from us).)

Sunayd said that Hajjaj said that Ibn Jurayj commented on this Ayah (2:102), "No one dares practice magic except a disbeliever. As for the Fitnah, it involves trials and freedom of choice."

Quran 2:140

$$أَمْ تَقُولُونَ إِنَّ إِبْرَاهِيمَ وَإِسْمَاعِيلَ وَإِسْحَاقَ وَيَعْقُوبَ وَالْأَسْبَاطَ كَانُوا هُودًا أَوْ نَصَارَى قُلْ ءَأَنتُمْ أَعْلَمُ أَمِ اللَّهُ وَمَنْ أَظْلَمُ مِمَّن كَتَمَ شَهَادَةً عِندَهُ مِنَ اللَّهِ وَمَا اللَّهُ بِغَافِلٍ عَمَّا تَعْمَلُونَ (١٤٠)$$

Or say you that Ibrâhim (Abraham), Ismâ'il (Ishmael), Ishâque (Isaac), Ya'qûb (Jacob) and Al-Asbât [the offspring twelve sons of Ya'qûb (Jacob)] were Jews or Christians? Say, "Do you know better or does Allâh (knows better... that they all were Muslims)? And who is more unjust than he who conceals the testimony [i.e. to believe in Prophet Muhammad when he comes, as is written in their Books.] he has from Allâh? And Allâh is not unaware of what you do." (140)

Allah criticized them in the claim that Ibrahim, the Prophets who came after him and the Asbat were following their religion, whether Judaism or Christianity. Allah said,

$$﴿قُلْ ءَأَنتُمْ أَعْلَمُ أَمِ اللَّهُ﴾$$

(Say, "Do you know better or does Allah") meaning, Allah has the best knowledge and He stated that they were neither Jews, nor Christians. Similarly, Allah said

مَا كَانَ إِبْرَهِيمُ يَهُودِيًّا وَلاَ نَصْرَانِيًّا وَلَكِن كَانَ حَنِيفًا مُّسْلِمًا وَمَا كَانَ مِنَ الْمُشْرِكِينَ

(Ibrahim was neither a Jew nor a Christian, but he was a true Muslim Hanifa (to worship none but Allah alone) and he was not of Al-Mushrikin) (3:67) and the following Ayat. Allah also said,

﴿وَمَنْ أَظْلَمُ مِمَّنْ كَتَمَ شَهَـدَةً عِندَهُ مِنَ اللَّهِ﴾

And who is more unjust than he who conceals the testimony he has from Allah Al-Hasan Al-Basri said, They used to recite the Book of Allah He sent to them that stated that the true religion is Islam and that Muhammad is the Messenger of Allah. Their Book also stated that Ibrahim, Ismail, Ishaaq, Yaqub and the tribes were neither Jews, nor Christians. They testified to these facts, yet hid them from the people. Allah s statement,

﴿وَمَا اللَّهُ بِغَفِلٍ عَمَّا تَعْمَلُونَ﴾

(And Allah is not unaware of what you do), is a threat and a warning that His knowledge encompasses every one's deeds, and He shall award each accordingly.

These verses criminalize concealing testimony as evil. This was not necessarily an action performed but it was the inaction of reporting the testimony Allah gave Jews and Christians in the actual scriptures which they failed to preserve and proclaim due to selfish desires. People often fall into this same trap thinking nobody will know if they fail to report something whether it is to report testimony of truth or report a crime but Allah knows and orders us to report the truth warning us of punishment for concealing testimony unjustly.

Zaid bin Khalid Al-Juhani narrated that the Messenger of Allah said:

"Shall l not inform you of the best of witnesses? The one who comes with his testimony before being asked for it."

Source: Jami` at-Tirmidhi 2295 Grade: Sahih

Quran 2:159-160

إِنَّ ٱلَّذِينَ يَكْتُمُونَ مَآ أَنزَلْنَا مِنَ ٱلْبَيِّنَٰتِ وَٱلْهُدَىٰ مِنۢ بَعْدِ مَا بَيَّنَّٰهُ لِلنَّاسِ فِى ٱلْكِتَٰبِ أُوْلَٰٓئِكَ يَلْعَنُهُمُ ٱللَّهُ وَيَلْعَنُهُمُ ٱللَّٰعِنُونَ (١٥٩) إِلَّا ٱلَّذِينَ تَابُواْ وَأَصْلَحُواْ وَبَيَّنُواْ فَأُوْلَٰٓئِكَ أَتُوبُ عَلَيْهِمْ وَأَنَا ٱلتَّوَّابُ ٱلرَّحِيمُ (١٦٠)

Verily, those who conceal the clear proofs, evidences and the guidance, which We have sent down, after We have made it clear for the people in the Book, they are the ones cursed by Allâh and cursed by the cursers. (159) Except those who repent and do righteous deeds, and openly declare (the truth which they concealed). These, I will accept their repentance. And I am the One Who accepts repentance, the Most Merciful. (160)

These verses sternly warn against those who hide the clear signs that the Messengers were sent with which guide to the correct path and beneficial guidance for the hearts, after Allah has made such aspects clear for His servants through the Books that He revealed to His Messengers. Abu Al-`Aliyah said that these Ayat, "were revealed about the People of the Scripture who hid the description of Muhammad ." Allah then states that everything curses such people for this evil act. Certainly, just as everything asks for forgiveness for the scholar, even the fish in the sea and the bird in the air, then those who hide knowledge are cursed by Allah and by the cursers. A Hadith in the Musnad, narrated through several chains of narrators, that strengthens the overall judgment of the Hadith, states that Abu Hurayrah narrated that Allah's Messenger said:

«مَنْ سُئِلَ عَنْ عِلْمٍ فَكَتَمَهُ، أَلْجِمَ يَوْمَ الْقِيَامَةِ بِلِجَامٍ مِنْ نَارٍ»

(Whoever was asked about knowledge that one has, but he hid it, then a bridle made of fire will be tied around his mouth on the Day of Resurrection.)

It is also recorded by Al-Bukhari that Abu Hurayrah said, "If it was not for an Ayah in Allah's Book, I would not have narrated a Hadith for anyone:

﴿إِنَّ الَّذِينَ يَكْتُمُونَ مَآ أَنزَلْنَا مِنَ الْبَيِّنَـتِ وَالْهُدَى﴾

(Verily, those who conceal the clear proofs, evidences and the guidance, which We have sent down,)"

Mujahid said, "When the earth is struck by drought, the animals say, `This is because of the sinners among the Children of Adam. May Allah curse the sinners among the Children of Adam.'"

Abu Al-`Aliyah, Ar-Rabi` bin Anas and Qatadah said that

﴿وَيَلْعَنُهُمُ اللَّـعِنُونَ﴾

(and cursed by the cursers) means that the angels and the believers will curse them. Moreover, a Hadith states that everything, including the fish in the sea, asks for forgiveness for the scholars. The Ayah (2:159 above) states that those who hide the knowledge will be cursed, (in this life and) on the Day of Resurrection, by Allah, the angels, all humanity, and those who curse (including the animals) each in its own distinct way. Allah knows best.

From this punishment, Allah excluded all who repent to Him:

﴿إِلاَّ الَّذِينَ تَابُواْ وَأَصْلَحُواْ وَبَيَّنُواْ﴾

(Except those who repent and do righteous deeds, and openly declare (the truth which they concealed).)

This Ayah refers to those who regret what they have been doing and correct their behavior and, thus, explain to the people what they have been hiding.

Firstly, the lesson is that concealing testimony is curse worthy and those who cover up crimes are cursed perhaps even more than the one guilty of doing the crime being covered up. To obtain a valid repentance from such one must snitch on oneself and those the circumstances require. So regarding some crimes snitching is the key to repentance and forgiveness and makes all the difference between being cursed by everything and blessed by the Creator of everything.

Quran 2:166-170

إِذْ تَبَرَّأَ ٱلَّذِينَ ٱتُّبِعُواْ مِنَ ٱلَّذِينَ ٱتَّبَعُواْ وَرَأَوُاْ ٱلْعَذَابَ وَتَقَطَّعَتْ بِهِمُ ٱلْأَسْبَابُ
(١٦٦) وَقَالَ ٱلَّذِينَ ٱتَّبَعُواْ لَوْ أَنَّ لَنَا كَرَّةً فَنَتَبَرَّأَ مِنْهُمْ كَمَا تَبَرَّءُواْ مِنَّا ۗ كَذَٰلِكَ يُرِيهِمُ ٱللَّهُ
أَعْمَـٰلَهُمْ حَسَرَٰتٍ عَلَيْهِمْ ۖ وَمَا هُم بِخَـٰرِجِينَ مِنَ ٱلنَّارِ (١٦٧) يَـٰٓأَيُّهَا ٱلنَّاسُ كُلُواْ مِمَّا فِى
ٱلْأَرْضِ حَلَٰلًا طَيِّبًا وَلَا تَتَّبِعُواْ خُطُوَٰتِ ٱلشَّيْطَـٰنِ ۚ إِنَّهُۥ لَكُمْ عَدُوٌّ مُّبِينٌ (١٦٨) إِنَّمَا
يَأْمُرُكُم بِٱلسُّوٓءِ وَٱلْفَحْشَآءِ وَأَن تَقُولُواْ عَلَى ٱللَّهِ مَا لَا تَعْلَمُونَ (١٦٩) وَإِذَا قِيلَ لَهُمُ
ٱتَّبِعُواْ مَآ أَنزَلَ ٱللَّهُ قَالُواْ بَلْ نَتَّبِعُ مَآ أَلْفَيْنَا عَلَيْهِ ءَابَآءَنَآ ۗ أَوَلَوْ كَانَ ءَابَآؤُهُمْ لَا يَعْقِلُونَ
شَيْئًا وَلَا يَهْتَدُونَ (١٧٠)

*When those who were followed, disown (declare themselves
innocent of) those who followed (them), and they see the
torment, then all their relations will be cut off from them.
(166) And those who followed will say: "If only we had one
more chance to return (to the worldly life), we would disown
(declare ourselves as innocent from) them as they have
disowned (declared themselves as innocent from) us." Thus
Allâh will show them their deeds as regrets for them. And they
will never get out of the Fire. (167) O mankind! Eat of that
which is lawful and good on the earth, and follow not the
footsteps of Shaitân (Satan). Verily, he is to you an open
enemy: (168) He [Shaitân (Satan)] commands you only what is
evil and Fahshâ (sinful), and that you should say against Allâh
what you know not. (169) When it is said to them: "Follow
what Allâh has sent down." They say: "Nay! We shall follow
what we found our fathers following." (Would they do that!)
even though their fathers did not understand anything nor were
they guided? (170)*

Allah said:

﴿وَقَالَ الَّذِينَ اتَّبَعُوا لَوْ أَنَّ لَنَا كَرَّةً فَنَتَبَرَّأَ مِنْهُمْ كَمَا تَبَرَّءُوا مِنَّا﴾

(And those who followed will say: "If only we had one
more chance to return (to the worldly life), we would

disown (declare ourselves as innocent from) them as they have disowned (declared themselves as innocent from) us.")

This Ayah means: `If we only had a chance to go back to the life so that we could disown them (their idols, leaders, etc.) shun their worship, ignore them and worship Allah Alone instead.' But they utter a lie in this regard, because if they were given the chance to go back, they would only return to what they were prohibited from doing.

After Allah stated that there is no deity worthy of worship except Him and that He Alone created the creation, He stated that He is the Sustainer for all His creation, and He mentioned a favor that He granted them; He has allowed them to eat any of the pure lawful things on the earth that do not cause harm to the body or the mind. He also forbade them from following the footsteps of Shaytan, meaning his ways and methods with which he misguides his followers, like prohibiting the Bahirah (a she-camel whose milk was spared for the idols and nobody was allowed to milk it), or Sa'ibah (a she-camel let loose for free pasture for the idols and nothing was allowed to be carried on it), or a Wasilah (a she-camel set free for idols because it has given birth to a she-camel at its first delivery and then again gives birth to a she-camel at its second delivery), and all of the other things that Shaytan made attractive to them during the time of Jahiliyyah. Muslim recorded `Iyad bin Himar saying that Allah's Messenger said that Allah the Exalted says,

يَقُولُ اللهُ تَعَالَى:إِنَّ كُلَّ مَالٍ مَنَحْتُهُ عِبَادِي فَهُوَ لَهُمْ حَلَالٌ، وَفِيهِ وَإِنِّي خَلَقْتُ عِبَادِي حُنَفَاءَ، فَجَاءَتْهُمُ الشَّيَاطِينُ فَاجْتَالَتْهُمْ عَنْ دِينِهِمْ، وَحَرَّمَتْ عَلَيْهِمْ مَا أَحْلَلْتُ لَهُمْ»

(`Every type of wealth I have endowed My servants is allowed for them...' (until), `I have created My servants Hunafa' (pure or upright), but the devils came to them and led them astray from their (true) religion and prohibited them from what I allowed for them. ')

Allah said:

﴿إِنَّهُ لَكُمْ عَدُوٌّ مُبِينٌ﴾

(...he is to you an open enemy.)

warning against Satan. Allah said in another instance:

﴿إِنَّ الشَّيْطَـنَ لَكُمْ عَدُوٌّ فَاتَّخِذُوهُ عَدُوّاً إِنَّمَا يَدْعُو حِزْبَهُ لِيَكُونُواْ مِنْ أَصْحَـبِ السَّعِيرِ ﴾

(Surely, Shaytan is an enemy to you, so take (treat) him as an enemy. He only invites his Hizb (followers) that they may become the dwellers of the blazing Fire.) (35:6), and:

﴿أَفَتَتَّخِذُونَهُ وَذُرِّيَّتَهُ أَوْلِيَآءَ مِن دُونِى وَهُمْ لَكُمْ عَدُوٌّ بِئْسَ لِلظَّـلِمِينَ بَدَلاً﴾

(Will you then take him (Iblis) and his offspring as protectors and helpers rather than Me while they are enemies to you What an evil is the exchange for the Zalimin (polytheists, and wrongdoers, etc).) (18:50)

Qatadah and As-Suddi commented on what Allah said:

﴿وَلاَ تَتَّبِعُواْ خُطُوَتِ الشَّيْطَـنِ﴾

(...and follow not the footsteps of Shaytan (Satan)):

Every act of disobedience to Allah is among the footsteps of Satan.

`Abd bin Humayd reported that Ibn `Abbas said: "Any vow or oath that one makes while angry, is among the footsteps of Shaytan and its expiation is that of the vow. " Allah's statement:

﴿إِنَّمَا يَأْمُرُكُم بِالسُّوءِ وَالْفَحْشَاءِ وَأَن تَقُولُواْ عَلَى اللَّهِ مَا لاَ تَعْلَمُونَ﴾

(He (Satan) commands you only what is evil and Fahsha (sinful), and that you should say about Allah what you know not.)

The verse means: `Your enemy, Satan, commands you to commit evil acts and what is worse than that, such as adultery and so forth. He commands you to commit what is even worse, that is, saying about Allah without knowledge.' So this includes every innovator and disbeliever.

Allah states that if the disbelievers and polytheists are called to follow what Allah has revealed to His Messenger and abandon the practices of misguidance and ignorance that they indulge in, they will say, "Rather. We shall follow what we found our fathers following," meaning, worshipping the idols and the false deities. Allah criticized their reasoning:

﴿أَوَلَوْ كَانَ ءَابَاؤُهُمْ﴾

((Would they do that!) even though their fathers), meaning, those whom they follow and whose practices they imitate, and:

$$\{ \lambda \ \text{يَعْقِلُونَ شَيْئًا وَلاَ يَهْتَدُونَ} \}$$

(...did not understand anything nor were they guided)
meaning, they had no sound understanding or guidance.
Ibn Ishaq reported that Ibn `Abbas said that this was
revealed about a group of Jews whom Allah's Messenger
called to Islam, but they refused, saying, "Rather, we shall
follow what we found our forefathers following."

The followers of falsehood will surely abandon those they
followed and those followed will surely abandoned those
who followed them on the day of Judgement, but not so
those who followed the Divine Revelation of Allah and
the prophets whom Allah has sent. Thus it is incumbent
on all to follow the prophetic guidance to avoid this
mutual disgraceful abandonment. Whether it is a gang
leader or a church preacher or a respected family member
anyone who is followed in misguidance will regret it both
the follower and followed and this includes those who
innovate in the religion of Islam as well as regular
disbelievers. Simply following the Islamic religion as
practiced by your parents is not equivalent to following
the religion the prophets taught. The only Islam valid
today is that which the Sahabah practiced as taught by
Muhammad. So the madhhab fanatics who blindly
follow certain shaikhs or the partisan political and non-
political groups as well as families, coworkers, cultures
and even national practices if they don't have a chain
linking them to the original prophetic teaching are
included in this "falsehood following". Regarding
snitching many dislike this aspect of the prophetic faith

and avoid it, especially if it must be done on friends, coworkers or family so instead of following prophetic injunctions they follow their desires. In reality though everyone who follows other than the prophetic standards is following their own desires in one way or the other, even if they follow reluctantly their following is out of a desire for other than prophetic guidance. This path is the path of the devil who has many followers under many different banners with few of them admitting they are following the devil, and some even falsely claim to follow the prophets while sincerely believing they are doing so. Yet prophets came with proof so it is a simple matter of proving you are following the prophets whereas the one who follows other than the prophets will have no proof to support their case though they may bring every excuse imaginable they will never come with authentic evidence that combines with correct interpreted knowledge to match. Some will indeed come with evidence to support their deviance, some may even use the Quran itself to back up their bida though the evidence is actually against them though they think it is for them. So do be careful in who you pledge your allegiance to via following because following in any aspect of religion is a type of allegiance. Take great concern to place each step on your path with alert sincere intentions that combine with proven prophetic good deeds whether others join you in this endeavor or not. Occasionally you may be alone in following the prophetic path in your particular locality but it should never matter whether you are in the majority or the minority for world faith fluctuates and we never follow the crowd even if the crowd is upon goodness because the path to paradise is in following the prophets regardless of the numbers of other parties. Lastly those who followed false prophets or false teachers/teachings will disown those they followed on the day they are judged and they promise if given the opportunity to return to earth they would disown in earth as well. Why? Because they will know they were supposed to disown the devil and his followers by disassociating in this worldly life rather than going along with their evil. If you are on good terms with everyone without enemies something is clearly wrong because the prophets had enemies, so if you don't that indicates you are on a path other than the prophets. The prophetic path is not without friendship, it just prioritizes the friendship of Allah, the angels and the righteous over that of all else. These verses also prove that unless such disassociation happens in this world it indicates one is indeed following a path of shaitan whether one knows it or not even if they are following those claiming to follow prophetic footsteps. Commonly Satan will beautify a path of misguidance by labeling it with alleged prophetic endorsement as an ultimate ruse to lead people to hell in the name of genuine prophets, hence false religions and false ways to practice the one prophetic religion of Islam. Thus taqlid in our era is only justified for the prophet Muhammad whom even Jesus will follow when he returns because salvation lies not in following any prophet one chooses but following the prophet Allah commands, when Allah commands, how Allah commands, for the reasons Allah commands, with sincere knowledgeable good actions until we meet Allah. Lastly Allah says "When it is said to them follow what Allah has sent down" this means someone has to do that job of telling the people to follow what Allah sent to us to clarify to the followers of falsehood that they are upon other than divine guidance. It's a tough job indeed but it's the job the prophets performed and left for their followers to inherit and successfully succeed in. If you aren't actively seeking knowledge of guidance and calling to guidance then your silence equates to you broadcasting the voice of Satan. Silence in the face of evil is the voice of Satan and so is speaking about God without prophetic knowledge.

Studying and advising go hand in hand and are done together throughout life to ensure one doesn't forget what prophetic proofs they are calling to. Because to forget the proofs and call to what you remember or think is right is the first step in following your desires which is ultimately to fall for the plot of the devil. Always remember the devil desires for you to follow what you desire in some way, shape or form. Entire false religions arose because of people being lazy in research and citation for prophetic evidence so they followed what others told them without fact checking for their faith. However if you don't fact check then your faith doesn't count. Be certain all you believe, say and do has prophetic precedence when it concerns religion and know that religious rulings pertain to everything, this is because we are judged by God for everything. Thus anyone who says there is an aspect of life that doesn't involve religion is a liar because even the mundane permissible deeds become worship based on sincerity and intentions. So each deed you do is always good or evil, for permissible is only a theoretical categorization. In reality on Judgement Day God will not say "That was a good deed, that was a evil deed and all of this stuff was permissible so its neither a good nor a evil deed, it was just free time you spent in life doing neutral living." Nothing is neutral because each second is a step either towards paradise or towards hellfire and even if you step in place without progress towards either place then such wasted time and effort amounts to negative progress which is lack of progress to paradise. Therefore doing "permissible things" in one's "free time" is known not to be virtuous but it is less known that it is blameworthy though not sinful. Just because something isn't sinful doesn't mean it is worth doing and just because the default general ruling indicates permissibility doesn't mean that is the case in your case if you overindulge in permissible actions to the point that obligations are neglected. Permissible can become forbidden for some due to intentions or timing. So know that following desires excessively indulging in lawful permissible deeds without pure prophetic motivation is not merely wasteful, it is riskily dangerous. For example imagine a Prophet telling God they wasted time during their mission doing permissible deeds? What would God say? Then imagine you telling God you are a follower of a prophet and are ready to enter paradise but you wasted some time in life doing permissible deeds. Let's not follow the permissible path to hellfire which Satan paves so well as he convinces many to waste time in wasting life following their desires under the guise of "permissible". Does a true slave of God have time to waste? Never.

Quran 2:282-283

يَـٰٓأَيُّهَا ٱلَّذِينَ ءَامَنُوٓاْ إِذَا تَدَايَنتُم بِدَيۡنٍ إِلَىٰٓ أَجَلٍ مُّسَمًّى فَٱكۡتُبُوهُ وَلۡيَكۡتُب بَّيۡنَكُمۡ كَاتِبُۢ بِٱلۡعَدۡلِ وَلَا يَأۡبَ كَاتِبٌ أَن يَكۡتُبَ كَمَا عَلَّمَهُ ٱللَّهُ فَلۡيَكۡتُبۡ وَلۡيُمۡلِلِ ٱلَّذِى عَلَيۡهِ ٱلۡحَقُّ وَلۡيَتَّقِ ٱللَّهَ رَبَّهُ وَلَا يَبۡخَسۡ مِنۡهُ شَيۡـًٔا فَإِن كَانَ ٱلَّذِى عَلَيۡهِ ٱلۡحَقُّ سَفِيهًا أَوۡ ضَعِيفًا أَوۡ لَا يَسۡتَطِيعُ أَن يُمِلَّ هُوَ فَلۡيُمۡلِلۡ وَلِيُّهُ بِٱلۡعَدۡلِ وَٱسۡتَشۡهِدُواْ شَهِيدَيۡنِ مِن رِّجَالِكُمۡ فَإِن لَّمۡ يَكُونَا رَجُلَيۡنِ فَرَجُلٌ وَٱمۡرَأَتَانِ مِمَّن تَرۡضَوۡنَ مِنَ ٱلشُّهَدَآءِ أَن تَضِلَّ إِحۡدَىٰهُمَا فَتُذَكِّرَ إِحۡدَىٰهُمَا ٱلۡأُخۡرَىٰ وَلَا يَأۡبَ ٱلشُّهَدَآءُ إِذَا مَا دُعُواْ وَلَا تَسۡـَٔمُوٓاْ أَن تَكۡتُبُوهُ صَغِيرًا أَوۡ كَبِيرًا إِلَىٰٓ أَجَلِهِ ذَٰلِكُمۡ أَقۡسَطُ عِندَ ٱللَّهِ وَأَقۡوَمُ لِلشَّهَٰدَةِ وَأَدۡنَىٰٓ أَلَّا تَرۡتَابُوٓاْ إِلَّآ أَن تَكُونَ تِجَٰرَةً حَاضِرَةً تُدِيرُونَهَا بَيۡنَكُمۡ فَلَيۡسَ عَلَيۡكُمۡ جُنَاحٌ أَلَّا تَكۡتُبُوهَا وَأَشۡهِدُوٓاْ إِذَا تَبَايَعۡتُمۡ وَلَا يُضَآرَّ كَاتِبٌ وَلَا شَهِيدٌ وَإِن تَفۡعَلُواْ فَإِنَّهُ فُسُوقٌۢ بِكُمۡ وَٱتَّقُواْ ٱللَّهَ وَيُعَلِّمُكُمُ ٱللَّهُ وَٱللَّهُ بِكُلِّ شَيۡءٍ عَلِيمٌ (٢٨٢) ۞ وَإِن كُنتُمۡ عَلَىٰ سَفَرٍ وَلَمۡ تَجِدُواْ كَاتِبًا فَرِهَٰنٌ مَّقۡبُوضَةٌ فَإِنۡ أَمِنَ بَعۡضُكُم بَعۡضًا فَلۡيُؤَدِّ ٱلَّذِى ٱؤۡتُمِنَ أَمَٰنَتَهُ وَلۡيَتَّقِ ٱللَّهَ رَبَّهُ وَلَا تَكۡتُمُواْ ٱلشَّهَٰدَةَ وَمَن يَكۡتُمۡهَا فَإِنَّهُ ءَاثِمٌ قَلۡبُهُ وَٱللَّهُ بِمَا تَعۡمَلُونَ عَلِيمٌ (٢٨٣)

O you who believe! When you contract a debt for a fixed period, write it down. Let a scribe write it down in justice between you. Let not the scribe refuse to write as Allâh has taught him, so let him write. Let him (the debtor) who incurs the liability dictate, and he must fear Allâh, his Lord, and diminish not anything of what he owes. But if the debtor is of poor understanding, or weak, or is unable to dictate for himself, then let his guardian dictate in justice. And get two witnesses out of your own men. And if there are not two men (available), then a man and two women, such as you agree for witnesses, so that if one of them (two women) errs, the other can remind her. And the witnesses should not refuse when they are called (for evidence). You should not become weary to write it (your contract), whether it be small or big, for its fixed term, that is more just with Allâh; more solid as evidence, and more convenient to prevent doubts among yourselves, save when it is a present trade which you carry out on the spot among yourselves, then there is no sin on you if you do not write it down. But take witnesses whenever you make a commercial contract. Let nither scribe nor witness suffer any harm, but if you do (such harm), it would be wickedness in you. So be afraid of Allah; and Allah teaches you. And Allah is the All-Knower of everything. (282) And if you are on a journey and cannot find a scribe, then let there be a pledge taken (mortgaging); then if one of you entrust the other, let the one who is entrusted discharge his trust (faithfully), and let him be afraid of Allâh, his Lord. And conceal not the evidence for he, who hides it, surely his heart is sinful. And Allâh is All-Knower of what you do. (283)

This Ayah is the longest in the Glorious Qur'an. Imam Abu Ja`far bin Jarir recorded that Sa`id bin Al-Musayyib said that he was told that the Ayah most recently revealed from above the Throne -- the last Ayah to be revealed in the Qur'an -- was the Ayah about debts.

Allah's statement,

﴿يَأَيُّهَا الَّذِينَ ءَامَنُواْ إِذَا تَدَايَنتُم بِدَيْنٍ إِلَى أَجَلٍ مُّسَمًّى فَاكْتُبُوهُ﴾

(O you who believe! When you contract a debt for a fixed period, write it down) directs Allah's believing servants to record their business transactions when their term is delayed, to preserve the terms and timing of these transactions, and the memory of witnesses, as mentioned at the end of the Ayah,

﴿ذَلِكُمْ أَقْسَطُ عِندَ اللهِ وَأَقْوَمُ لِلشَّهَدَةِ وَأَدْنَى أَلاَّ تَرْتَابُواْ﴾

(that is more just with Allah; more solid as evidence, and more convenient to prevent doubts among yourselves.)

The Two Sahihs recorded that Ibn `Abbas said, "Allah's Messenger came to Al-Madinah, while the people were in the habit of paying in advance for fruits to be delivered within one or two years. The Messenger of Allah said,

«مَنْ أَسْلَفَ، فَلْيُسْلِفْ فِي كَيْلٍ مَعْلُومٍ، وَوَزْنٍ مَعْلُومٍ، إِلَى أَجَلٍ مَعْلُوم»

(Whoever pays money in advance (for dates to be delivered later) should pay it for known specified measure and weight (of the dates) for a specified date.)

Allah's statement,

﴿فَاكْتُبُوهُ﴾

(write it down) is a command from Him to record such transactions to endorse and preserve their terms. Ibn Jurayj said, "Whoever borrowed should write the terms, and whoever bought should have witnesses." Abu Sa`id, Ash-Sha`bi, Ar-Rabi` bin Anas, Al-Hasan, Ibn Jurayj and Ibn Zayd said that recording such transactions was necessary before, but was then abrogated by Allah's statement,

﴿فَإِنْ أَمِنَ بَعْضُكُم بَعْضًا فَلْيُوَدِّ الَّذِى اؤْتُمِنَ أَمَـٰنَتَهُ﴾

(Then if one of you entrusts the other, let the one who is entrusted discharge his trust (faithfully).)

Allah's statement,

﴿وَلْيَكْتُب بَّيْنَكُم كَاتِبٌ بِالْعَدْلِ﴾

(Let a scribe write it down in justice between you) and in truth. Therefore, the scribe is not allowed to cheat any party of the contract and is to only record what the parties of the contract agreed to, without addition or deletion. Allah's statement,

﴿وَلاَ يَأْبَ كَاتِبٌ أَن يَكْتُبَ كَمَا عَلَّمَهُ اللهُ فَلْيَكْتُبْ﴾

(Let not the scribe refuse to write, as Allah has taught him, so let him write) means, "Those who know how to write should not refrain from writing transaction contracts when asked to do so." Further, let writing such contracts be a type of charity from the scribe for those who are not lettered, just as Allah taught him what he knew not. Therefore, let him write, just as the Hadith stated,

«إِنَّ مِنَ الصَّدَقَةِ أَنْ تُعِينَ صَانِعًا، أَوْ تَصْنَعَ لِأَخْرَق»

(It is a type of charity to help a worker and to do something for a feeble person.)

In another Hadith, the Prophet said,

«مَنْ كَتَمَ عِلْمًا يَعْلَمُهُ، أَلْجِمَ يَوْمَ الْقِيَامَةِ بِلِجَامٍ مِنْ نَار»

(Whoever kept knowledge to himself will be restrained by a bridle made of fire on the Day of Resurrection.) Mujahid and `Ata' said that if asked to do so, "The scribe is required to record."

Allah's statement,

﴿وَلْيُمْلِلِ الَّذِى عَلَيْهِ الْحَقُّ وَلْيَتَّقِ اللَّهَ رَبَّهُ﴾

(Let him (the debtor) who incurs the liability dictate, and he must have Taqwa of Allah, his Lord) indicates that the debtor should dictate to the scribe what he owes, so let him fear Allah,

﴿وَلاَ يَبْخَسْ مِنْهُ شَيْئاً﴾

(And diminish not anything of what he owes,) meaning, not hide any portion of what he owes.

﴿فَإِن كَانَ الَّذِى عَلَيْهِ الْحَقُّ سَفِيهًا﴾

(But if the debtor is of poor understanding) and is not allowed to decide on such matters, because he used to waste money, for instance,

﴿أَوْ ضَعِيفًا﴾

(Or weak), such as being too young or insane,

﴿أَوْ لاَ يَسْتَطِيعُ أَن يُمِلَّ هُوَ﴾

(Or is unable to dictate for himself) because of a disease, or ignorance about such matters,

﴿فَلْيُمْلِلْ وَلِيُّهُ بِالْعَدْلِ﴾

(then let his guardian dictate in justice.)

Allah said,

﴿وَاسْتَشْهِدُواْ شَهِيدَيْنِ مِّن رِّجَالِكُمْ﴾

(And get two witnesses out of your own men) requiring witnesses to attend the dictation of contracts to further preserve the contents,

﴿فَإِن لَّمْ يَكُونَا رَجُلَيْنِ فَرَجُلٌ وَامْرَأَتَانِ﴾

(And if there are not two men (available), then a man and
two women) this requirement is only for contracts that
directly or indirectly involve money. Allah requires that
two women take the place of one man as witness, because
of the woman's shortcomings, as the Prophet described.
Muslim recorded in his Sahih that Abu Hurayrah said
that the Messenger of Allah said,

«يَا مَعْشَرَ النِّسَاءِ تَصَدَّقْنَ وَأَكْثِرْنَ الِاسْتِغْفَارَ، فَإِنِّي رَأَيْتُكُنَّ أَكْثَرَ أَهْلِ النَّارِ»

(O women! Give away charity and ask for forgiveness, for
I saw that you comprise the majority of the people of the
Fire.)

One eloquent woman said, "O Messenger of Allah! Why
do we comprise the majority of the people of the Fire" He
said,

«تُكْثِرْنَ اللَّعْنَ، وَتَكْفُرْنَ الْعَشِيرَ، وَمَا رَأَيْتُ مِنْ نَاقِصَاتِ عَقْلٍ وَدِينٍ، أَغْلَبَ لِذِي لُبَ
مِنْكُنَّ»

(You curse a lot and you do not appreciate your mate. I
have never seen those who have shortcoming in mind
and religion controlling those who have sound minds,
other than you.) She said, "O Messenger of Allah! What is
this shortcoming in mind and religion" He said,

«أَمَّا نُقْصَانُ عَقْلِهَا، فَشَهَادَةُ امْرَأَتَيْنِ تَعْدِلُ شَهَادَةَ رَجُلٍ، فَهَذَا نُقْصَانُ الْعَقْلِ، وَتَمْكُثُ
اللَّيَالِي لَا تُصَلِّي وَتُفْطِرُ فِي رَمَضَانَ، فَهَذَا نُقْصَانُ الدِّينِ»

(As for the shortcoming in her mind, the testimony of two
women equals the testimony of one man, and this is the
shortcoming in the mind. As for the shortcoming in the

religion, woman remains for nights at a time when she does not pray and breaks the fast in Ramadan)

Allah's statement,

﴿مِمَّن تَرْضَوْنَ مِنَ الشُّهَدَآءِ﴾

(such as you agree for witnesses) requires competency in the witnesses. Further, Allah's statement,

﴿أَن تَضِلَّ إِحْدَاهُمَا﴾

(so that if one of them errs) refers to the two women witnesses; whenever one of them forgets a part of the testimony,

﴿فَتُذَكِّرَ إِحْدَاهُمَا الأُخْرَى﴾

(the other can remind her) meaning, the other woman's testimony mends the shortcoming of forgetfulness in the first woman.

Allah's statement,

﴿وَلاَ يَأْبَ الشُّهَدَآءُ إِذَا مَا دُعُواْ﴾

(And the witnesses should not refuse when they are called) means, when people are called to be witnesses, they should agree, as Qatadah and Ar-Rabi` bin Anas stated. Similarly, Allah said,

﴿وَلاَ يَأْبَ كَاتِبٌ أَن يَكْتُبَ كَمَا عَلَّمَهُ اللهُ فَلْيَكْتُبْ﴾

(Let not the scribe refuse to write as Allah has taught him,

»أَمَّا نُقْصَانُ عَقْلِهَا، فَشَهَادَةُ امْرَأَتَيْنِ تَعْدِلُ شَهَادَةَ رَجُلٍ، فَهَذَا نُقْصَانُ الْعَقْلِ، وَتَمْكُثُ اللَّيَالِيَ لَا تُصَلِّي وَتُفْطِرُ فِي رَمَضَانَ، فَهَذَا نُقْصَانُ الدِّينِ«

(As for the shortcoming in her mind, the testimony of two women equals the testimony of one man, and this is the shortcoming in the mind. As for the shortcoming in the religion, woman remains for nights at a time when she does not pray and breaks the fast in Ramadan)

Allah's statement,

﴿مِمَّن تَرْضَوْنَ مِنَ الشُّهَدَآءِ﴾

(such as you agree for witnesses) requires competency in the witnesses. Further, Allah's statement,

﴿أَن تَضِلَّ إْحْدَاهُمَا﴾

(so that if one of them errs) refers to the two women witnesses; whenever one of them forgets a part of the testimony,

﴿فَتُذَكِّرَ إِحْدَاهُمَا الإِخْرَى﴾

(the other can remind her) meaning, the other woman's testimony mends the shortcoming of forgetfulness in the first woman.

Allah's statement,

﴿وَلاَ يَأْبَ الشُّهَدَآءُ إِذَا مَا دُعُواْ﴾

(And the witnesses should not refuse when they are called) means, when people are called to be witnesses, they should agree, as Qatadah and Ar-Rabi` bin Anas stated. Similarly, Allah said,

﴿وَلاَ يَأْبَ كَاتِبٌ أَن يَكْتُبَ كَمَا عَلَّمَهُ اللَّهُ فَلْيَكْتُبْ﴾

(Let not the scribe refuse to write as Allah has taught him, so let him write.)

Some say that this Ayah indicates that agreeing to become a witness is Fard Kifayah (required on at least a part of the Muslim Ummah). However, the majority of the scholars say that the Ayah,

﴿وَلاَ يَأْبَ الشُّهَدَآءُ إِذَا مَا دُعُواْ﴾

(And the witnesses should not refuse when they are called) is referring to testifying to what the witnesses actually witnessed, thus befitting their description of being `witnesses'. Therefore, when the witness is called to testify to what he witnessed, he is required to give testimony, unless this obligation was already fulfilled, in which case such testimony becomes Fard Kifayah. Mujahid and Abu Mijlaz said, "If you are called to be a witness, then you have the choice to agree. If you witnessed and were called to testify, then come forward." It was reported that Ibn `Abbas and Al-Hasan Al-Basri said that the obligation includes both cases, agreeing to be a witness and testifying to what one witnessed.

Allah's statement,

﴿وَلاَ تَسْئَمُواْ أَن تَكْتُبُوهُ صَغِيرًا أَوْ كَبِيرًا إِلَى أَجَلِهِ﴾

(You should not become weary to write it (your contract), whether it be small or large, for its fixed term) perfects this direction from Allah by commanding that the debt be written, whether the amount is large or small. Allah said,

﴿وَلاَ تَسْئَمُواْ﴾

(You should not become weary) meaning, do not be discouraged against writing transactions and their terms, whether the amount involved is large or small. Allah's statement,

﴿ذَلِكُمْ أَقْسَطُ عِندَ اللَّهِ وَأَقْوَمُ لِلشَّهَدَةِ وَأَدْنَى أَلاَّ تَرْتَابُواْ﴾

(that is more just with Allah; more solid as evidence, and more convenient to prevent doubts among yourselves) means, writing transactions that will be fulfillled at a later date is more just with Allah meaning better and more convenient in order to preserve the terms of the contract. Therefore, recording such agreements helps the witnesses, when they see their handwriting - or signatures - later on and thus remember what they witnessed, for it is possible that the witnesses might forget what they witnessed.

﴿وَأَدْنَى أَلاَّ تَرْتَابُواْ﴾

(And more convenient to prevent doubts among yourselves) meaning, this helps repel any doubt. Since if you need to then refer to the contract that you wrote and the doubt will end.

Allah's statement,

﴿إِلاَّ أَن تَكُونَ تِجَرَةً حَاضِرَةً تُدِيرُونَهَا بَيْنَكُمْ فَلَيْسَ عَلَيْكُمْ جُنَاحٌ أَلاَّ تَكْتُبُوهَا﴾

(save when it is a present trade which you carry out on the spot among yourselves, then there is no sin on you if you do not write it down) indicates that if the transaction will be fulfilled immediately, then there is no harm if it is not recorded.

As for requiring witnesses to be present in trading transactions, Allah said,

﴿وَأَشْهِدُواْ إِذَا تَبَايَعْتُمْ﴾

(But take witnesses whenever you make a commercial contract.)

However, this command was abrogated by,

﴿فَإِنْ أَمِنَ بَعْضُكُم بَعْضًا فَلْيُؤَدِّ الَّذِى اؤْتُمِنَ أَمَـنَتَهُ﴾

(Then if one of you entrusts the other, let the one who is entrusted discharge his trust (faithfully).)

Or, it could be that having witnesses in such cases is only recommended and not obligatory, as evident from the Hadith that Khuzaymah bin Thabit Al-Ansari narrated which Imam Ahmad collected. `Umarah bin Khuzaymah Al-Ansari said that his uncle, who was among the Prophet's Companions, told him that the Prophet was making a deal for a horse with a bedouin man. The Prophet asked the bedouin to follow him so that he could pay him the price of the horse. The Prophet went ahead of the bedouin. The bedouin met several men who tried to buy his horse, not knowing if the Prophet was actually determined to buy it. Some people offered more money for the horse than the Prophet had. The bedouin man said to the Prophet , "If you want to buy this horse, then buy it or I will sell it to someone else." When he heard the bedouin man's words, the Prophet stood up and said, "Have I not bought that horse from you" The bedouin said, "By Allah! I have not sold it to you." The Prophet said, "Rather, I did buy it from you." The people gathered around the Prophet and the Bedouin while they were disputing, and the bedouin said, "Bring forth a witness who testifies that I sold you the horse." Meanwhile, the Muslims who came said to the bedouin, "Woe to you! The Prophet only says the truth." When Khuzaymah bin Thabit came and heard the dispute between the Prophet and the bedouin who was saying, "Bring forth a witness who testifies that I sold you the horse, " Khuzaymah said, "I bear witness that you sold him the horse." The Prophet said to Khuzaymah, "What is the basis of your testimony" Khuzaymah said, "That I entrusted you, O Messenger of Allah!" Therefore, the Messenger made Khuzaymah's testimony equal to the testimony of two men. This was also recorded by Abu Dawud and An-Nasai

Allah's statement,

﴿وَلاَ يُضَآرَّ كَاتِبٌ وَلاَ شَهِيدٌ﴾

(Let neither scribe nor witness suffer (or cause) any harm) also indicates that the scribe and the witness must not cause any harm, such as, when the scribe writes other than what he is being dictated, or the witness testifies to other than what he heard or conceals his testimony. This is the explanation of Al-Hasan and Qatadah."

Allah's statement,

﴿وَإِن تَفْعَلُواْ فَإِنَّهُ فُسُوقٌ بِكُمْ﴾

(But if you do (such harm), it would be wickedness in you) means, "If you defy what you were commanded and commit what you were prohibited, then it is because of the sin that resides and remains with you; sin that you never release or rid yourselves from."

Allah said,

$$﴿وَإِن كُنتُمْ عَلَى سَفَرٍ﴾$$

(And if you are on a journey) meaning, traveling and some of you borrowed some money to be paid at a later date,

$$﴿وَلَمْ تَجِدُواْ كَاتِبًا﴾$$

(and cannot find a scribe) who would record the debt for you. Ibn `Abbas said, "And even if they find a scribe, but did not find paper, ink or pen." Then,

$$﴿فَرِهَـٰنٌ مَّقْبُوضَةٌ﴾$$

(let there be a pledge taken (mortgaging)) given to the creditor in lieu of writing the transaction. The Two Sahihs recorded that Anas said that the Messenger of Allah died while his shield was mortgaged with a Jew in return for thirty Wasq (approximately 180 kg) of barley, which the Prophet bought on credit as provisions for his household. In another narration, the Hadith stated that this Jew was among the Jews of Al-Madinah.

Allah said,

$$﴿فَإِنْ أَمِنَ بَعْضُكُم بَعْضًا فَلْيُؤَدِّ الَّذِى اؤْتُمِنَ أَمَـٰنَتَهُ﴾$$

(then if one of you entrusts the other, let the one who is entrusted discharge his trust (faithfully).)

Ibn Abi Hatim recorded, with a sound chain of narration, that Abu Sa`id Al-Khudri said, "This Ayah abrogated what came before it (i.e. that which required recording the transaction and having witnesses present)." Ash-Sha`bi said, "If you trust each other, then there is no harm if you do not write the loan or have witnesses present." Allah's statement,

﴿وَلْيَتَّقِ اللَّهَ رَبَّهُ﴾

(And let him have Taqwa of Allah) means, the debtor.

Imam Ahmad and the Sunan recorded that Qatadah said that Al-Hasan said that Samurah said that the Messenger of Allah said,

«عَلَى الْيَدِ مَا أَخَذَتْ، حَتَّى تُؤَدِّيَه»

(The hand (of the debtor) will carry the burden of what it took until it gives it back.)

Allah's statement,

﴿وَلاَ تَكْتُمُواْ الشَّهَدَةَ﴾

(And conceal not the evidence) means, do not hide it or refuse to announce it. Ibn `Abbas and other scholars said, "False testimony is one of the worst of the major sins, and such is the case with hiding the true testimony. This is why Allah said,

﴿وَمَن يَكْتُمْهَا فَإِنَّهُ ءَاثِمٌ قَلْبُهُ﴾

(For he who hides it, surely, his heart is sinful).

As-Suddi commented, "Meaning he is a sinner in his heart."

This is similar to Allah's statement,

﴿وَلاَ نَكْتُمُ شَهَدَةَ اللَّهِ إِنَّآ إِذاً لَّمِنَ الأُثِمِينَ﴾

(We shall not hide testimony of Allah, for then indeed we should be of the sinful) 5}:106{.

Allah said,

﴿يَـأَيُّهَا الَّذِينَ ءَامَنُواْ كُونُواْ قَوَّامِينَ بِالْقِسْطِ شُهَدَاءِ للَّهِ وَلَوْ عَلَى أَنفُسِكُمْ أَوِ الْوَلِدَيْنِ وَالاُقْرَبِينَ إِن يَكُنْ غَنِيّاً أَوْ فَقِيراً فَاللَّهُ أَوْلَى بِهِمَا فَلاَ تَتَّبِعُواْ الْهَوَى أَن تَعْدِلُواْ وَإِن تَلْوُواْ أَوْ تُعْرِضُواْ فَإِنَّ اللَّهَ كَانَ بِمَا تَعْمَلُونَ خَبِيراً﴾

(O you who believe! Stand out firmly for justice, as witnesses to Allah, even though it be against yourselves, or your parents, or your kin, be he rich or poor, Allah is a better Protector to both (than you). So follow not the lusts (of your hearts), lest you avoid justice; and if you distort your witness or refuse to give it, verily, Allah is Ever Well-Acquainted with what you do) 4}:135 {and in this Ayah 2}:283 {He said,

﴿وَلاَ تَكْتُمُواْ الشَّهَدَةَ وَمَن يَكْتُمْهَا فَإِنَّهُ ءَاثِمٌ قَلْبُهُ وَاللَّهُ بِمَا تَعْمَلُونَ عَلِيمٌ﴾

(And conceal not the evidence, for he who hides it, surely, his heart is sinful. And Allah is All-Knower of what you do.)

These verses stipulate it is a crime to harm the witnesses for their testimony to contracts/wills and that it is sinful for them to falsely testify. Since the criminality of harming witnesses is so great then how much greater is the crime of harming witnesses/snitches who truthfully testify about crimes rather than contracts? Of course, false testimony is known as lying and as such is illegal and punishable but for snitches/witnesses to fear the repercussions of snitching is backwards. The matter should rightfully be that the criminals fear snitches more than the snitches fear backlash from criminals for testifying to the truth. Therefore it takes courage to fight crime correctly fulfilling the duty to the divine without committing crime when doing so.

Quran 3:3-4

نَزَّلَ عَلَيْكَ ٱلْكِتَـٰبَ بِٱلْحَقِّ مُصَدِّقًا لِّمَا بَيْنَ يَدَيْهِ وَأَنزَلَ ٱلتَّوْرَىٰةَ وَٱلْإِنجِيلَ (٣) مِن قَبْلُ هُدًى لِّلنَّاسِ وَأَنزَلَ ٱلْفُرْقَانَّ إِنَّ ٱلَّذِينَ كَفَرُواْ بِـَٔايَـٰتِ ٱللَّهِ لَهُمْ عَذَابٌ شَدِيدٌّ وَٱللَّهُ عَزِيزٌ ذُو ٱنتِقَامٍ (٤)

It is He Who has sent down the Book (the Qur'ân) to you (Muhammad) with truth, confirming what came before it. And he sent down the Taurât (Torah) and the Injeel (3) Aforetime, as a guidance to mankind, And He sent down the criterion [of judgement between right and wrong (this Qur'ân)]. Truly, those who disbelieve in the Ayât (proofs, evidences, verses, lessons, signs, revelations, etc.) of Allâh, for them there is a severe torment; and Allâh is All-Mighty, All-Able of Retribution. (4)

﴿نَزَّلَ عَلَيْكَ الْكِتَـٰبَ بِالْحَقِّ﴾

(It is He Who has sent down the Book to you with truth,) means, revealed the Qur'an to you, O Muhammad, in truth, meaning there is no doubt or suspicion that it is revealed from Allah. Verily, Allah revealed the Qur'an with His knowledge, and the angels testify to this fact, Allah is sufficient as a Witness. Allah's statement,

﴿مُصَدِّقاً لِّمَا بَيْنَ يَدَيْهِ﴾

(Confirming what came before it) means, from the previous divinely revealed Books, sent to the servants and Prophets of Allah. These Books testify to the truth of the Qur'an, and the Qur'an also testifies to the truth these Books contained, including the news and glad tidings of Muhammad's prophethood and the revelation of the Glorious Qur'an.

Allah said,

﴿وَأَنزَلَ التَّوْرَاةَ﴾

(And He sent down the Tawrah) to Musa (Musa) son of `Imran,

﴿وَالإِنجِيلَ﴾

(And the Injil), to `Isa, son of Mary,

﴿مِن قَبْلُ﴾

(Aforetime) meaning, before the Qur'an was revealed,

﴿هُدًى لِّلنَّاسِ﴾

(As a guidance to mankind) in their time.

﴿وَأَنزَلَ الْفُرْقَانَ﴾

(And He sent down the criterion) which is the distinction between misguidance, falsehood and deviation on one hand, and guidance, truth and piety on the other hand.

This is because of the indications, signs, plain evidences and clear proofs that it contains, and because of its explanations, clarifications, etc.

Allah's statement,

$$﴿إِنَّ الَّذِينَ كَفَرُواْ بِأَيَـتِ اللَّهِ﴾$$

(Truly, those who disbelieve in the Ayat of Allah) means they denied, refused and unjustly rejected them,

$$﴿لَهُمْ عَذَابٌ شَدِيدٌ﴾$$

(For them there is a severe torment) on the Day of Resurrection,

$$﴿وَاللَّهُ عَزِيزٌ﴾$$

(And Allah is All-Mighty) meaning, His grandeur is invincible and His sovereignty is infinite,

$$﴿ذُو انتِقَامٍ﴾$$

(All-Able of Retribution.) from those who reject His Ayat and defy His honorable Messengers and great Prophets.

These verses inform us that the Scripture/Revelations sent down by God clarify what is right and wrong. Meaning it's not up to us or our environment or historical/political norms to choose what is criminal or not that would merit snitching or not or whether snitching is good or bad. So the snitching action as well as what is snitched on overall is determined by the criteria set forth by God via texts of revelation. It is the Creator of the Universe who determines virtue and vice and the greatest testimony is the testimony exposing the falsehood of false religions and the true correctness of the prophetic faith. Yet this testimony is incomplete if merely denoted as speech without the actions to verify and confirm it. Thus in a very real sense the call to believe is in fact a snitching on all the falsehood contrived by Satan. All the prophets snitched on Satan's greatest crimes.

Quran 3:7

هُوَ ٱلَّذِىٓ أَنزَلَ عَلَيْكَ ٱلْكِتَٰبَ مِنْهُ ءَايَٰتٌ مُّحْكَمَٰتٌ هُنَّ أُمُّ ٱلْكِتَٰبِ وَأُخَرُ مُتَشَٰبِهَٰتٌ فَأَمَّا ٱلَّذِينَ فِى قُلُوبِهِمْ زَيْغٌ فَيَتَّبِعُونَ مَا تَشَٰبَهَ مِنْهُ ٱبْتِغَآءَ ٱلْفِتْنَةِ وَٱبْتِغَآءَ تَأْوِيلِهِۦ وَمَا يَعْلَمُ تَأْوِيلَهُۥٓ إِلَّا ٱللَّهُ وَٱلرَّٰسِخُونَ فِى ٱلْعِلْمِ يَقُولُونَ ءَامَنَّا بِهِۦ كُلٌّ مِّنْ عِندِ رَبِّنَا وَمَا يَذَّكَّرُ إِلَّآ أُو۟لُوا۟ ٱلْأَلْبَٰبِ (٧)

It is He Who has sent down to you (Muhammad) the Book (this Qur'ân). In it are Verses that are entirely clear, they are the foundations of the Book [and those are the Verses of Al-Ahkâm (commandments), Al-Farâ'id (obligatory duties) and Al-Hudud (legal laws for the punishment of thieves, adulterers)]; and others not entirely clear. So as for those in whose hearts there is a deviation (from the truth) they follow that which is not entirely clear thereof, seeking Al-Fitnah (polytheism and trials), and seeking for its hidden meanings, but none knows its hidden meanings save Allâh. And those who are firmly grounded in knowledge say: "We believe in it; the whole of it (clear and unclear Verses) are from our Lord." And none receive admonition except men of understanding. (7)

Allah states that in the Qur'an, there are Ayat that are Muhkamat, entirely clear and plain, and these are the foundations of the Book which are plain for everyone. And there are Ayat in the Qur'an that are Mutashabihat not entirely clear for many, or some people. So those who refer to the Muhkam Ayat to understand the Mutashabih Ayat, will have acquired the correct guidance, and vice versa. This is why Allah said,

﴿هُنَّ أُمُّ الْكِتَـبِ﴾

(They are the foundations of the Book), meaning, they are the basis of the Qur'an, and should be referred to for clarification, when warranted,

﴿وَأُخَرُ مُتَشَـبِهَـتٌ﴾

(And others not entirely clear) as they have several meanings, some that agree with the Muhkam and some that carry other literal indications, although these meaning might not be desired.

The Muhkamat are the Ayat that explain the abrogating rulings, the allowed, prohibited, laws, limits, obligations and rulings that should be believed in and implemented. As for the Mutashabihat Ayat, they include the abrogated Ayat, parables, oaths, and what should be believed in, but not implemented.

Muhammad bin Ishaq bin Yasar commented on,

﴿مِنْهُ آيَـتٌ مُّحْكَمَـتٌ﴾

(In it are verses that are entirely clear) as "Containing proof of the Lord, immunity for the servants and a refutation of opponents and of falsehood. They cannot be changed or altered from what they were meant for." He also said, "As for the unclear Ayat, they can (but must not) be altered and changed, and this is a test from Allah to the servants, just as He tested them with the allowed and prohibited things. So these Ayat must not be altered to imply a false meaning or be distorted from the truth."

Therefore, Allah said,

﴿فَأَمَّا الَّذِينَ فِى قُلُوبِهِمْ زَيْغٌ﴾

(So as for those in whose hearts there is a deviation) meaning, those who are misguided and deviate from truth to falsehood,

﴿فَيَتَّبِعُونَ مَا تَشَبَهَ مِنْهُ﴾

(they follow that which is not entirely clear thereof) meaning, they refer to the Mutashabih, because they are able to alter its meanings to conform with their false interpretation since the wordings of the Mutashabihat encompass such a wide area of meanings. As for the Muhkam Ayat, they cannot be altered because they are clear and, thus, constitute unequivocal proof against the misguided people. This is why Allah said,

﴿ابْتِغَاءَ الْفِتْنَةِ﴾

(seeking Al-Fitnah) meaning, they seek to misguide their following by pretending to prove their innovation by relying on the Qur'an -- the Mutashabih of it -- but, this is proof against and not for them. For instance, Christians might claim that ﴿Isa is divine because ﴿the Qur'an states that he is Ruhullah and His Word, which He gave to Mary, all the while ignoring Allah's statements,

﴿إِنْ هُوَ إِلاَّ عَبْدٌ أَنْعَمْنَا عَلَيْهِ﴾

(He ﴾`Isa ﴿ was not more than a servant. We granted Our favor to him.) 43﴾:59﴿, and,

﴿ إِنَّ مَثَلَ عِيسَى عِندَ اللَّهِ كَمَثَلِ ءَادَمَ خَلَقَهُ مِن تُرَابٍ ثُمَّ قَالَ لَهُ كُن فَيَكُونُ ﴾

(Verily, the likeness of `Isa before Allah is the likeness of Adam. He created him from dust, then (He) said to him: "Be!" and he was.) 3﴾:59﴿.

There are other Ayat that clearly assert that `Isa is but one of Allah's creatures and that he is the servant and Messenger of Allah, among other Messengers.

Allah's statement,

﴿ وَابْتِغَاءَ تَأْوِيلِهِ ﴾

(And seeking for its Ta'wil,) to alter them as they desire. Imam Ahmad recorded that `A'ishah said, "The Messenger of Allah recited,

﴿ هُوَ الَّذِى أَنزَلَ عَلَيْكَ الْكِتَـبَ مِنْهُ آيَـتٌ مُّحْكَمَـتٌ هُنَّ أُمُّ الْكِتَـبِ وَأُخَرُ مُتَشَـبِهَـتٌ ﴾

(It is He Who has sent down to you the Book. In it are verses that are entirely clear, they are the foundations of the Book; and others not entirely clear,), until,

﴿ أُوْلُواْ الأَلْبَـبِ ﴾

(Men of understanding) and he said,

« فَإِذَا رَأَيْتُمُ الَّذِينَ يُجَادِلُونَ فِيهِ، فَهُمُ الَّذِينَ عَنَى اللهُ، فَاحْذَرُوهُمْ »

(When you see those who argue in it (using the Mutashabihat), then they are those whom Allah meant. Therefore, beware of them.)"

Al-Bukhari recorded a similar Hadith in the Tafsir of this Ayah, as did Muslim in the book of Qadar (the Divine Will) in his Sahih, and Abu Dawud in the Sunnah section of his Sunan, from `A'ishah; "The Messenger of Allah recited this Ayah,

﴿هُوَ الَّذِى أَنزَلَ عَلَيْكَ الْكِتَبَ مِنْهُ آيَتٌ مُّحْكَمَتٌ﴾

(It is He Who has sent down to you the Book. In it are verses that are entirely clear,) until,

﴿وَمَا يَذَّكَّرُ إِلاَّ أُوْلُواْ الأَلْبَـبِ﴾

(And none receive admonition except men of understanding.)

He then said,

«فَإِذَا رَأَيْتِ الَّذِينَ يَتَّبِعُونَ مَا تَشَابَهَ مِنْهُ؛ فَأُولئِكَ الَّذِينَ سَمَّى اللهُ، فَاحْذَرُوهُم»

(When you see those who follow what is not so clear of the Qur'an, then they are those whom Allah described, so beware of them.)"

This is the wording recorded by Al-Bukhari.

Allah said,

﴿وَمَا يَعْلَمُ تَأْوِيلَهُ إِلاَّ اللَّهُ﴾

(But none knows its Ta'wil except Allah.)

Similarly, as preceded in what has been reported from Ibn `Abbas, "Tafsir is of four types: Tafsir that the Arabs know in their language; Tafsir that no one is excused of being ignorant of; Tafsir that the scholars know; and Tafsir that only Allah knows." Scholars of Qur'an recitation have different opinions about pausing at Allah's Name in this Ayah. This stop was reported from `A'ishah, `Urwah, Abu Ash-Sha`tha' and Abu Nahik.

Some pause after reciting,

﴿وَالرَسِخُونَ فِي الْعِلْمِ﴾

(And those who are firmly grounded in knowledge) saying that the Qur'an does not address the people with what they cannot understand. Ibn Abi Najih said that Mujahid said that Ibn `Abbas said, "I am among those who are firmly grounded in its Ta'wil interpretation." The Messenger of Allah supplicated for the benefit of Ibn `Abbas,

«اللَّهُمَّ فَقِّهْهُ فِي الدِّينِ وَعَلِّمْهُ التَّأْوِيلَ»

(O Allah! Bestow on him knowledge in the religion and teach him the Ta'wil (interpretation).)

Ta'wil has two meanings in the Qur'an, the true reality of things, and what they will turn out to be. For instance, Allah said,

﴿وَقَالَ يأَبَتِ هَذَا تَأْوِيلُ رُؤْيَـى مِن قَبْلُ﴾

(And he said: "O my father! This is the Ta'wil of my dream aforetime!".), and,

﴿هَلْ يَنظُرُونَ إِلاَّ تَأْوِيلَهُ يَوْمَ يَأْتِى تَأْوِيلُهُ﴾

(Await they just for it's Ta'wil On the Day (Day of Resurrection) it's Ta'wil is finally fulfillled.)(7:53) refers to the true reality of Resurrection that they were told about. If this is the meaning desired in the Ayah above, then pausing after reciting Allah's Name is warranted, because only Allah knows the true reality of things. In this case, Allah's statement,

﴿وَالرَّسِخُونَ فِي الْعِلْمِ﴾

(And those who are firmly grounded in knowledge) is connected to His statement,

﴿يَقُولُونَ ءَامَنَّا بِهِ﴾

(say: "We believe in it") If the word Ta'wil means the second meaning, that is, explaining and describing, such as what Allah said,

﴿نَبِّئْنَا بِتَأْوِيلِهِ﴾

((They said): "Inform us of the Ta'wil of this") meaning its explanation, then pausing after reciting,

﴿وَالرَّسِخُونَ فِي الْعِلْمِ﴾

(And those who are firmly grounded in knowledge) is warranted. This is because the scholars have general knowledge in, and understand what they were addressed with, even though they do not have knowledge of the true reality of things. Therefore, Allah's statement,

﴿يَقُولُونَ ءَامَنَّا بِهِ﴾

(say: "We believe in it") describes the conduct of the scholars. Similarly, Allah said,

﴿وَجَآءَ رَبُّكَ وَالْمَلَكُ صَفًّا صَفًّا﴾

(And your Lord comes, and the angels, in rows.) means, your Lord will come, and the angels will come in rows.

Allah's statement that the knowledgeable people proclaim,

$$﴿يَقُولُونَ ءَامَنَّا بِهِ﴾$$

(We believe in it) means, they believe in the Mutashabih.

$$﴿كُلٌّ مِّنْ عِندِ رَبِّنَا﴾$$

(all of it is from our Lord) meaning, both the Muhkam and the Mutashabih are true and authentic, and each one of them testifies to the truth of the other.

All of the revelation of the Quran is from the Creator and therefore relevant for us and to be believed in. As has been said before, belief includes actions and to disbelieve in any part of revelation is to disbelieve period. Thus while this book is specialized around snitching this verse labels all verses as meriting our adherence to. Therefore there is no such thing as believing in the Quran but simultaneously being anti-snitching because believing in the Quran involves the snitching aspect as well or else one doesn't really believe in all of the Quran. Yet how many believe and claim to believe in all of the Quran and then want others to act instead of themselves while maintaining they believe and act accordingly? Such is indicative of a trait of hypocrisy because one either does or doesn't there is no middle ground between belief and disbelief or half credit. If you believe in all of it then you act accordingly to all of it or at the least are working towards acting accordingly hoping to die successful upon that endeavor. Perfection and 100% adherence 100% of the time is impossible but it's not required, however the intentions are required. Meaning one must intend to be perfectly in compliance with the commands of God and then the sincerity will eventually turn to reality once blessed and aided towards the path of guidance by God.

Quran 3:23

أَلَمْ تَرَ إِلَى ٱلَّذِينَ أُوتُواْ نَصِيبًا مِّنَ ٱلْكِتَبِ يُدْعَوْنَ إِلَىٰ كِتَبِ ٱللَّهِ لِيَحْكُمَ بَيْنَهُمْ ثُمَّ يَتَوَلَّىٰ فَرِيقٌ مِّنْهُمْ وَهُم مُّعْرِضُونَ (٢٣)

Have you not seen those who have been given a portion of the Scripture? They are being invited to the Book of Allâh to settle their dispute, then a party of them turn away, and they are averse. (23)

Allah criticizes the Jews and Christians who claim to follow their Books, the Tawrah and the Injil, because when they are called to refer to these Books where Allah commanded them to follow Muhammad, they turn away with aversion. This censure and criticism from Allah was all because of their defiance and rejection.

This verse stipulates those who turn away from the Book of Allah, ie the Quran, are averse. Meaning anyone who turns away from Quranic resolutions is averse even if they claim to be Muslim following Islam and doing deeds of Islam to match. Thus when we have a dispute regarding something in this world it is incumbent upon believers to refer accordingly to resolve it rather than use secular laws or laws of other false religions. So regarding the issue of snitching the only important information on the subject is the prophetic revelation of the Quran and Sunnah which form the Shariah and anything else is irrelevant and should not be a factor worth consideration. Because otherwise one is averse to Allah and being averse is equivalent to being an enemy of God aka non-Muslim. You may wonder why write a book on snitching? It's because this overlooked aspect is really that important. People disagree on snitching and turn away from the Islamic injunctions regarding its obligation instead choosing to follow their desires knowingly or unknowingly and this is wrong for all who do so. Hence a microscopic type of analysis on the issue is necessary to clarify and I hope to be helped to prove the virtue and necessity of the practice to revive the goodness inshallah.

Quran 3:104-105

وَلْتَكُن مِّنكُمْ أُمَّةٌ يَدْعُونَ إِلَى ٱلْخَيْرِ وَيَأْمُرُونَ بِٱلْمَعْرُوفِ وَيَنْهَوْنَ عَنِ ٱلْمُنكَرِ ۚ وَأُوْلَٰٓئِكَ هُمُ ٱلْمُفْلِحُونَ (١٠٤) وَلَا تَكُونُواْ كَٱلَّذِينَ تَفَرَّقُواْ وَٱخْتَلَفُواْ مِنْ بَعْدِ مَا جَآءَهُمُ ٱلْبَيِّنَٰتُ ۚ وَأُوْلَٰٓئِكَ لَهُمْ عَذَابٌ عَظِيمٌ (١٠٥)

Let there arise out of you a group of people inviting to all that is good (Islâm), enjoining Al-Ma'rûf (i.e. Islâmic Monotheism and all that Islâm orders one to do) and forbidding Al-Munkar (polytheism and disbelief and all that Islâm has forbidden). And it is they who are the successful. (104) And be not as those who divided and differed among themselves after the clear proofs had come to them. It is they for whom there is an awful torment. (105)

Allah said,

﴿وَلْتَكُن مِّنْكُمْ أُمَّةٌ﴾

(Let there arise out of you a group of people)

that calls to righteousness, enjoins all that is good and forbids evil in the manner Allah commanded,

$$﴿وَأُوْلَـئِكَ هُمُ الْمُفْلِحُونَ﴾$$

(And it is they who are the successful.)

Ad-Dahhak said, "They are a special group of the Companions and a special group of those after them, that is those who perform Jihad and the scholars."

The objective of this Ayah is that there should be a segment of this Muslim Ummah fulfilling this task, even though it is also an obligation on every member of this Ummah, each according to his ability. Muslim recorded that Abu Hurayrah said that the Messenger of Allah said,

$$«مَنْ رَأَى مِنْكُمْ مُنْكَرًا فَلْيُغَيِّرْهُ بِيَدِهِ، فَإِنْ لَمْ يَسْتَطِعْ فَبِلِسَانِهِ، فَإِنْ لَمْ يَسْتَطِعْ فَبِقَلْبِهِ، وَذلِكَ أَضْعَفُ الْإِيمَانِ»$$

(Whoever among you witnesses an evil, let him change it with his hand. If he is unable, then let him change it with his tongue. If he is unable, then let him change it with his heart, and this is the weakest faith.) In another narration, The Prophet said,

$$«وَلَيْسَ وَرَاءَ ذَلِكَ مِنَ الْإِيمَانِ حَبَّةُ خَرْدَل»$$

(There is no faith beyond that, not even the weight of a mustard seed.)

Imam Ahmad recorded that Hudhayfah bin Al-Yaman said that the Prophet said,

$$«وَالَّذِي نَفْسِي بِيَدِهِ، لَتَأْمُرُنَّ بِالْمَعْرُوفِ، وَلَتَنْهَوُنَّ عَنِ الْمُنْكَرِ، أَوْ لَيُوشِكَنَّ اللهُ أَنْ يَبْعَثَ عَلَيْكُمْ عِقَابًا مِنْ عِنْدِهِ، ثُمَّ لَتَدْعُنَّـهُ فَلَا يَسْتَجِيبَ لَكُمْ»$$

(By He in Whose Hand is my soul! You will enjoin righteousness and forbid evil, or Allah shall send down a punishment from Him to you. Then, you will supplicate to Him, but He will not accept your supplication.)

At-Tirmidhi also collected this Hadith and said, "Hasan". There are many other Hadiths and Ayat on this subject, which will be explained later.

Allah said,

﴿وَلاَ تَكُونُواْ كَالَّذِينَ تَفَرَّقُواْ وَاخْتَلَفُواْ مِن بَعْدِ مَا جَاءَهُمُ الْبَيِّنَـتُ﴾

(And be not as those who divided and differed among themselves after the clear proofs had come to them)

In this Ayah, Allah forbids this Ummah from imitating the division and discord of the nations that came before them. These nations also abandoned enjoining righteousness and forbidding evil, although they had proof of its necessity.

Imam Ahmad recorded that Abu `Amir `Abdullah bin Luhay said, "We performed Hajj with Mu`awiyah bin Abi Sufyan. When we arrived at Makkah, he stood up after praying Zuhr and said, `The Messenger of Allah said,

«إِنَّ أَهْلَ الْكِتَابَيْنِ افْتَرَقُوا فِي دِينِهِمْ عَلَى ثِنْتَيْنِ وَسَبْعِينَ مِلَّةً، وَإِنَّ هَذِهِ الْأُمَّةَ سَتَفْتَرِقُ عَلَى ثَلَاثٍ وَسَبْعِينَ مِلَّةً يَعْنِي الْأَهْوَاءَ كُلُّهَا فِي النَّارِ إِلَّا وَاحِدَةً وَهِيَ الْجَمَاعَةُ وَإِنَّهُ سَيَخْرُجُ فِي أُمَّتِي أَقْوَامٌ تَجَارَى بِهِمْ تِلْكَ الْأَهْوَاءُ كَمَا يَتَجَارَى الْكَلَبُ بِصَاحِبِهِ، لَا يَبْقَى مِنْهُ عِرْقٌ وَلَا مَفْصِلٌ إِلَّا دَخَلَهُ»

(The People of the Two Scriptures divided into seventy-two sects. This Ummah will divide into seventy-three sects, all in the Fire except one, that is, the Jama`ah. Some of my Ummah will be guided by desire, like one who is infected by rabies; no vein or joint will be saved from these desires.)

Mu`awiyah said next: By Allah, O Arabs! If you do not adhere to what came to you from your Prophet then other people are even more prone not to adhere to it. " Similar was recorded by Abu Dawud from Ahmad bin Hanbal and Muhammad bin Yahya.

This verse as well as the next verse instructs us that the successful faithful are those who enjoin what is good and forbid what is evil, in all-encompassing totality, without dividing into partisan sectarian divisions or differing about what is good and what is evil. Whereas snitching is a type of forbidding what is evil.

Quran 3:114

يُؤْمِنُونَ بِٱللَّهِ وَٱلْيَوْمِ ٱلْءَاخِرِ وَيَأْمُرُونَ بِٱلْمَعْرُوفِ وَيَنْهَوْنَ عَنِ ٱلْمُنكَرِ وَيُسَـٰرِعُونَ فِى ٱلْخَيْرَٰتِ وَأُوْلَـٰئِكَ مِنَ ٱلصَّـٰلِحِينَ (١١٤)

They believe in Allâh and the Last Day; they enjoin Al-Ma'rûf (Islâmic Monotheism, and following Prophet Muhammad) and forbid Al-Munkar (polytheism, disbelief and opposing Prophet Muhammad); and they hasten in (all) good works; and they are among the righteous. (114)

Quran 4:58-66

۞ إِنَّ ٱللَّهَ يَأْمُرُكُمْ أَن تُؤَدُّواْ ٱلْأَمَـٰنَـٰتِ إِلَىٰٓ أَهْلِهَا وَإِذَا حَكَمْتُم بَيْنَ ٱلنَّاسِ أَن تَحْكُمُواْ بِٱلْعَدْلِ إِنَّ ٱللَّهَ نِعِمَّا يَعِظُكُم بِهِۦٓ إِنَّ ٱللَّهَ كَانَ سَمِيعًا بَصِيرًا (٥٨) يَـٰٓأَيُّهَا ٱلَّذِينَ ءَامَنُوٓاْ أَطِيعُواْ ٱللَّهَ وَأَطِيعُواْ ٱلرَّسُولَ وَأُوْلِى ٱلْأَمْرِ مِنكُمْ فَإِن تَنَـٰزَعْتُمْ فِى شَىْءٍ فَرُدُّوهُ إِلَى ٱللَّهِ وَٱلرَّسُولِ إِن كُنتُمْ تُؤْمِنُونَ بِٱللَّهِ وَٱلْيَوْمِ ٱلْءَاخِرِ ذَٰلِكَ خَيْرٌ وَأَحْسَنُ تَأْوِيلاً (٥٩) أَلَمْ تَرَ

إِلَى ٱلَّذِينَ يَزْعُمُونَ أَنَّهُمْ ءَامَنُواْ بِمَآ أُنزِلَ إِلَيْكَ وَمَآ أُنزِلَ مِن قَبْلِكَ يُرِيدُونَ أَن يَتَحَاكَمُوٓاْ إِلَى ٱلطَّٰغُوتِ وَقَدْ أُمِرُوٓاْ أَن يَكْفُرُواْ بِهِۦ وَيُرِيدُ ٱلشَّيْطَٰنُ أَن يُضِلَّهُمْ ضَلَٰلاً بَعِيدًا (٦٠) وَإِذَا قِيلَ لَهُمْ تَعَالَوْاْ إِلَىٰ مَآ أَنزَلَ ٱللَّهُ وَإِلَى ٱلرَّسُولِ رَأَيْتَ ٱلْمُنَٰفِقِينَ يَصُدُّونَ عَنكَ صُدُودًا (٦١) فَكَيْفَ إِذَآ أَصَٰبَتْهُم مُّصِيبَةٌۢ بِمَا قَدَّمَتْ أَيْدِيهِمْ ثُمَّ جَآءُوكَ يَحْلِفُونَ بِٱللَّهِ إِنْ أَرَدْنَآ إِلَّآ إِحْسَٰنًا وَتَوْفِيقًا (٦٢) أُوْلَٰٓئِكَ ٱلَّذِينَ يَعْلَمُ ٱللَّهُ مَا فِى قُلُوبِهِمْ فَأَعْرِضْ عَنْهُمْ وَعِظْهُمْ وَقُل لَّهُمْ فِىٓ أَنفُسِهِمْ قَوْلاَۢ بَلِيغًا (٦٣) وَمَآ أَرْسَلْنَا مِن رَّسُولٍ إِلَّا لِيُطَاعَ بِإِذْنِ ٱللَّهِ وَلَوْ أَنَّهُمْ إِذ ظَّلَمُوٓاْ أَنفُسَهُمْ جَآءُوكَ فَٱسْتَغْفَرُواْ ٱللَّهَ وَٱسْتَغْفَرَ لَهُمُ ٱلرَّسُولُ لَوَجَدُواْ ٱللَّهَ تَوَّابًا رَّحِيمًا (٦٤) فَلَا وَرَبِّكَ لَا يُؤْمِنُونَ حَتَّىٰ يُحَكِّمُوكَ فِيمَا شَجَرَ بَيْنَهُمْ ثُمَّ لَا يَجِدُواْ فِىٓ أَنفُسِهِمْ حَرَجًا مِّمَّا قَضَيْتَ وَيُسَلِّمُواْ تَسْلِيمًا (٦٥) وَلَوْ أَنَّا كَتَبْنَا عَلَيْهِمْ أَنِ ٱقْتُلُوٓاْ أَنفُسَكُمْ أَوِ ٱخْرُجُواْ مِن دِيَٰرِكُم مَّا فَعَلُوهُ إِلَّا قَلِيلٌ مِّنْهُمْ وَلَوْ أَنَّهُمْ فَعَلُواْ مَا يُوعَظُونَ بِهِۦ لَكَانَ خَيْرًا لَّهُمْ وَأَشَدَّ تَثْبِيتًا (٦٦)

Verily! Allâh commands that you should render back the trusts to those, to whom they are due; and that when you judge between men, you judge with justice. Verily, how excellent is the teaching which He (Allâh) gives you! Truly, Allâh is Ever All¬Hearer, All¬Seer. (58) O you who believe! Obey Allâh and obey the Messenger (Muhammad), and those of you (Muslims) who are in authority. (And) if you differ in anything amongst yourselves, refer it to Allâh and His Messenger, if you believe in Allâh and in the Last Day. That is better and more suitable for final determination. (59) Have you seen those (hypocrites) who claim that they believe in that which has been sent down to you, and that which was sent down before you, and they wish to go for judgement (in their disputes) to the Tâghût (false judges) while they have been ordered to reject them. But Shaitân (Satan) wishes to lead them far astray.(60) And when it is said to them: "Come to what Allâh has sent down and to the Messenger (Muhammad)," you (Muhammad) see the hypocrites turn away from you (Muhammad) with aversion (61) How then, when a catastrophe befalls them because of what their hands have sent forth, they come to you swearing by

Allâh, "We meant no more than goodwill and conciliation!"
(62) They (hypocrites) are those of whom Allâh knows what is
in their hearts; so turn aside from them (do not punish them)
but admonish them, and speak to them an effective word (i.e. to
believe in Allâh, worship Him, obey Him, and be afraid of Him)
to reach their inner selves (63) We sent no Messenger, but to be
obeyed by Allâh's Leave. If they (hypocrites), when they had
been unjust to themselves, had come to you (Muhammad) and
begged Allâh's Forgiveness, and the Messenger had begged
forgiveness for them: indeed, they would have found Allâh All-
Forgiving (One Who forgives and accepts repentance), Most
Merciful. (64) But no, by your Lord, they can have no Faith,
until they make you (O Muhammad) judge in all disputes
between them, and find in themselves no resistance against
your decisions, and accept (them) with full submission.
(65) And if We had ordered them (saying), "Kill yourselves (i.e.
the innocent ones kill the guilty ones) or leave your homes,"
very few of them would have done it; but if they had done what
they were told, it would have been better for them, and would
have strengthened their (Faith); (66)

Allah commands that the trusts be returned to their
rightful owners. Al-Hasan narrated that Samurah said
that the Messenger of Allah said,

«أَدِّ الْأَمَانَةَ إِلى مَنِ انْتَمَنَكَ، وَلَا تَخُنْ مَنْ خَانَكَ»

(Return the trust to those who entrusted you, and do not
betray those who betrayed you.) Imam Ahmad and the
collectors of Sunan recorded this Hadith. This command
refers to all things that one is expected to look after, such
as Allah's rights on His servants: praying, Zakah, fasting,

penalties for sins, vows and so forth. The command also includes the rights of the servants on each other, such as what they entrust each other with, including the cases that are not recorded or documented. Allah commands that all types of trusts be fulfilled. Those who do not implement this command in this life, it will be extracted from them on the Day of Resurrection. It is recorded in the Sahih that the Messenger of Allah said,

«لَتُؤَدَّنَّ الْحُقُوقُ إِلَى أَهْلِهَا حَتَّى يُقْتَصَّ لِلشَّاةِ الْجَمَّاءِ مِنَ الْقَرْنَاءِ»

(The rights will be rendered back to those to whom they are due, and even the sheep that does not have horns will take revenge from the horned sheep.) Ibn Jarir recorded that Ibn Jurayj said about this Ayah, "It was revealed concerning `Uthman bin Talhah from whom the Messenger of Allah took the key of the Ka`bah and entered it on the Day of the victory of Makkah. When the Prophet went out, he was reciting this Ayah,

﴿إِنَّ اللَّهَ يَأْمُرُكُمْ أَن تُؤدُّواْ الاحَمَـنَـتِ إِلَى أَهْلِهَا﴾

(Verily, Allah commands that you should render back the trusts to those, to whom they are due). He then called `Uthman and gave the key back to him." Ibn Jarir also narrated that `Umar bin Al-Khattab said, "When the Messenger of Allah went out of the Ka`bah, he was reciting this Ayah,

﴿إِنَّ اللَّهَ يَأْمُرُكُمْ أَن تُؤدُّواْ الاحَمَـنَـتِ إِلَى أَهْلِهَا﴾

(Verily, Allah commands that you should render back the trusts to those, to whom they are due). May I sacrifice my father and mother for him, I never heard him recite this Ayah before that." It is popular that this is the reason behind revealing the Ayah (4:58). Yet, the application of the Ayah is general, and this is why Ibn `Abbas and Muhammad bin Al-Hanafiyyah said, "This Ayah is for the righteous and wicked," meaning it is a command that encompasses everyone.

Allah said,

﴿وَإِذَا حَكَمْتُم بَيْنَ النَّاسِ أَن تَحْكُمُواْ بِالْعَدْلِ﴾

(and that when you judge between men, you judge with justice.) commanding justice when judging between people. Muhammad bin Ka`b, Zayd bin Aslam and Shahr bin Hawshab said; "This Ayah was revealed about those in authority", meaning those who judge between people. A Hadith states,

«إِنَّ اللهَ مَعَ الْحَاكِمِ مَا لَمْ يَجُرْ، فَإِذَا جَارَ وَكَلَهُ اللهُ إِلَى نَفْسِه»

(Allah is with the judge as long as he does not commit injustice, for when he does, Allah will make him reliant on himself.) A statement goes, "One day of justice equals forty years of worship." Allah said,

﴿إِنَّ اللَّهَ نِعِمَّا يَعِظُكُم بِهِ﴾

(Verily, how excellent is the teaching which He (Allah) gives you!) meaning, His commands to return the trusts to their owners, to judge between people with justice, and all of His complete, perfect and great commandments and laws.

Al-Bukhari recorded that Ibn `Abbas said that the Ayah,

﴿أَطِيعُواْ اللَّهَ وَأَطِيعُواْ الرَّسُولَ وَأُوْلِى الأٌمْرِ مِنْكُمْ﴾

(Obey Allah and obey the Messenger, and those of you who are in authority.) "Was revealed about `Abdullah bin Hudhafah bin Qays bin `Adi, who the Messenger of Allah sent on a military expedition." This statement was collected by the Group, with the exception of Ibn Majah At-Tirmidhi said, "Hasan, Gharib". Imam Ahmad recorded that `Ali said, "The Messenger of Allah sent a troop under the command of a man from Al-Ansar. When they left, he became angry with them for some reason and said to them, `Has not the Messenger of Allah commanded you to obey me' They said, `Yes.' He said, `Collect some wood,' and then he started a fire with the wood, saying, `I command you to enter the fire.' The people almost entered the fire, but a young man among them said, `You only ran away from the Fire to Allah's Messenger. Therefore, do not rush until you go back to Allah's Messenger, and if he commands you to enter it, then enter it.' When they went back to Allah's Messenger, they told him what had happened, and the Messenger said,

«لَوْ دَخَلْتُمُوهَا مَا خَرَجْتُمْ مِنْهَا أَبَدًا، إِنَّمَا الطَّاعَةُ فِي الْمَعْرُوفِ»

(Had you entered it, you would never have departed from it. Obedience is only in righteousness.)" This Hadith is recorded in the Two Sahihs. Abu Dawud recorded that `Abdullah bin `Umar said that the Messenger of Allah said,

«السَّمْعُ وَالطَّاعَةُ عَلَى الْمَرْءِ الْمُسْلِمِ فِيمَا أَحَبَّ وَكَرِهَ، مَا لَمْ يُؤْمَرْ بِمَعْصِيَةٍ، فَإِذَا أُمِرَ بِمَعْصِيَةٍ فَلَا سَمْعَ وَلَا طَاعَةَ»

(The Muslim is required to hear and obey in that which he likes and dislikes, unless he was commanded to sin. When he is commanded with sin, then there is no hearing or obeying.) This Hadith is recorded in the Two Sahihs. `Ubadah bin As-Samit said, "We gave our pledge to Allah's Messenger to hear and obey (our leaders), while active and otherwise, in times of ease and times of difficulty, even if we were deprived of our due shares, and to not dispute this matter (leadership) with its rightful people. The Prophet said,

«إِلَّا أَنْ تَرَوْا كُفْرًا بَوَاحًا، عِنْدَكُمْ فِيهِ مِنَ اللهِ بُرْهَان»

(Except when you witness clear Kufr about which you have clear proof from Allah.)" This Hadith is recorded in the Two Sahihs. Another Hadith narrated by Anas states that the Messenger of Allah said,

«اسْمَعُوا وَأَطِيعُوا، وَإِنْ أُمِّرَ عَلَيْكُمْ عَبْدٌ حَبَشِيٌّ كَأَنَّ رَأْسَهُ زَبِيبَة»

(Hear and obey (your leaders), even if an Ethiopian slave whose head is like a raisin, is made your chief.) Al-Bukhari recorded this Hadith. Umm Al-Husayn said that she heard the Messenger of Allah giving a speech during the Farewell Hajj, in which he said;

«وَلَوِ اسْتُعْمِلَ عَلَيْكُمْ عَبْدٌ يَقُودُكُمْ بِكِتَابِ اللهِ، اسْمَعُوا لَهُ وَأَطِيعُوا»

(Even if a slave was appointed over you, and he rules you with Allah's Book, then listen to him and obey him.)

Muslim recorded this Hadith. In another narration with Muslim, the Prophet said,

«عَبْدًا حَبَشِيًّا مَجْدُوعًا»

(Even if an Ethiopian slave, whose nose was mutilated...) In the Two Sahihs, it is recorded that Abu Hurayrah said that the Messenger of Allah said,

«مَنْ أَطَاعَنِي فَقَدْ أَطَاعَ اللهَ، وَمَنْ عَصَانِي فَقَدْ عَصَى اللهَ، وَمَنْ أَطَاعَ أَمِيرِي فَقَدْ أَطَاعَنِي، وَمَنْ عَصَى أَمِيرِي فَقَدْ عَصَانِي»

(Whoever obeys me, obeys Allah, and whoever disobeys me, disobeys Allah. Whoever obeys my commander, obeys me, and whoever disobeys my commander, disobeys me.) This is why Allah said,

﴿أَطِيعُواْ اللَّهَ﴾

(Obey Allah), adhere to His Book,

﴿وَأَطِيعُواْ الرَّسُولَ﴾

(and obey the Messenger), adhere to his Sunnah,

﴿وَأُوْلِى الأّمْرِ مِنْكُمْ﴾

(And those of you who are in authority) in the obedience to Allah which they command you, not what constitutes disobedience of Allah, for there is no obedience to anyone in disobedience to Allah, as we mentioned in the authentic Hadith,

«إِنَّمَا الطَّاعَةُ فِي الْمَعْرُوفِ»

(Obedience is only in righteousness.)

Allah said,

$$﴿فَإِن تَنَازَعْتُمْ فِى شَىْءٍ فَرُدُّوهُ إِلَى اللَّهِ وَالرَّسُولِ﴾$$

((And) if you differ in anything amongst yourselves, refer it to Allah and His Messenger). Mujahid and several others among the Salaf said that the Ayah means, "(Refer) to the Book of Allah and the Sunnah of His Messenger." This is a command from Allah that whatever areas the people dispute about, whether major or minor areas of the religion, they are required to refer to the Qur'an and Sunnah for judgment concerning these disputes. In another Ayah, Allah said,

$$﴿وَمَا اخْتَلَفْتُمْ فِيهِ مِن شَىْءٍ فَحُكْمُهُ إِلَى اللَّهِ﴾$$

(And in whatsoever you differ, the decision thereof is with Allah). Therefore, whatever the Book and Sunnah decide and testify to the truth of, then it, is the plain truth. What is beyond truth, save falsehood This is why Allah said, u

$$﴿إِن كُنتُمْ تُؤْمِنُونَ بِاللَّهِ وَالْيَوْمِ الأَّخِرِ﴾$$

(if you believe in Allah and in the Last Day.) meaning, refer the disputes and conflicts that arise between you to the Book of Allah and the Sunnah of His Messenger for judgment. Allah's statement,

$$﴿إِن كُنتُمْ تُؤْمِنُونَ بِاللَّهِ وَالْيَوْمِ الأُّخِرِ﴾$$

(if you believe in Allah and in the Last Day.) indicates that those who do not refer to the Book and Sunnah for judgment in their disputes, are not believers in Allah or the Last Day.

Allah chastises those who claim to believe in what Allah has sent down to His Messenger and to the earlier Prophets, yet they refer to other than the Book of Allah and the Sunnah of His Messenger for judgment in various disputes. It was reported that the reason behind revealing this Ayah was that a man from the Ansar and a Jew had a dispute, and the Jew said, "Let us refer to Muhammad to judge between us." However, the Muslim man said, "Let us refer to Ka`b bin Al-Ashraf (a Jew) to judge between us." It was also reported that the Ayah was revealed about some hypocrites who pretended to be Muslims, yet they sought to refer to the judgment of Jahiliyyah. Other reasons were also reported behind the revelation of the Ayah. However, the Ayah has a general meaning, as it chastises all those who refrain from referring to the Qur'an and Sunnah for judgment and prefer the judgment of whatever they chose of falsehood, which befits the description of Taghut here. Thus Allah said,

$$﴿يُرِيدُونَ أَن يَتَحَاكَمُواْ إِلَى الطَّـغُوتِ﴾$$

(and they wish to go for judgment to the Taghut) until the end of the Ayah. Allah's statement,

$$﴿يَصُدُّونَ عَنكَ صُدُوداً﴾$$

(turn away from you with aversion) means, they turn away from you in arrogance, just as Allah described the polytheists,

$$﴿وَإِذَا قِيلَ لَهُمُ اتَّبِعُواْ مَا أَنزَلَ اللَّهُ قَالُواْ بَلْ نَتَّبِعُ مَا وَجَدْنَا عَلَيْهِ ءَابَآءَنَا﴾$$

(When it is said to them: "Follow what Allah has sent down." They say: "Nay! We shall follow what we found our fathers following.") This is different from the conduct of the faithful believers, whom Allah describes as,

﴿إِنَّمَا كَانَ قَوْلَ الْمُؤْمِنِينَ إِذَا دُعُواْ إِلَى اللَّهِ وَرَسُولِهِ لِيَحْكُمَ بَيْنَهُمْ أَن يَقُولُواْ سَمِعْنَا وَأَطَعْنَا﴾

(The only saying of the faithful believers, when they are called to Allah and His Messenger, to judge between them, is that they say: "We hear and we obey.")

Chastising the hypocrites, Allah said,

﴿فَكَيْفَ إِذَآ أَصَـبَتْهُمْ مُّصِيبَةٌ بِمَا قَدَّمَتْ أَيْدِيهِمْ﴾

(How then, when a catastrophe befalls them because of what their hands have sent forth,) meaning, how about it if they feel compelled to join you because of disasters that they suffer due to their sins, then they will be in need of you.

﴿ثُمَّ جَآءُوكَ يَحْلِفُونَ بِاللَّهِ إِنْ أَرَدْنَآ إِلاَّ إِحْسَاناً وَتَوْفِيقاً﴾

(They come to you swearing by Allah, "We meant no more than goodwill and conciliation!") apologizing and swearing that they only sought goodwill and reconciliation when they referred to other than the Prophet for judgment, not that they believe in such alternative judgment, as they claim. Allah describes these people to us further in His statement,

﴿فَتَرَى الَّذِينَ فِى قُلُوبِهِم مَّرَضٌ يُسَـرِعُونَ فِيهِمْ يَقُولُونَ نَخْشَى﴾

(And you see those in whose hearts there is a disease (of hypocrisy), they hurry to their friendship, saying: "We fear"), until,

﴿فَيُصْبِحُواْ عَلَى مَآ أَسَرُّواْ فِى أَنفُسِهِمْ نَـٰدِمِينَ﴾

(Then they will become regretful for what they have been keeping as a secret in themselves). At-Tabarani recorded that Ibn `Abbas said, "Abu Barzah Al-Aslami used to be a soothsayer who judged between the Jews in their disputes. When some Muslims came to him to judge between them, Allah sent down,

﴿أَلَمْ تَرَ إِلَى الَّذِينَ يَزْعُمُونَ أَنَّهُمْ ءَامَنُواْ بِمَآ أُنزِلَ إِلَيْكَ وَمَآ أُنزِلَ مِن قَبْلِكَ﴾

(Have you not seen those (hypocrites) who claim that they believe in that which has been sent down to you, and that which was sent down before you), until,

﴿إِنْ أَرَدْنَآ إِلاَّ إِحْسَاناً وَتَوْفِيقاً﴾

("We meant no more than goodwill and conciliation!") Allah then said,

﴿أُوْلَـٰئِكَ الَّذِينَ يَعْلَمُ اللهُ مَا فِى قُلُوبِهِمْ﴾

(They (hypocrites) are those of whom Allah knows what is in their hearts;) These people are hypocrites, and Allah knows what is in their hearts and will punish them accordingly, for nothing escapes Allah's watch. Consequently, O Muhammad! Let Allah be sufficient for you in this regard, because He has perfect knowledge of their apparent and hidden affairs. This is why Allah said,

﴿فَأَعْرِضْ عَنْهُمْ﴾

(so turn aside from them (do not punish them)) meaning, do not punish them because of what is in their hearts.

﴿وَعِظْهُمْ﴾

(but admonish them) means, advise them against the hypocrisy and evil that reside in their hearts,

﴿وَقُل لَّهُمْ فِى أَنفُسِهِمْ قَوْلاً بَلِيغاً﴾

(and speak to them an effective word to reach their inner selves) advise them, between you and them, using effective words that might benefit them.

Allah said,

﴿وَمَا أَرْسَلْنَا مِن رَّسُولٍ إِلاَّ لِيُطَاعَ﴾

(We sent no Messenger, but to be obeyed) meaning, obeying the Prophet was ordained for those to whom Allah sends the Prophet. Allah's statement,

﴿بِإِذْنِ اللَّهِ﴾

(by Allah's leave) means, "None shall obey, except by My leave," according to Mujahid. This Ayah indicates that the Prophets are only obeyed by whomever Allah directs to obedience. In another Ayah, Allah said,

﴿وَلَقَدْ صَدَقَكُمُ اللَّهُ وَعْدَهُ إِذْ تَحُسُّونَهُم بِإِذْنِهِ﴾

(And Allah did indeed fulfill His promise to you when you were killing them (your enemy) with His permission) meaning, by His command, decree, will and because He granted you superiority over them. Allah's statement,

﴿وَلَوْ أَنَّهُمْ إِذ ظَّلَمُواْ أَنفُسَهُمْ﴾

(If they (hypocrites), when they had been unjust to themselves,) directs the sinners and evildoers, when they commit errors and mistakes, to come to the Messenger , so that they ask Allah for forgiveness in his presence and ask him to supplicate to Allah to forgive them. If they do this, Allah will forgive them and award them His mercy and pardon. This is why Allah said,

﴿لَوَجَدُواْ اللَّهَ تَوَّاباً رَّحِيماً﴾

(they would have found Allah All-Forgiving (One Who forgives and accepts repentance), Most Merciful).

Allah said,

﴿فَلاَ وَرَبِّكَ لاَ يُؤْمِنُونَ حَتَّى يُحَكِّمُوكَ فِيمَا شَجَرَ بَيْنَهُمْ﴾

(But no, by your Lord, they can have no faith, until they make you judge in all disputes between them,) Allah swears by His Glorious, Most Honorable Self, that no one shall attain faith until he refers to the Messenger for judgment in all matters. Thereafter, whatever the Messenger commands, is the plain truth that must be submitted to inwardly and outwardly. Allah said,

﴿ثُمَّ لاَ يَجِدُواْ فِى أَنفُسِهِمْ حَرَجاً مِّمَّا قَضَيْتَ وَيُسَلِّمُواْ تَسْلِيماً﴾

(and find in themselves no resistance against your decisions, and accept (them) with full submission.) meaning: they adhere to your judgment, and thus do not feel any hesitation over your decision, and they submit to it inwardly and outwardly. They submit to the Prophet's decision with total submission without any rejection, denial or dispute. Al-Bukhari recorded that `Urwah said,

"Az-Zubayr quarreled with a man about a stream which both of them used for irrigation. Allah's Messenger said to Az-Zubayr,

«اسْقِ يَا زُبَيْرُ ثُمَّ أَرْسِلِ الْمَاءَ إلى جَارِك»

(O Zubayr! Irrigate (your garden) first, and then let the water flow to your neighbor.) The Ansari became angry and said, `O Allah's Messenger! Is it because he is your cousin' On that, the face of Allah's Messenger changed color (because of anger) and said,

«اسْقِ يَا زُبَيْرُ ثُمَّ احْبِسِ الْمَاءَ حَتَّى يَرْجِعَ إلَى الْجَدْرِ، ثُمَّ أَرْسِلِ الْمَاءَ إلى جَارِك»

(Irrigate (your garden), O Zubayr, and then withhold the water until it reaches the walls (surrounding the palms). Then, release the water to your neighbor.) So, Allah's Messenger gave Az-Zubayr his full right when the Ansari made him angry. Before that, Allah's Messenger had given a generous judgment, beneficial for Az-Zubayr and the Ansari. Az-Zubayr said, `I think the following verse was revealed concerning that case,

﴿فَلاَ وَرَبِّكَ لاَ يُؤْمِنُونَ حَتَّى يُحَكِّمُوكَ فِيمَا شَجَرَ بَيْنَهُمْ﴾

(But no, by your Lord, they can have no faith, until they make you (O Muhammad) judge in all disputes between them.)'" Another Reason In his Tafsir, Al-Hafiz Abu Ishaq Ibrahim bin `Abdur-Rahman bin Ibrahim bin Duhaym recorded that Damrah narrated that two men took their dispute to the Prophet , and he gave a judgment to the benefit of whoever among them had the right. The person who lost the dispute said, "I do not agree." The other person asked him, "What do you want then" He said, "Let us go to Abu Bakr As-Siddiq." They went to Abu Bakr and the person who won the dispute said, "We went to the Prophet with our dispute and he issued a decision in my favor." Abu Bakr said, "Then the decision is that which the Messenger of Allah issued." The person who lost the dispute still rejected the decision and said, "Let us go to `Umar bin Al-Khattab." When they went to `Umar, the person who won the dispute said, "We took our dispute to the Prophet and he decided in my favor, but this man refused to submit to the decision." `Umar bin Al-Khattab asked the second man and he concurred. `Umar went to his house and emerged from it holding aloft his sword. He struck the head of the man who rejected the Prophet's decision with the sword and killed him.

Allah states that even if the people were commanded to commit what they were prohibited from doing, most of them would not submit to this command, for their wicked nature is such that they dispute orders. Allah has complete knowledge of what has not occurred, and how it would be if and when it did occur. This is why Allah said,

﴿وَلَوْ أَنَّا كَتَبْنَا عَلَيْهِمْ أَنِ اقْتُلُواْ أَنفُسَكُمْ﴾

(And if We had ordered them (saying), "Kill yourselves (i.e. the innocent ones kill the guilty ones)) until the end of the Ayah. This is why Allah said,

﴿وَلَوْ أَنَّهُمْ فَعَلُواْ مَا يُوعَظُونَ بِهِ﴾

(but if they had done what they were told,) meaning, if they do what they were commanded and refrain from what they were prohibited,

$$﴿لَكَانَ خَيْراً لَّهُمْ﴾$$

(it would have been better for them,) than disobeying the command and committing the prohibition

These verses highlight the order to judge with justice in all affairs and that those who don't do so, even if they claim to have good intentions are wreaking havoc and opposition to the prophetic teachings/laws and are not actual believers despite what they may say. Many lessons can be drawn from this, as it pertains to the topic you cannot just snitch on what you think is right or wrong and even when snitching you must do so justly not for personal reasons such as revenge or other than that. It is better to judge by Islamic Shariah because that is the best way of life which is legislated by the Creator of all life who has wisdom beyond measure. Sadly others in trying to please other than the Creator agree to sacrifice the Shariah to judge by other than it and fall into error and potentially disbelief depending on the extent of such error. As governing is a separate and more controversial topic than snitching I will limit myself to snitching and remind the reader how gossiping or backbiting against rulers is sinful and reportable to the rulers so justice can be done. Thus while many may think it pertinent to comment on rulers implementing Shariah I will stick to the topic at hand as snitching is a rule implementable by everyone and everyone is a ruler in some capacity even if only over oneself. Whereas oftentimes we are prejudiced towards ourself when we judge ourselves to be good in comparison to others which is a manifest example of judging unjustly using a criteria other than the Shariah.

Quran 4:83

وَإِذَا جَاءَهُمْ أَمْرٌ مِّنَ ٱلْأَمْنِ أَوِ ٱلْخَوْفِ أَذَاعُوا بِهِ ۖ وَلَوْ رَدُّوهُ إِلَى ٱلرَّسُولِ وَإِلَىٰ أُولِى ٱلْأَمْرِ مِنْهُمْ لَعَلِمَهُ ٱلَّذِينَ يَسْتَنۢبِطُونَهُ مِنْهُمْ ۗ وَلَوْلَا فَضْلُ ٱللَّهِ عَلَيْكُمْ وَرَحْمَتُهُ لَٱتَّبَعْتُمُ ٱلشَّيْطَٰنَ إِلَّا قَلِيلًا (٨٣)

When there comes to them some matter touching (public) safety or fear, they make it known (among the people), if only they had referred it to the Messenger or to those charged with authority among them, the proper investigators would have understood it from them (directly). Had it not been for the Grace and Mercy of Allâh upon you, you would have followed Shaitân (Satan), save a few of you. (83)

Allah said,

﴿وَإِذَا جَاءَهُمْ أَمْرٌ مِّنَ الأُمْنِ أَو الْخَوْفِ أَذَاعُواْ بِهِ﴾

(When there comes to them some matter touching (public) safety or fear, they make it known (among the people);) chastising those who indulge in things before being sure of their truth, disclosing them, making them known and spreading their news, even though such news might not be true at all. In the introduction to his Sahih, Imam Muslim recorded that Abu Hurayrah said that the Prophet said,

»كَفَى بِالْمَرْءِ كَذِبًا أَنْ يُحَدِّثَ بِكُلِّ مَا سَمِع«

(Narrating everything one hears is sufficient to make a person a liar.) This is the same narration collected by Abu Dawud in the section of Adab (manners) in his Sunan. In the Two Sahihs, it is recorded that Al-Mughirah bin Shu`bah said that the Messenger of Allah prohibited, "It was said," and, "So-and-so said." This Hadith refers to those who often convey the speech that people utter without investigating the reliability and truth of what he is disclosing. The Sahih also records,

«مَنْ حَدَّثَ بِحَدِيثٍ وَهُوَ يُرَى أَنَّهُ كَذِبٌ، فَهُوَ أَحَدُ الْكَاذِبَيْنِ»

(Whoever narrates a Hadith while knowing it is false, then he is one of the two liars (who invents and who spreads the lie).) We should mention here the Hadith of `Umar bin Al-Khattab collected in the Two Sahihs. When `Umar was informed that the Messenger of Allah divorced his wives, he came from his house, entered the Masjid and found the people talking about this news. He could not wait and went to the Prophet to ask him about what had truly happened, asking him, "Have you divorced your wives" The Prophet said, "No." `Umar said, "I said, Allahu Akbar..." and mentioned the rest of the Hadith. In the narration that Muslim collected, `Umar said, "I asked, `Have you divorced them' He said, `No.' So, I stood by the door of the Masjid and shouted with the loudest voice, `The Messenger of Allah did not divorce his wives.' Then, this Ayah was revealed,

﴿وَإِذَا جَاءَهُمْ أَمْرٌ مِّنَ الأُمْنِ أَوِ الْخَوْفِ أَذَاعُواْ بِهِ وَلَوْ رَدُّوهُ إِلَى الرَّسُولِ وَإِلَى أُوْلِى الأُمْرِ مِنْهُمْ لَعَلِمَهُ الَّذِينَ يَسْتَنْبِطُونَهُ مِنْهُمْ﴾

(When there comes to them some matter touching (public) safety or fear, they make it known (among the people), if only they had referred it to the Messenger or to those charged with authority among them, the proper investigators would have understood it from them (directly).) So I properly investigated that matter." This Ayah refers to proper investigation, or extraction of matters from their proper resources.

It is actually an obligation to properly investigate and snitch to the authorities per these verses. Yet where do most people get the information we discuss most often? Improper businesses who sell news stories or unverifiable internet sources. Then we chit-chat tit for tat in clear violation of this golden principle of proper investigation and reporting to leaders who will further investigate, analyze, act and inform us of the reality and what we should do. Instead we hear unclear data and jump to our own conclusions about the reality and what is to be done about it. Fundamentally this methodology is sinful and a path of the devil that leads many to ruination. Most news actually need not be known at all and much is irrelevant to us anyways. People fail to understand news is being sold rather than told and that reporting is an act of worship. How many reporters actually intend and knowingly perform the ritual of reporting news according to the prophetic rules? Nearly none and this is a disaster. Not everyone needs to know everything and for some it is dangerous for them to know things because they can't react appropriately to the news they learn. Referring to authority figures is vital for societal health and the proliferation of news on traditional sources as well as innovative sources such as social media is a poison that results in many skipping steps the Shariah specifies as crucial to societal stability and success. It is only disbelievers who believe in a free open press market where anything and everything is shared at all times with everyone on all topics sinful and frivolous they may be. A free non-governmental controlled press not only is an illusion yet to be realized anywhere but it is a satanic concept we should prevent rather than promote. When prophets ruled communities they did not institute free unrestricted media outlets. So, that there is a trend in that direction today indicates a turn for the worse. Prophetically news is disseminated scholastically and responsibly by authority figures. Today few state-controlled media outlets exist but nearly none are scholastic or disseminate news in a manner consistent with prophetic teaching concerning dress code, vocabulary, imagery and many other factors which prophets taught for news reporting. People often believe the prophets came with rules for life and then completely disregard the rules for spreading news the prophets taught us despite a constant consumption of news media. So know that believing in God and his prophets requires adherence to media rules for news dissemination as well and that reporting/snitching news to authority figures is divinely commanded. Personally the less time you waste on news consumption the better your life is likely to be anyways, especially if sins are involved in that news media such as seeing members of the opposite gender clothed inappropriately, listening to music or gossip. Even the fundamental fact that the news is non-scholastic desensitizes you to a non-scholastic standard and is a way of dumbing down the populace so they treat news media as a reliable standard of information when it doesn't adhere to scholastic methods of accurate information conveyance. Therefore I advise limiting your exposure to news media because honestly most of it just wastes time you could use doing better things of which we will all be judged for every second we lived and learning the latest news is known to not be a virtuous habit and if it leads you to sin in any way then it is a serious sinful habit.

Quran 4:107-112

وَلَا تُجَٰدِلْ عَنِ ٱلَّذِينَ يَخْتَانُونَ أَنفُسَهُمْ إِنَّ ٱللَّهَ لَا يُحِبُّ مَن كَانَ خَوَّانًا أَثِيمًا (١٠٧) يَسْتَخْفُونَ مِنَ ٱلنَّاسِ وَلَا يَسْتَخْفُونَ مِنَ ٱللَّهِ وَهُوَ مَعَهُمْ إِذْ يُبَيِّتُونَ مَا لَا يَرْضَىٰ مِنَ ٱلْقَوْلِ وَكَانَ ٱللَّهُ بِمَا يَعْمَلُونَ مُحِيطًا (١٠٨) هَٰٓأَنتُمْ هَٰٓؤُلَآءِ جَٰدَلْتُمْ عَنْهُمْ فِى ٱلْحَيَوٰةِ ٱلدُّنْيَا فَمَن يُجَٰدِلُ ٱللَّهَ عَنْهُمْ يَوْمَ ٱلْقِيَٰمَةِ أَم مَّن يَكُونُ عَلَيْهِمْ وَكِيلاً (١٠٩) وَمَن يَعْمَلْ سُوٓءًا أَوْ يَظْلِمْ نَفْسَهُ ثُمَّ يَسْتَغْفِرِ ٱللَّهَ يَجِدِ ٱللَّهَ غَفُورًا رَّحِيمًا (١١٠) وَمَن يَكْسِبْ إِثْمًا فَإِنَّمَا يَكْسِبُهُ عَلَىٰ نَفْسِهِ وَكَانَ ٱللَّهُ عَلِيمًا حَكِيمًا (١١١) وَمَن يَكْسِبْ خَطِيٓئَةً أَوْ إِثْمًا ثُمَّ يَرْمِ بِهِ بَرِيٓئًا فَقَدِ ٱحْتَمَلَ بُهْتَٰنًا وَإِثْمًا مُّبِينًا (١١٢)

And argue not on behalf of those who deceive themselves. Verily, Allâh does not like anyone who is a betrayer of his trust, and sinner. (107) They may hide (their crimes) from men, but they cannot hide (them) from Allâh, for He is with them (by His Knowledge), when they plot by night in words that He does not approve, And Allâh ever encompasses what they do. (108) Lo! You are those who have argued for them in the life of this world, but who will argue for them on the Day of Resurrection against

Allâh, or who will then be their defender? (109) And whoever does evil or wrongs himself but afterwards seeks Allâh's Forgiveness, he will find Allâh Oft¬Forgiving, Most Merciful. (110) And whoever earns sin, he earns it only against himself. And Allâh is Ever All-Knowing, All-Wise. (111) And whoever earns a fault or a sin and then throws it on to someone innocent, he has indeed burdened himself with falsehood and a manifest sin. (112)

The most important verse in the previous sample of Quranic verses is 4:112 in that whoever sins and lays the blame on another or falsely snitches is in big time trouble for a major sin. This is because a sin is one thing but to sin and then blame another is a compounded sin on top of a sin especially if the innocent is punished for your crime. Everyone agrees if you do the crime you deserve the sentence of punishment for your actions, its called liable responsibility. Yet as bad as the aforementioned is entire religions such as Christianity revolve around others such as Jesus being punished for the sins of others. Even if Jesus were divine/semi-divine or if crucified, none of which is accurate, this would be a manifest sin compounded not a means of salvation. Which is why even the least sinful Christian is always more sinful than the most sinful Muslim by default because the sin of disbelief and this sin of burdening Jesus with their sins falsely is a crime against God, Jesus and religion itself.

Quran 4:123

لَّيْسَ بِأَمَانِيِّكُمْ وَلَا أَمَانِيِّ أَهْلِ ٱلْكِتَـٰبِۗ مَن يَعْمَلْ سُوٓءًا يُجْزَ بِهِۦ وَلَا يَجِدْ لَهُۥ مِن دُونِ ٱللَّهِ وَلِيًّا وَلَا نَصِيرًا (١٢٣)

It will not be in accordance with your desires (Muslims), nor those of the people of the Scripture (Jews and Christians), whosoever works evil, will have the recompense thereof, and he will not find any protector or helper besides Allâh. (123)

Qatadah said, "We were told that the Muslims and the People of the Scriptures mentioned their own virtues to each other. People of the Scriptures said, `Our Prophet came before your Prophet and our Book before your Book. Therefore, we should have more right to Allah than you have.' Muslims said, `Rather, we have more right to Allah than you, our Prophet is the Final Prophet and our Book supersedes all the Books before it.' Allah sent down,

﴿لَّيْسَ بِأَمَانِيِّكُمْ وَلاَ أَمَانِيِّ أَهْلِ الْكِتَـبِ مَن يَعْمَلْ سُوءًا يُجْزَ بِهِ﴾

(It will not be in accordance with your desires (Muslims), nor those of the People of the Scripture (Jews and Christians), whosoever works evil, will have the recompense thereof),

﴿وَمَنْ أَحْسَنُ دِيناً مِّمَّنْ أَسْلَمَ وَجْهَهُ لله وَهُوَ مُحْسِنٌ﴾

(And who can be better in religion than one who submits his face (himself) to Allah; and he is a Muhsin.) Allah then supported the argument of the Muslims against their opponents of the other religions." Similar statements were attributed to As-Suddi, Masruq, Ad-Dahhak and Abu Salih. Al-`Awfi reported that Ibn `Abbas commented on this Ayah 4:123 "The followers of various religions disputed, the people of the Tawrah said, `Our Book is the best Book and our Prophet (Musa) is the best Prophet. ' The people of the Injil said similarly, the people of Islam said, `There is no religion except Islam, our Book has abrogated every other Book, our Prophet is the Final Prophet, and you were commanded to believe in your Books and adhere to our Book.' Allah judged between them, saying:

$$﴿لَّيْسَ بِأَمَانِيِّكُمْ وَلا أَمَانِيِّ أَهْلِ الْكِتَـبِ مَن يَعْمَلْ سُوءًا يُجْزَ بِهِ﴾$$

(It will not be in accordance with your desires, nor those of the People of the Scripture, whosoever works evil, will have the recompense thereof)." This Ayah indicates that the religion is not accepted on account of wishful thinking or mere hopes. Rather, the accepted religion relies on what resides in the heart and which is made truthful through actions. It is not true that when one utters a claim to something, he attains it merely on account of his claim. It is not true that every person who claims to be on the truth is considered as such, merely on account of his words, until his claim gains merit with proof from Allah. Hence Allah's statement,

$$﴿لَّيْسَ بِأَمَانِيِّكُمْ وَلا أَمَانِيِّ أَهْلِ الْكِتَـبِ مَن يَعْمَلْ سُوءًا يُجْزَ بِهِ﴾$$

(It will not be in accordance with your desires, nor those of the People of the Scripture, whosoever works evil, will have the recompense thereof), meaning safety will not be acquired by you or them just by wishful thinking. Rather, the key is in obeying Allah and following what He has legislated through the words of His honorable Messengers.

That the matter is not upon our desires applies to snitching as well because the Shariah itself which is the religion does not come under the influence of creatures. The law is clear and unchanged not in accordance to desires and fanciful hopes or dreams so just as one says the final decision is up to Allah regarding paradise or hell then the decision on snitching is up to Allah as well.

Quran 4:135

۞ يَـٰٓأَيُّهَا ٱلَّذِينَ ءَامَنُوا۟ كُونُوا۟ قَوَّٰمِينَ بِٱلْقِسْطِ شُهَدَآءَ لِلَّهِ وَلَوْ عَلَىٰٓ أَنفُسِكُمْ أَوِ ٱلْوَٰلِدَيْنِ وَٱلْأَقْرَبِينَ إِن يَكُنْ غَنِيًّا أَوْ فَقِيرًا فَٱللَّهُ أَوْلَىٰ بِهِمَا فَلَا تَتَّبِعُوا۟ ٱلْهَوَىٰٓ أَن تَعْدِلُوا۟ وَإِن تَلْوُۥٓا۟ أَوْ تُعْرِضُوا۟ فَإِنَّ ٱللَّهَ كَانَ بِمَا تَعْمَلُونَ خَبِيرًا (١٣٥)

O you who believe! Stand out firmly for justice, as witnesses to Allâh, even though it be against yourselves, or your parents, or your kin, be he rich or poor, Allâh is a Better Protector to both (than you). So follow not the lusts (of your hearts), lest you avoid justice, and if you distort your witness or refuse to give it, verily, Allâh is Ever Well¬Acquainted with what you do. (135)

Allah commands His believing servants to stand up for justice and fairness and not to deviate from it, right or left. They should not fear the blame of anyone or allow anyone to prevent them from doing something for the sake of Allah. They are also required to help, support and aid each other for Allah's sake. Allah's statement,

﴿شُهَدَآءِ لِلَّهِ﴾

(as witnesses to Allah) is similar to His statement,

﴿وَأَقِيمُوا۟ ٱلشَّهَـٰدَةَ لِلَّهِ﴾

(And establish the testimony for Allah). Testimony should be delivered precisely, for the sake of Allah, thus making the testimony correct, truly just, and free of alterations, changes or deletions. This is why Allah said,

﴿وَلَوْ عَلَى أَنفُسِكُمْ﴾

(even though it be against yourselves,) meaning, give correct testimony, and say the truth when you are asked about it, even if harm will effect you as a consequence. Indeed, Allah shall make a way out and give relief for those who obey Him in every matter. Allah's statement,

﴿أَوِ الْوَلِدَيْنِ وَالأَقْرَبِينَ﴾

(or your parents, or your kin,) means, even if you have to testify against your parents and kin, do not compromise for their sake. Rather, give the correct and just witness even if they are harmed in the process, for the truth presides above everyone and is preferred to everyone. Allah's statement,

﴿إِن يَكُنْ غَنِيّاً أَوْ فَقَيراً فَاللَّهُ أَوْلَى بِهِمَا﴾

(be he rich or poor, Allah is a better Protector to both.) means, do not favor someone (in your testimony) because he is rich, or feel pity for him because he is poor, for Allah is their caretaker, a better Protector of them than you, and has better knowledge of what is good for them. Allah's statement,

﴿فَلاَ تَتَّبِعُواْ الْهَوَى أَن تَعْدِلُواْ﴾

(So follow not the lusts, lest you may avoid justice;) means, let not desire, lust or the hatred you have against others, lure you into injustice in your affairs. Rather, stand for justice in all situations. Allah said;

﴿وَلاَ يَجْرِمَنَّكُمْ شَنَآنُ قَوْمٍ عَلَى أَلاَّ تَعْدِلُواْ اعْدِلُواْ هُوَ أَقْرَبُ لِلتَّقْوَى﴾

(And let not the enmity and hatred of others make you avoid justice. Be just: that is nearer to piety) when the Prophet sent `Abdullah bin Rawahah to collect the tax on the fruits and produce of the Jews of Khaybar, they offered him a bribe so that he would go easy on them. He said; "By Allah! I have come to you from the dearest of the creation to me (Muhammad), and you are more hated by me than an equivalent number of apes and swine. However, my love for him (the Prophet) and hatred for you shall not prevent me from being just with you." On that, they said, "This (justice) is the basis which the heavens and earth were created. " Allah's statement afterwards,

﴿وَإِن تَلْوُواْ أَوْ تُعْرِضُواْ﴾

(and if you Talwu or Tu`ridu) means, "Distort your testimony and change it", according to Mujahid and several others among the Salaf. Talwu, includes distortion and intentional lying. For instance, Allah said,

﴿وَإِنَّ مِنْهُمْ لَفَرِيقًا يَلْوُونَ أَلْسِنَتَهُم بِالْكِتَـبِ﴾

(And verily, among them is a party who Yalwuna (distort) the Book with their tongues (as they read)). Tu`ridu, includes hiding and withholding the testimony. Allah said,

﴿وَمَن يَكْتُمْهَا فَإِنَّهُ ءَاثِمٌ قَلْبُهُ﴾

(Who hides it, surely, his heart is sinful) The Prophet said,

«خَيْرُ الشُّهَدَاءِ الَّذِي يَأْتِي بِشَهَادَتِهِ قَبْلَ أَنْ يُسْأَلَهَا»

(The best witness is he who discloses his testimony before being asked to do so.) Allah then warned,

﴿فَإِنَّ اللَّهَ كَانَ بِمَا تَعْمَلُونَ خَبِيراً﴾

(Verily, Allah is Ever Well-Acquainted with what you do.) and will reward or punish you accordingly.

This verse 4:135 is perhaps the strongest proof supporting snitches in the Quran. It explains that nobody is immune from being snitched on, not even yourself by yourself and in fact sometimes snitching on yourself becomes a duty though it is typically relabeled as a confession rather than self-snitching. Firmness in truthful testimony is ordered and punishment from Allah is alluded to for those who fail to testify to crimes done by anyone even kin for whatever reason. There is no wiggle room to escape the fact that snitching on guilty criminals is enjoined in Islam.

Quran 4:148

۞ لَّا يُحِبُّ ٱللَّهُ ٱلْجَهْرَ بِٱلسُّوٓءِ مِنَ ٱلْقَوْلِ إِلَّا مَن ظُلِمَ وَكَانَ ٱللَّهُ سَمِيعًا عَلِيمًا (١٤٨)

Allâh does not like that the evil should be uttered in public except by him who has been wronged. And Allâh is Ever All¬Hearer, All¬Knower. (148)

Ali bin Abi Talhah said that Ibn `Abbas commented on the Ayah,

﴿لاَّ يُحِبُّ اللَّهُ الْجَهْرَ بِالسُّوءِ مِنَ الْقَوْلِ﴾

(Allah does not like that the evil should be uttered in public) "Allah does not like that any one should invoke Him against anyone else, unless one was wronged. In this case, Allah allows one to invoke Him against whoever wronged him. Hence Allah's statement,

﴿إِلاَّ مَن ظُلَمَ﴾

(except by him who has been wronged.) Yet, it is better for one if he observes patience." Al-Hasan Al-Basri commented, "One should not invoke Allah (for curses) against whoever wronged him. Rather, he should supplicate, `O Allah! Help me against him and take my right from him.'" In another narration, Al-Hasan said, "Allah has allowed one to invoke Him against whoever wronged him without transgressing the limits." `Abdul-Karim bin Malik Al-Jazari said about this Ayah; "When a man curses you, you could curse him in retaliation. But if he lies about you, you may not lie about him.

﴿وَلَمَنِ انتَصَرَ بَعْدَ ظُلْمِهِ فَأُوْلَـئِكَ مَا عَلَيْهِمْ مِّن سَبِيلٍ ﴾

(And indeed whosoever takes revenge after he has suffered wrong, for such there is no way (of blame) against them.)" Abu Dawud recorded that Abu Hurayrah said that the Messenger of Allah said,

«الْمُسْتَبَّانِ مَا قَالاَ، فَعَلَى الْبَادِئ مِنْهُمَا مَا لَمْ يَعْتَدِ الْمَظْلُومُ»

(Whatever words are uttered by those who curse each other, then he who started it will carry the burden thereof, unless the one who was wronged transgresses the limit.)

As it applies to snitching many get confused and mislabel snitching as gossiping or backbiting but there is a difference especially if the snitch was directly harmed as a result of the crime they are snitching about. Which in reality all are harmed by crime because it lowers the standards for society and incurs the potential collective punishment of the community by God. Yet whether directly or indirectly harmed by crime, the snitch has a duty to tell the truth to rectify society and pursue justice. It falls under reporting to authority figures and enjoining good or forbidding evil so never fall for the excuse criminals and accessories to crime may cite deceptively guilt-tripping you into concealing testimony for fear of it being sinful to speak out against the satanic sins. There is no sin in Shariah compliant snitching, on the contrary it is an ordained good deed in certain circumstances.

Quran 5:25

قَالَ رَبِّ إِنِّى لَا أَمْلِكُ إِلَّا نَفْسِى وَأَخِى ۖ فَٱفْرُقْ بَيْنَنَا وَبَيْنَ ٱلْقَوْمِ ٱلْفَٰسِقِينَ (٢٥)

He [Mûsa (Moses)] said: "O my Lord! I have power only over myself and my brother, so separate us from the people who are the Fâsiqûn (rebellious and disobedient to Allâh)!" (25)

Musa said,

﴿قَالَ رَبِّ إِنِّى لا أَمْلِكُ إلاَّ نَفْسِى وَأَخِى فَافْرُقْ بَيْنَنَا وَبَيْنَ الْقَوْمِ الْفَـسِقِينَ ﴾

("O my Lord! I have power only over myself and my brother, so separate us from the rebellious people!") When the Children of Israel refused to fight, Musa became very angry with them and supplicated to Allah against them,

﴿رَبِّ إِنِّى لاَ أَمْلِكُ إِلاَّ نَفْسِى وَأَخِى﴾

(O my Lord! I have power only over myself and my brother') meaning, only I and my brother Harun among them will obey, implement Allah's command and accept the call,

﴿فَافْرُقْ بَيْنَنَا وَبَيْنَ الْقَوْمِ الْفَـسِقِينَ﴾

(So Ifruq us from the rebellious people!) Al-`Awfi reported that Ibn `Abbas said, "Meaning, judge between us and them." `Ali bin Abi Talhah reported similarly from him. Ad-Dahhak said that the Ayah means, "Judge and decide between us and them." Other scholars said that the Ayah means, "Separate between us and them."

Moses himself snitched to God what God already knew a prayer to be free from the crimes of his people which he was sent to and thus couldn't legally abandon or depart from. While snitching generally involves human legal systems, it is important to know that sometimes instead of referring to creatures God is the only authority one can report to because the creatures may not care or may be the criminals themselves or unwilling to do justice. Nevertheless it is a practice of the prophets so regardless of the situation the first resort should be to seek help with Allah in the issue of snitching and that first step is the best of all steps. Despite Allah not being ignorant of your case the act of reporting to Allah itself merits accolades.

Quran 5:44-52

إِنَّا أَنزَلْنَا ٱلتَّوْرَىٰةَ فِيهَا هُدًى وَنُورٌ يَحْكُمُ بِهَا ٱلنَّبِيُّونَ ٱلَّذِينَ أَسْلَمُوا۟ لِلَّذِينَ هَادُوا۟ وَٱلرَّبَّـٰنِيُّونَ وَٱلْأَحْبَارُ بِمَا ٱسْتُحْفِظُوا۟ مِن كِتَـٰبِ ٱللَّهِ وَكَانُوا۟ عَلَيْهِ شُهَدَآءَ فَلَا تَخْشَوُا۟ ٱلنَّاسَ وَٱخْشَوْنِ وَلَا تَشْتَرُوا۟ بِـَٔايَـٰتِى ثَمَنًا قَلِيلًا وَمَن لَّمْ يَحْكُم بِمَآ أَنزَلَ ٱللَّهُ فَأُو۟لَـٰٓئِكَ هُمُ ٱلْكَـٰفِرُونَ (٤٤) وَكَتَبْنَا عَلَيْهِمْ فِيهَآ أَنَّ ٱلنَّفْسَ بِٱلنَّفْسِ وَٱلْعَيْنَ بِٱلْعَيْنِ وَٱلْأَنفَ بِٱلْأَنفِ وَٱلْأُذُنَ بِٱلْأُذُنِ وَٱلسِّنَّ بِٱلسِّنِّ وَٱلْجُرُوحَ قِصَاصٌ فَمَن تَصَدَّقَ بِهِۦ فَهُوَ كَفَّارَةٌ لَّهُۥ وَمَن لَّمْ يَحْكُم بِمَآ أَنزَلَ ٱللَّهُ فَأُو۟لَـٰٓئِكَ هُمُ ٱلظَّـٰلِمُونَ (٤٥) وَقَفَّيْنَا عَلَىٰٓ ءَاثَـٰرِهِم بِعِيسَى ٱبْنِ مَرْيَمَ مُصَدِّقًا لِّمَا بَيْنَ يَدَيْهِ مِنَ ٱلتَّوْرَىٰةِ وَءَاتَيْنَـٰهُ ٱلْإِنجِيلَ فِيهِ هُدًى وَنُورٌ وَمُصَدِّقًا لِّمَا بَيْنَ يَدَيْهِ مِنَ ٱلتَّوْرَىٰةِ وَهُدًى وَمَوْعِظَةً لِّلْمُتَّقِينَ (٤٦) وَلْيَحْكُمْ أَهْلُ ٱلْإِنجِيلِ بِمَآ أَنزَلَ ٱللَّهُ فِيهِ وَمَن لَّمْ يَحْكُم بِمَآ أَنزَلَ ٱللَّهُ فَأُو۟لَـٰٓئِكَ هُمُ ٱلْفَـٰسِقُونَ (٤٧) وَأَنزَلْنَآ إِلَيْكَ ٱلْكِتَـٰبَ بِٱلْحَقِّ مُصَدِّقًا لِّمَا بَيْنَ يَدَيْهِ مِنَ ٱلْكِتَـٰبِ وَمُهَيْمِنًا عَلَيْهِ فَٱحْكُم بَيْنَهُم بِمَآ أَنزَلَ ٱللَّهُ وَلَا تَتَّبِعْ أَهْوَآءَهُمْ عَمَّا جَآءَكَ مِنَ ٱلْحَقِّ لِكُلٍّ جَعَلْنَا مِنكُمْ شِرْعَةً وَمِنْهَاجًا وَلَوْ شَآءَ ٱللَّهُ لَجَعَلَكُمْ أُمَّةً وَٰحِدَةً وَلَـٰكِن لِّيَبْلُوَكُمْ فِى مَآ ءَاتَىٰكُمْ فَٱسْتَبِقُوا۟ ٱلْخَيْرَٰتِ إِلَى ٱللَّهِ مَرْجِعُكُمْ جَمِيعًا فَيُنَبِّئُكُم بِمَا كُنتُمْ فِيهِ تَخْتَلِفُونَ (٤٨) وَأَنِ ٱحْكُم بَيْنَهُم بِمَآ أَنزَلَ ٱللَّهُ وَلَا تَتَّبِعْ أَهْوَآءَهُمْ وَٱحْذَرْهُمْ أَن يَفْتِنُوكَ عَنۢ بَعْضِ مَآ أَنزَلَ ٱللَّهُ إِلَيْكَ فَإِن تَوَلَّوْا۟ فَٱعْلَمْ أَنَّمَا يُرِيدُ ٱللَّهُ أَن يُصِيبَهُم بِبَعْضِ ذُنُوبِهِمْ وَإِنَّ كَثِيرًا مِّنَ ٱلنَّاسِ لَفَـٰسِقُونَ (٤٩) أَفَحُكْمَ ٱلْجَـٰهِلِيَّةِ يَبْغُونَ وَمَنْ أَحْسَنُ مِنَ ٱللَّهِ حُكْمًا لِّقَوْمٍ يُوقِنُونَ (٥٠) ۞ يَـٰٓأَيُّهَا ٱلَّذِينَ ءَامَنُوا۟ لَا تَتَّخِذُوا۟ ٱلْيَهُودَ وَٱلنَّصَـٰرَىٰٓ أَوْلِيَآءَ بَعْضُهُمْ أَوْلِيَآءُ بَعْضٍ وَمَن يَتَوَلَّهُم مِّنكُمْ فَإِنَّهُۥ مِنْهُمْ إِنَّ ٱللَّهَ لَا يَهْدِى ٱلْقَوْمَ ٱلظَّـٰلِمِينَ (٥١) فَتَرَى ٱلَّذِينَ فِى قُلُوبِهِم مَّرَضٌ يُسَـٰرِعُونَ فِيهِمْ يَقُولُونَ نَخْشَىٰٓ أَن تُصِيبَنَا دَآئِرَةٌ فَعَسَى ٱللَّهُ أَن يَأْتِىَ بِٱلْفَتْحِ أَوْ أَمْرٍ مِّنْ عِندِهِۦ فَيُصْبِحُوا۟ عَلَىٰ مَآ أَسَرُّوا۟ فِىٓ أَنفُسِهِمْ نَـٰدِمِينَ (٥٢)

Verily, We did send down the Taurât (Torah) [to Mûsa (Moses)], therein was guidance and light, by which the Prophets, who submitted themselves to Allâh's Will, judged for the Jews. And the rabbis and the priests [too judged for the Jews by the Taurât (Torah) after those Prophets] for to them was entrusted the protection of Allâh's Book, and they were witnesses thereto. Therefore fear not men but fear Me (O Jews) and sell not My Verses for a miserable price. And whosoever does not judge by what Allâh has revealed, such are the Kâfirûn (i.e. disbelievers - of a lesser degree as they do not act on Allâh's

Laws). (44) And We ordained therein for them: "Life for life, eye for eye, nose for nose, ear for ear, tooth for tooth, and wounds equal for equal." But if anyone remits the retaliation by way of charity, it shall be for him an expiation. And whosoever does not judge by that which Allâh has revealed, such are the Zâlimûn (polytheists and wrong¬doers - of a lesser degree). (45) And in their footsteps, We sent 'Īsā (Jesus), son of Maryam (Mary), confirming the Taurât (Torah) that had come before him, and We gave him the Injeel (Gospel), in which was guidance and light and confirmation of the Taurât (Torah) that had come before it, a guidance and an admonition for Al-Muttaqûn (the pious). (46) Let the people of the Injeel judge by what Allâh has revealed therein. And whosoever does not judge by what Allâh has revealed (then) such (people) are the Fâsiqûn (the rebellious i.e. disobedient (of a lesser degree) to Allâh. (47) And We have sent down to you (O Muhammad) the Book (this Qur'ân) in truth, confirming the Scripture that came before it and Muhaymin (trustworthy in highness and a witness) over it (old Scriptures). So judge among them by what Allâh has revealed, and follow not their vain desires, diverging away from the truth that has come to you. To each among you, We have prescribed a law and a clear way. If Allâh had willed, He would have made you one nation, but that (He) may test you in what He has given you; so compete in good deeds. The return of you (all) is to Allâh; then He will inform you about that in which you used to differ (48) And so judge (you O Muhammad) among them by what Allâh has revealed and follow not their vain desires, but beware of them lest they turn you (O Muhammad) far away from some of that which Allâh has sent down to you. And if they turn away, then know that

Allâh's Will is to punish them for some sins of theirs. And truly, most of men are Fâsiqûn (rebellious and disobedient to Allâh). (49) Do they then seek the judgement of (the days of) Ignorance? And who is better in judgement than Allâh for a people who have firm Faith. (50) O you who believe! Take not the Jews and the Christians as Auliyâ' (friends, protectors, helpers), they are but Auliyâ' of each other. And if any amongst you takes them (as Auliyâ'), then surely he is one of them. Verily, Allâh guides not those people who are the Zâlimûn (polytheists and wrong-doers and unjust). (51) And you see those in whose hearts there is a disease (of hypocrisy), they hurry to their friendship, saying: "We fear lest some misfortune of a disaster may befall us." Perhaps Allâh may bring a victory or a decision according to His Will. Then they will become regretful for what they have been keeping as a secret in themselves. (52)

Allah praises the Tawrah that He sent down to His servant and Messenger Musa, son of `Imran,

﴿إِنَّآ أَنزَلْنَا التَّوْرَاةَ فِيهَا هُدًى وَنُورٌ يَحْكُمُ بِهَا النَّبِيُّونَ الَّذِينَ أَسْلَمُواْ لِلَّذِينَ هَادُواْ﴾

(Verily, We did send down the Tawrah) to Musa(therein was guidance and light, by which the Prophets who submitted themselves to Allah's will, judged the Jews.) and these Prophets did not deviate from the law of the Tawrah, change or alter it,

﴿وَالرَّبَّانِيُّونَ وَالأَّحْبَارُ﴾

(And (also) the Rabbaniyyun and the Ahbar...) wherein Rabbaniyyun refers to the worshippers who are learned and religious, and Ahbar refers to the scholars,

﴿بِمَا اسْتُحْفِظُوا مِن كِتَـبِ اللَّهِ﴾

(for to them was entrusted the protection of Allah's Book,) meaning, they were entrusted with the Book of Allah, and they were commanded to adhere to it and not hide any part of,

﴿وَكَانُوا عَلَيْهِ شُهَدَآءَ فَلاَ تَخْشَوُا النَّاسَ وَاخْشَوْنِ وَلاَ تَشْتَرُوا بِـَايَـتِى ثَمَناً قَلِيلاً وَمَن لَّمْ يَحْكُم بِمَآ أَنزَلَ اللَّهُ فَأُوْلَـئِكَ هُمُ الْكَـفِرُونَ﴾

(and they were witnesses thereto. Therefore fear not men but fear Me and sell not My verses for a miserable price. And whosoever does not judge by what Allah has revealed, such are the disbelievers.) There are two ways to explain this Ayah and we will mention the later.

Imam Ahmad recorded that Ibn `Abbas said, "Allah sent down the Ayat,

﴿وَمَن لَّمْ يَحْكُم بِمَآ أَنزَلَ اللَّهُ فَأُوْلَـئِكَ هُمُ الْكَـفِرُونَ﴾

(And whosoever does not judge by what Allah has revealed, such are the disbelievers,)

﴿فَأُوْلَـئِكَ هُمُ الظَّـلِمُونَ﴾

(Such are the unjust,) and,

﴿فَأُوْلَـئِكَ هُمُ الْفَـسِقُونَ﴾

(Such are the rebellious.) about two groups among the Jews. During the time of Jahiliyyah, one of them had defeated the other. As a result, they made a treaty that they would pay blood money totaling fifty Wasaq }of gold {(each Wasaq approx. 3 kg) for every dead person from the defeated group killed by the victors, and a hundred Wasaq for every dead person the defeated group killed from the victors. This treaty remained in effect until the Prophet came to Al-Madinah and both of these groups became subservient under the Prophet . Yet, when the mighty group once suffered a casualty at the hands of the weaker group, the mighty group sent a delegation demanding the hundred Wasaq. The weaker group said, `How can two groups who have the same religion, one ancestral lineage and a common land, have a Diyah that for some of them is half of that of the others We only agreed to this because you oppressed us and because we feared you. Now that Muhammad has come, we will not give you what you asked.' So war was almost rekindled between them, but they agreed to seek Muhammad's judgement in their dispute. The mighty group among them said among themselves "By Allah! Muhammad will never give you double the Diyah that you pay to them compared to what they pay to you. They have said the truth anyway, for they only gave us this amount because we oppressed and overpowered them. Therefore, send someone to Muhammad who will sense what his judgement will be. If he agrees to give you what you demand, accept his judgment, and if he does not give you what you seek, do not refer to him for judgement." So they sent some hypocrites to the Messenger of Allah to try and find out the Messenger's judgement. When they came to the Messenger , Allah informed him of their matter and of their plot. Allah sent down,

﴿يأَيُّهَا الرَّسُولُ لاَ يَحْزُنكَ الَّذِينَ يُسَارِعُونَ فِى الْكُفْرِ﴾

(O Messenger! Let not those who hurry to fall into disbelief grieve you,) until,

﴾الْفَـسِقُونَ﴾

(Such are the rebellious.) By Allah! It is because of their problem that Allah sent down these verses and it is they whom Allah meant." Abu Dawud collected a similar narration for this Hadith. Abu Ja`far Ibn Jarir recorded that Ibn `Abbas said that the Ayah in Surat Al-Ma'idah,

﴾فَاحْكُم بَيْنَهُمْ أَوْ أَعْرِضْ عَنْهُمْ﴾

(either judge between them, or turn away from them...) until,

﴾الْمُقْسِطِينَ﴾

(Those who act justly.) was revealed concerning the problem of blood money between Bani An-Nadir and Bani Qurayzah. The dead of Bani An-Nadir were being honored more and they received the full amount of Diyah, while Qurayzah received half the Diyah for their dead. So they referred to the Messenger of Allah for judgement and Allah sent down these verses about them. The Messenger of Allah compelled them to adhere to the true judgement in this matter and made the Diyah the same for both groups and Allah knows best about that matter." Ahmad, Abu Dawud and An-Nasa'i also recorded this Hadith from Abu Ishaq. Al-`Awfi and `Ali bin Abi Talhah reported that Ibn `Abbas said that these Ayat were revealed about the two Jews who committed adultery. It appears that both of these were the reasons behind revealing these Ayat, and Allah knows best. This is why Allah said afterwards,

﴿وَكَتَبْنَا عَلَيْهِمْ فِيهَآ أَنَّ النَّفْسَ بِالنَّفْسِ وَالْعَيْنَ بِالْعَيْنِ﴾

(And We ordained therein for them: Life for life, eye for eye) until the end of the Ayah, which strengthens the opinion that the story of the Diyah was behind revealing the Ayat as we explained above. Allah knows best. Allah said,

﴿وَمَن لَّمْ يَحْكُم بِمَآ أَنزَلَ اللَّهُ فَأُوْلَـئِكَ هُمُ الْكَـفِرُونَ﴾

(And whosoever does not judge by what Allah has revealed, such are the disbelievers.) Al-Bara' bin `Azib, Hudhayfah bin Al-Yaman, Ibn `Abbas, Abu Mijlaz, Abu Raja' Al-`Utaridi, `Ikrimah, `Ubaydullah bin `Abdullah, Al-Hasan Al-Basri and others said that this Ayah was revealed about the People of the Book. Al-Hasan Al-Basri added that this Ayah also applies to us. `Abdur-Razzaq said that Ath-Thawri said that Mansur said that Ibrahim said that these Ayat, "Were revealed about the Children of Israel, and Allah accepted them for this Ummah." Ibn Jarir recorded this statement. `Ali bin Abi Talhah also stated that Ibn `Abbas commented on Allah's statement,

﴿وَمَن لَّمْ يَحْكُم بِمَآ أَنزَلَ اللَّهُ فَأُوْلَـئِكَ هُمُ الْكَـفِرُونَ﴾

(And whosoever does not judge by what Allah has revealed, such are the disbelievers,) "Whoever rejects what Allah has revealed, will have committed Kufr, and whoever accepts what Allah has revealed, but did not rule by it, is a Zalim (unjust) and a Fasiq (rebellious) and a sinner." Ibn Jarir recorded this statement. `Abdur-Razzaq said, "Ma`mar narrated to us that Tawus said that Ibn `Abbas was asked about Allah's statement,

﴿وَمَن لَّمْ يَحْكُم﴾

(And whosoever does not judge...) He said, `It is an act of Kufr.' Ibn Tawus added, `It is not like those who disbelieve in Allah, His angels, His Books and His Messengers.' Ath-Thawri narrated that Ibn Jurayj said that `Ata' said, `There is Kufr and Kufr less than Kufr, Zulm and Zulm less than Zulm, Fisq and Fisq less than Fisq.'" Waki` said that Sa`id Al-Makki said that Tawus said that,

﴿وَمَن لَّمْ يَحْكُم بِمَآ أَنزَلَ اللَّهُ فَأُوْلَـئِكَ هُمُ الْكَـفِرُونَ﴾

(And whosoever does not judge by what Allah has revealed, such are the disbelievers,) "This is not the Kufr that annuls one's religion."

A Hadith that An-Nasa'i recorded states that the Messenger of Allah had this statement written in the book that he gave `Amr bin Hazm,

«أَنَّ الرَّجُلَ يُقْتَلُ بِالْمَرْأَةِ»

(The man is killed for the woman (whom he kills).) In another Hadith, the Messenger said,

«الْمُسْلِمُونَ تَتَكَافَأُ دِمَاؤُهُم»

(Muslims are equal regarding the sanctity of their blood.) This is also the opinion of the majority of the scholars. What further supports what Ibn As-Sabbagh said is the

Hadith that Imam Ahmad recorded that Anas bin Malik said, "Ar-Rabi` (his aunt) broke the tooth of a girl, and the relatives of Ar-Rabi` requested the girl's relatives to forgive (the offender), but they refused. So, they went to the Prophet who ordered them to bring about retaliation. Anas bin An-Nadr, her brother, asked, `O Allah's Messenger! Will the tooth of Ar-Rabi` be broken' The Messenger of Allah said, `O Anas! The Book of Allah prescribes retaliation.' Anas said, `No, by Him Who has sent you with the Truth, her tooth will not be broken.' Later the relatives of the girl agreed to forgive Ar-Rabi` and forfeit their right to retaliation. The Messenger of Allah said,

«إن من عباد الله من لو أقسم على الله لأبره»

(There are some of Allah's servants who, if they take an oath by Allah, Allah fullfils them.)" It was recorded in the Two Sahihs.

Allah said,

﴿وَالْجُرُوحَ قِصَاصٌ﴾

(and wounds equal for equal.) `Ali bin Abi Talhah reported that Ibn `Abbas said, "Life for life, an eye for an eye, a nose, if cut off, for a nose, a tooth broken for a tooth and wounds equal for wound." The free Muslims, men and women, are equal in this matter. And their slaves, male and female, are equal in this matter. And this ruling is the same regarding intentional murder and lesser offenses, as Ibn Jarir and Ibn Abi Hatim recorded.

The retaliation for wounds should not be implemented until the wounds of the victim heal. If retaliation occurs before the wound heals, and then the wound becomes aggravated, the victim will have no additional rights in this case. The proof for this ruling is what Imam Ahmad narrated from `Amr bin Shu`ayb, from his father, from his grandfather that a man once stabbed another man in his leg using a horn. The victim came to the Prophet asking for retaliation, and the Prophet said,

«حَتَّى تَبْرَأ»

(Not until you heal.) The man again came to the Prophet and asked for equality in retaliation and the Prophet allowed him that. Later on, that man said, "O Messenger of Allah! I limp now." The Messenger said,

«قَدْ نَهَيْتُكَ فَعَصَيْتَنِي، فَأَبْعَدَكَ اللهُ وَبَطَلَ عَرَجُك»

(I had asked you to wait, but you disobeyed me. Therefore, Allah cast you away and your limp has no compensation.) Afterwards, the Messenger of Allah forbade that the wound be retaliated for until the wound of the victim heals. If the victim is allowed to retaliate for his wound caused by the aggressor and the aggressor dies as a result, there is no compensation in this case, according to the majority of the Companions and their followers.

Allah said,

﴿فَمَن تَصَدَّقَ بِهِ فَهُوَ كَفَّارَةٌ لَّهُ﴾

(But if anyone remits the retaliation by way of charity, it shall be for him an expiation.) `Ali bin Abi Talhah reported that Ibn `Abbas commented that

﴿فَمَن تَصَدَّقَ بِهِ﴾

(But if anyone remits the retaliation by way of charity) means; "If one pardons by way of charity, it will result in expiation for the aggressor and reward for the victim." Sufyan Ath-Thawri said that `Ata' bin As-Sa'ib said that Sa`id bin Jubayr said that Ibn `Abbas said, `He who pardons the retaliation by way of charity, it will be an expiation for the aggressor and a reward for the victim with Allah." Ibn Abi Hatim recorded this statement. Jabir bin `Abdullah said that Allah's statement,

﴿فَمَن تَصَدَّقَ بِهِ فَهُوَ كَفَّارَةٌ لَّهُ﴾

(But if anyone remits the retaliation by way of charity, it shall be for him an expiation,) "For the victim." This is also the opinion of Al-Hasan Al-Basri, Ibrahim An-Nakha`i and Abu Ishaq Al-Hamdani. Imam Ahmad recorded that `Ubadah bin As-Samit said, "I heard the Messenger of Allah saying,

«مَا مِنْ رَجُلٍ يُجْرَحُ مِنْ جَسَدِهِ جَرَاحَةً فَيَتَصَدَّقُ بِهَا، إِلَّا كَفَّرَ اللهُ عَنْهُ مِثْلَ مَا تَصَدَّقَ بِهِ»

(Any man who suffers a wound on his body and forfeits his right of retaliation as way of charity, then Allah will pardon him that which is similar to what he forfeited.) An-Nasa'i and Ibn Jarir recorded this Hadith

Allah said,

﴿وَقَفَّيْنَا﴾

(and We sent...) meaning, We sent

﴿عَلَى ءَاثَـٰرِهِمْ﴾

(in their footsteps) meaning the Prophets of the Children of Israel,

﴿بِعِيسَى ابْنِ مَرْيَمَ مُصَدِّقاً لِّمَا بَيْنَ يَدَيْهِ مِنَ التَّوْرَاةِ﴾

(Jesus, son of Maryam, confirming the Tawrah that had come before him,) meaning, he believed in it and ruled by it.

﴿وَءَاتَيْنَـٰهُ الإِنجِيلَ فِيهِ هُدًى وَنُورٌ﴾

(and We gave him the Injil, in which was guidance and light) a guidance that directs to the truth and a light that removes the doubts and solves disputes,

﴿وَمُصَدِّقاً لِّمَا بَيْنَ يَدَيْهِ مِنَ التَّوْرَاةِ﴾

(and confirmation of the Tawrah that had come before it,) meaning, he adhered to the Tawrah, except for the few instances that clarified the truth where the Children of Israel differed. Allah states in another Ayah that `Jesus said to the Children of Israel,

﴿وَلأُحِلَّ لَكُم بَعْضَ الَّذِي حُرِّمَ عَلَيْكُمْ﴾

(...and to make lawful to you part of what was forbidden to you.) So the scholars say that the Injil abrogated some of the rulings of the Tawrah. Allah's statement,

﴿وَهُدًى وَمَوْعِظَةٌ لِّلْمُتَّقِينَ﴾

(a guidance and an admonition for those who have Taqwa.) means, We made the Injil guidance and an admonition that prohibits committing sins and errors, for those who have Taqwa of Allah and fear His warning and torment. Allah said next,

﴿وَلْيَحْكُمْ أَهْلُ الإِنجِيلِ بِمَآ أَنزَلَ اللَّهُ فِيهِ﴾

(Let the people of the Injil judge by what Allah has revealed therein.) meaning, so that He judges the people of the Injil by it in their time. Or, the Ayah means, so that they believe in all that is in it and adhere to all its commands, including the good news about the coming of Muhammad and the command to believe in and follow him when he is sent. Allah said in other Ayat,

﴿قُلْ يَـأَهْلَ الْكِتَـبِ لَسْتُمْ عَلَى شَىْءٍ حَتَّى تُقِيمُواْ التَّوْرَاةَ وَالإِنجِيلَ وَمَا أُنزِلَ إِلَيْكُم مِّن رَّبِّكُمْ﴾

(Say "O People of the Scripture! You have nothing (guidance) until you act according to the Tawrah, the Injil, and what has been sent down to you from your Lord.") and,

﴿الَّذِينَ يَتَّبِعُونَ الرَّسُولَ النَّبِىَّ الأُمِّىَّ الَّذِى يَجِدُونَهُ مَكْتُوبًا عِندَهُمْ فِى التَّوْرَاةِ﴾

(Those who follow the Messenger, the Prophet who can neither read nor write whom they find written with them in the Tawrah...) until,

﴿الْمُفْلِحُونَ﴾

(...successful.) Here, Allah said,

﴿وَمَن لَّمْ يَحْكُم بِمَآ أَنزَلَ اللَّهُ فَأُوْلَـئِكَ هُمُ الْفَـسِقُونَ﴾

(And whosoever does not judge by what Allah has revealed, such are the rebellious.) meaning, the rebellious and disobedient of Allah who prefer falsehood and abandon truth.

Allah mentioned the Tawrah that He sent down to His Prophet Musa, the one whom He spoke directly to, praising it, commanding that it should be implemented, before it was abrogated. Allah then mentioned the Injil, praised it and commanded its people to adhere to it and follow it, as we stated. He next mentioned the Glorious Qur'an that He sent down to His honorable servant and Messenger. Allah said,

﴿وَأَنزَلْنَا إِلَيْكَ الْكِتَـبَ بِالْحَقّ﴾

(And We have sent down to you the Book in truth...) meaning, with the truth that, no doubt, is coming from Allah,

﴿مُصَدِّقاً لِّمَا بَيْنَ يَدَيْهِ مِنَ الْكِتَـبِ﴾

(confirming the Scripture that came before it) meaning, the Divinely Revealed Books that praised the Qur'an and mentioned that it would be sent down from Allah to His servant and Messenger Muhammad . The Qur'an was revealed as was foretold in the previous Scriptures. This fact increased faith in the previous Scriptures for the sincere who have knowledge of these Scriptures, those who adhered to Allah's commands and Laws and believed in His Messengers. Allah said,

﴿قُلْ ءَامِنُواْ بِهِ أَوْ لاَ تُؤْمِنُواْ إِنَّ الَّذِينَ أُوتُواْ الْعِلْمَ مِن قَبْلِهِ إِذَا يُتْلَى عَلَيْهِمْ يَخِرُّونَ لِلأَذْقَانِ سُجَّدَا - وَيَقُولُونَ سُبْحَانَ رَبِّنَا إِن كَانَ وَعْدُ رَبِّنَا لَمَفْعُولاً ﴾

(Say: "Believe in it or do not believe (in it). Verily, those who were given knowledge before it, when it is recited to them, fall down on their faces in humble prostration." And they say: "Glory be to our Lord! Truly, the promise of our Lord must be fulfilled.") meaning that they say, the promise of our Lord, concerning the coming of Muhammad by the words of His previous Messengers, will certainly be fulfilled. Allah's statement,

﴿وَمُهَيْمِناً عَلَيْهِ﴾

(and Muhayminan over it) means entrusted over it, according to Sufyan Ath-Thawri who narrated it from Abu Ishaq from At-Tamimi from Ibn `Abbas. `Ali bin Abi Talhah reported that Ibn `Abbas said, "Muhaymin is, `the Trustworthy'. Allah says that the Qur'an is trustworthy over every Divine Book that preceded it." This was reported from `Ikrimah, Sa`id bin Jubayr, Mujahid, Muhammad bin Ka`b, `Atiyyah, Al-Hasan, Qatadah, `Ata' Al-Khurasani, As-Suddi and Ibn Zayd. Ibn Jarir said, "The Qur'an is trustworthy over the Books that preceded it. Therefore, whatever in these previous Books conforms to the Qur'an is true, and whatever disagrees with the Qur'an is false." Al-Walibi said that Ibn `Abbas said that Muhayminan means, `Witness'. Mujahid, Qatadah and As-Suddi said the same. Al-`Awfi said that Ibn `Abbas said that Muhayminan means, `dominant over the previous Scriptures'. These meanings are similar, as the word Muhaymin includes them all. Consequently, the Qur'an is trustworthy, a witness, and dominant over every Scripture that preceded it. This Glorious Book, which Allah revealed as the Last and Final Book, is the most encompassing, glorious and perfect Book of all times. The Qur'an includes all the good aspects of previous Scriptures and even more, which no previous Scripture ever contained. This is why Allah made it trustworthy, a witness and dominant over all Scriptures. Allah promised that He will protect the Qur'an and swore by His Most Honorable Self,

﴿إِنَّا نَحْنُ نَزَّلْنَا الذِّكْرَ وَإِنَّا لَهُ لَحَـٰفِظُونَ﴾

(Verily, We, it is We Who have sent down the Dhikr and surely, We will guard it (from corruption).) Allah said,

﴿فَاحْكُم بَيْنَهُم بِمَآ أَنزَلَ اللَّهُ﴾

(So judge between them by what Allah has revealed.) The Ayah commands: O Muhammad! Rule between the people, Arabs and non-Arabs, lettered and unlettered, by what Allah has revealed to you in this Glorious Book and what it approves of for you from the Law of the previous Prophets, as Ibn Jarir said. Ibn Abi Hatim reported that Ibn `Abbas said, "The Prophet had the choice to judge between them or to turn away from them and refer them to their own Law. Then this Ayah was revealed,

﴿وَأَنِ احْكُم بَيْنَهُمْ بِمَآ أَنزَلَ اللَّهُ وَلاَ تَتَّبِعْ أَهْوَآءَهُمْ﴾

(So judge between them by what Allah has revealed, and follow not their vain desires. ..) and he was commanded to judge between them by our Book.". Allah's statement

﴿وَلاَ تَتَّبِعْ أَهْوَآءَهُمْ﴾

(and follow not their vain desires...) This means the ideas they promote, because of which they turned away from what Allah revealed to His Messengers. This is why Allah said,

﴿وَلاَ تَتَّبِعْ أَهْوَآءَهُمْ عَمَّا جَآءَكَ مِنَ الْحَقِّ﴾

(And follow not their vain desires, diverging away from the truth that has come to you.) The Ayah commands: Do not diverge from the truth that Allah has ordained for you, to the vain desires of these miserable, ignorant people. Allah's statement,

﴿لِكُلٍّ جَعَلْنَا مِنكُمْ شِرْعَةً وَمِنْهَاجاً﴾

(To each among you, We have prescribed a law and a clear way.)

﴿لِكُلٍّ جَعَلْنَا مِنكُمْ شِرْعَةً﴾

(To each among you, We have prescribed a law) Shir`at meaning, a clear path, as Ibn Abi Hatim recorded from Ibn `Abbas.

﴿وَلَوْ شَآءَ اللَّهُ لَجَعَلَكُمْ أُمَّةً وَحِدَةً﴾

(If Allah willed, He would have made you one nation.) This is a general proclamation to all nations informing them of Allah's mighty ability. If Allah wills, He would make all mankind follow one religion and one Law, that would never be abrogated. Allah decided that every Prophet would have his own distinct law that is later abrogated partially or totally with the law of a latter Prophet. Later on, all previous laws were abrogated by the Law that Allah sent with Muhammad , His servant and Messenger, whom Allah sent to the people of earth as the Final Prophet. Allah said,

﴿وَلَوْ شَآءَ اللَّهُ لَجَعَلَكُمْ أُمَّةً وَحِدَةً وَلَـكِن لِّيَبْلُوَكُمْ فِى مَآ ءَاتَـكُمْ﴾

(If Allah willed, He would have made you one nation, but that (He) may test you in what He has given you.) This Ayah means, Allah has instituted different laws to test His servants' obedience to what He legislates for them, thus, He rewards or punishes them according to their actions and what they intend. `Abdullah bin Kathir said that the Ayah,

﴿فِى مَآ ءَاتَـكُمْ﴾

(In what He has given you.) means, of the Book. Next, Allah encouraged rushing to perform good deeds,

﴿فَاسْتَبِقُواْ الْخَيْرَتِ﴾

(so strive as in a race in good deeds.) which are obedience to Allah, following His Law that abrogated the laws that came before it, and believing in His Book, the Qur'an, which is the Final Book that He revealed. Allah said next,

﴿إِلَى الله مَرْجِعُكُمْ﴾

(The return of you (all) is to Allah;) Therefore, O people, your return and final destination is to Allah on the Day of Resurrection,

﴿فَيُنَبِّئُكُم بِمَا كُنتُمْ فِيهِ تَخْتَلِفُونَ﴾

(then He will inform you about that in which you used to differ.) Allah will inform you about the truth in which you used to differ and will reward the sincere, as compensation for their sincerity, and will punish the disbelieving, rebellious people who rejected the truth and deviated from it to other paths, without proof or evidence to justify their actions. Rather, they have rejected the clear evidences, unequivocal proofs and established signs. Ad-Dahhak said that,

﴿فَاسْتَبِقُواْ الْخَيْرَتِ﴾

(So strive as in a race in good deeds.) is directed at the Ummah of Muhammad , but the first view is more apparent. Allah's statement,

﴿وَأَنِ احْكُم بَيْنَهُم بِمَا أَنزَلَ اللَّهُ وَلاَ تَتَّبِعْ أَهْوَاءَهُمْ﴾

(And so judge between them by what Allah has revealed and follow not their vain desires,) emphasizes this command and forbids ignoring it. Allah said next,

﴿وَاحْذَرْهُمْ أَن يَفْتِنُوكَ عَن بَعْضِ مَا أَنزَلَ اللَّهُ إِلَيْكَ﴾

(but beware of them lest they turn you far away from some of that which Allah has sent down to you.) meaning; beware of the Jews, your enemies, lest they distort the truth for you in what they convey to you.

Therefore, do not be deceived by them, for they are liars, treacherous and disbelievers.

﴿فَإِن تَوَلَّوْاْ﴾

(And if they turn away,) from the judgement that you pass in their disputes, and they defy Allah's Law,

﴿فَاعْلَمْ أَنَّمَا يُرِيدُ اللَّهُ أَن يُصِيبَهُم بِبَعْضِ ذُنُوبِهِمْ﴾

(then know that Allah's will is to punish them for some sins of theirs.) meaning, know that this will occur according to the decree of Allah, and because out of His wisdom they have deviated from the truth, and because of their previous sins.

﴿وَإِنَّ كَثِيراً مِّنَ النَّاسِ لَفَـسِقُونَ﴾

(And truly, most men are rebellious.) Therefore, the majority of humans are disobedient to their Lord, defiant of the truth and deviate away from it. Allah said in other Ayat,

﴿وَمَآ أَكْثَرُ النَّاسِ وَلَوْ حَرَصْتَ بِمُؤْمِنِينَ ﴾

(And most people will not believe even if you desire it eagerly,) and,

﴿وَإِن تُطِعْ أَكْثَرَ مَن فِى الأَرْضِ يُضِلُّوكَ عَن سَبِيلِ اللَّهِ﴾

(And if you obey most of those on the earth they will mislead you far away from Allah's path.) Muhammad bin Ishaq reported that Ibn `Abbas said, "Ka`b bin Asad, Ibn Saluba, `Abdullah bin Surya and Shas bin Qays said to each other, `Let us go to Muhammad to try and misguide him from his religion.' So they went to the Prophet and said, `O Muhammad! You know that we are the scholars, noblemen and chiefs of the Jews. If we follow you, the Jews will follow suit and will not contradict us. But, there is enmity between us and some of our people, so we will refer to you for judgement in this matter, and you should rule in our favor against them and we will believe in you.' The Messenger of Allah refused the offer and Allah sent down these Ayat about them,

﴿وَأَنِ احْكُم بَيْنَهُمْ بِمَآ أَنزَلَ اللَّهُ وَلاَ تَتَّبِعْ أَهْوَآءَهُمْ وَاحْذَرْهُمْ أَن يَفْتِنُوكَ عَن بَعْضِ مَآ أَنزَلَ اللَّهُ إِلَيْكَ﴾

(And so judge between them by what Allah has revealed and follow not their vain desires, but beware of them lest they turn you far away from some of that which Allah has sent down to you.) until,

﴿لِقَوْمٍ يُوقِنُونَ﴾

(for a people who have firm faith.)" Ibn Jarir and Ibn Abi Hatim recorded this Hadith. Allah continues,

﴿أَفَحُكْمَ الْجَـهِلِيَّةِ يَبْغُونَ وَمَنْ أَحْسَنُ مِنَ اللَّهِ حُكْماً لِّقَوْمٍ يُوقِنُونَ﴾

(Do they then seek the judgement of (the days of) ignorance And who is better in judgement than Allah for a people who have firm faith) Allah criticizes those who ignore Allah's commandments, which include every type of righteous good thing and prohibit every type of evil, but they refer instead to opinions, desires and customs that people themselves invented, all of which have no basis in Allah's religion. During the time of Jahiliyyah, the people used to abide by the misguidance and ignorance that they invented by sheer opinion and lusts. The Tatar (Mongols) abided by the law that they inherited from their king Genghis Khan who wrote Al-Yasiq, for them. This book contains some rulings that were derived from various religions, such as Judaism, Christianity and Islam. Many of these rulings were derived from his own opinion and desires. Later on, these rulings became the followed law among his children, preferring them to the Law of the Book of Allah and the Sunnah of His Messenger . Therefore, whoever does this, he is a disbeliever who deserves to be fought against, until he reverts to Allah's and His Messenger's decisions, so that no law, minor or major, is referred to except by His Law. Allah said,

$$\text{﴿أَفَحُكْمَ الْجَـٰهِلِيَّةِ يَبْغُونَ﴾}$$

(Do they then seek the judgement of (the days of) ignorance) meaning, they desire and want this and ignore Allah's judgement,

$$\text{﴿وَمَنْ أَحْسَنُ مِنَ اللَّهِ حُكْماً لِّقَوْمٍ يُوقِنُونَ﴾}$$

(And who is better in judgement than Allah for a people who have firm faith) Who is more just in decision than Allah for those who comprehend Allah's Law, believe in Him, who are certain that Allah is the best among those who give decisions and that He is more merciful with His creation than the mother with her own child Allah has perfect knowledge of everything, is able to do all things, and He is just in all matters. Al-Hafiz Abu Al-Qasim At-Tabarani recorded that Ibn `Abbas said that the Messenger of Allah said,

«أَبْغَضُ النَّاسِ إِلَى اللهِ عَزَّ وَجَلَّ، مَنْ يَبْتَغِي فِي الْإِسْلَامِ سُنَّةَ الْجَاهِلِيَّةِ، وَطَالِبُ دَمِ امْرِىءٍ بِغَيْرِ حَقٍّ لِيُرِيقَ دَمَهُ»

(The most hated person to Allah is the Muslim who seeks the ways of the days of ignorance and he who seeks to shed the blood of a person without justification.) Al-Bukhari recorded Abu Al-Yaman narrating a similar Hadith, with some addition.

Allah forbids His believing servants from having Jews and Christians as friends, because they are the enemies of Islam and its people, may Allah curse them. Allah then states that they are friends of each other and He gives a warning threat to those who do this,

﴿وَمَن يَتَوَلَّهُم مِّنكُمْ فَإِنَّهُ مِنْهُمْ﴾

(And if any among you befriends them, then surely he is one of them.) Ibn Abi Hatim recorded that `Umar ordered Abu Musa Al-Ash`ari to send him on one sheet of balance the count of what he took in and what he spent. Abu Musa then had a Christian scribe, and he was able to comply with `Umar's demand. `Umar liked what he saw and exclaimed, "This scribe is proficient. Would you read in the Masjid a letter that came to us from Ash-Sham" Abu Musa said, `He cannot." `Umar said, "Is he not pure" Abu Musa said, "No, but he is Christian." Abu Musa said, "So `Umar admonished me and poked my thigh (with his finger), saying, `Drive him out (from Al-Madinah).' He then recited,

﴿يَـٰأَيُّهَا الَّذِينَ ءَامَنُواْ لاَ تَتَّخِذُواْ الْيَهُودَ وَالنَّصَـٰرَى أَوْلِيَآءَ﴾

(O you who believe! Take not the Jews and the Christians as friends...)" Then he reported that `Abdullah bin `Utbah said, "Let one of you beware that he might be a Jew or a Christian, while unaware." The narrator of this statement said, "We thought that he was referring to the Ayah,

﴿يَـٰٓأَيُّهَا الَّذِينَ ءَامَنُواْ لاَ تَتَّخِذُواْ الْيَهُودَ وَالنَّصَـٰرَىٰ أَوْلِيَآءَ﴾

(O you who believe! Take not the Jews and the Christians as friends,)" Allah said,

﴿فَتَرَى الَّذِينَ فِى قُلُوبِهِم مَّرَضٌ﴾

(And you see those in whose hearts there is a disease...) A disease of doubt, hesitation and hypocrisy.

﴿يُسَـٰرِعُونَ فِيهِمْ﴾

(they hurry to their friendship,) meaning, they rush to offer them their friendship and allegiances in secret and in public,

﴿يَقُولُونَ نَخْشَىٰ أَن تُصِيبَنَا دَآئِرَةٌ﴾

(saying: "We fear lest some misfortune of a disaster may befall us.") They thus offer this excuse for their friendship and allegiances to the disbelievers, saying that they fear that the disbelievers might defeat the Muslims, so they want to be in favor with the Jews and Christians, to use this favor for their benefit in that eventuality! Allah replied,

﴿فَعَسَى اللَّهُ أَن يَأْتِىَ بِالْفَتْحِ﴾

(Perhaps Allah may bring a victory...) referring to the conquering of Makkah, according to As-Suddi.

﴾أَوْ أَمْرٍ مِّنْ عِندِهِ﴿

(or a decision according to His will) requiring the Jews and Christians to pay the Jizyah, as As-Suddi stated,

﴾فَيُصْبِحُواْ﴿

(Then they will become) meaning, the hypocrites who gave their friendship to the Jews and Christians, will become,

﴾عَلَى مَآ أَسَرُّواْ فِى أَنفُسِهِمْ﴿

(for what they have been keeping as a secret in themselves) of allegiances,

﴾نَـٰدِمِينَ﴿

(regretful,) for their friendship with the Jews and Christians which did not benefit them or protect them from any harm. Rather, it was nothing but harm, as Allah exposed their true reality to His faithful servants in this life, although they tried to conceal it. When the signs that exposed their hypocrisy were compiled against them, their matter became clear to Allah's faithful servants. So the believers were amazed at these hypocrites who pretended to be believers, swearing to their faithfulness, yet their claims were all lies and deceit.

This section focuses on legalistic history of judgements according to the Tawrah revealed to Moses and Injil revealed to Jesus and the command to now judge everything according to the revelation sent to Muhammad peace be upon them all. Those who seek justice elsewhere are falling into ignorance and sin. The top excuse for those who do so, usually under the guise of interfaith or tolerance, is fear of calamity striking them if they were to strictly adhere to and advocate the justice of Allah's Shariah. This error of judging by other than the law of Allah is mentioned alongside interfaith friendship because they often go hand in hand on the road to hell. Though it also symbolizes that those who refer to other laws, abrogated or innovations, are in a sense befriending kuffar via their imitation. So you don't necessarily have to be companions with a kafir to have befriended them for by adopting their laws or lifestyles or holidays or mannerisms or dress one is essentially being friendly to the enemies of God. So judging is not restricted to legal affairs, it applies to individual personal judgement in everything. Concerning snitching disliking it or aligning with anti-snitching movements are similar to erroneously judging in opposition to the Shariah's promotion of snitching. While that example is one aspect of judging correctly or incorrectly the principle applies to all aspects of life in that any evaluation of something must stick to the parameters of Prophetic laws.

Quran 5:54

يَـٰٓأَيُّهَا ٱلَّذِينَ ءَامَنُوا۟ مَن يَرْتَدَّ مِنكُمْ عَن دِينِهِۦ فَسَوْفَ يَأْتِى ٱللَّهُ بِقَوْمٍ يُحِبُّهُمْ وَيُحِبُّونَهُۥٓ أَذِلَّةٍ عَلَى ٱلْمُؤْمِنِينَ أَعِزَّةٍ عَلَى ٱلْكَـٰفِرِينَ يُجَـٰهِدُونَ فِى سَبِيلِ ٱللَّهِ وَلَا يَخَافُونَ لَوْمَةَ لَآئِمٍ ذَٰلِكَ فَضْلُ ٱللَّهِ يُؤْتِيهِ مَن يَشَآءُ وَٱللَّهُ وَٰسِعٌ عَلِيمٌ (٥٤)

O you who believe! Whoever from among you turns back from his religion (Islâm), Allâh will bring a people whom He will love and they will love Him; humble towards the believers, stern towards the disbelievers, fighting in the Way of Allâh, and never fear of the blame of the blamers. That is the Grace of Allâh which He bestows on whom He wills. And Allâh is All-Sufficient for His creatures' needs, All-Knower. (54)

Allah emphasizes His mighty ability and states that whoever reverts from supporting His religion and establishing His Law, then Allah will replace them with whomever is better, mightier and more righteous in Allah's religion and Law. Allah said in other Ayat,

﴿الْفُقَرَآءُ وَإِن تَتَوَلَّوْاْ يَسْتَبْدِلْ قَوْماً غَيْرَكُمْ ثُمَّ لاَ يَكُونُواْ﴾

(And if you turn away, He will exchange you for some other people and they will not be your likes.) and,

﴿أَلَمْ تَرَ أَنَّ اللَّهَ خَلَقَ السَّمَـوَتِ وَالأَرْضَ بِالْحقِّ إِن يَشَأْ يُذْهِبْكُمْ وَيَأْتِ بِخَلْقٍ جَدِيدٍ - وَمَا ذَلِكَ عَلَى اللَّهِ بِعَزِيزٍ ﴾

(Do you not see that Allah has created the heavens and the earth with truth If He will, He can remove you and bring (in your place) a new creation! And for Allah that is not hard or difficult.)14 :19-20 Verily this is not difficult or hard on Allah. Allah said here,

﴿يَأَيُّهَا الَّذِينَ ءَامَنُواْ مَن يَرْتَدَّ مِنكُمْ عَن دِينِهِ﴾

(O you who believe! Whoever from among you turns back from his religion...) and turns back from the truth to falsehood, from now until the commencement of the Last Hour. Allah said next,

﴿أَذِلَّةٍ عَلَى الْمُؤْمِنِينَ أَعِزَّةٍ عَلَى الْكَفِرِينَ﴾

(humble towards the believers, stern towards the disbelievers.) These are the qualities of perfect believers, as they are humble with their believing brothers and allies, stern with their enemies and adversaries. In another Ayah, Allah said,

﴿مُّحَمَّدٌ رَّسُولُ اللَّهِ وَالَّذِينَ مَعَهُ أَشِدَّآءُ عَلَى الْكُفَّارِ رُحَمَآءُ بَيْنَهُمْ﴾

(Muhammad is the Messenger of Allah. And those who are with him are severe against disbelievers, and merciful among themselves.) The Prophet is described as the smiling fighter, smiling to his allies and fighting his enemies. Allah's statement,

﴿يُجَـهِدُونَ فِى سَبِيلِ اللَّهِ وَلاَ يَخَـفُونَ لَوْمَةَ لائِمٍ﴾

(Fighting in the way of Allah, and never fearing the blame of the blamers.) Nothing prevents them from obeying Allah, establishing His Law, fighting His enemies, enjoining righteousness and forbidding evil. Certainly, nothing prevents them from taking this path, neither someone who seeks to hinder them, nor one who blames or chastises them. Imam Ahmad recorded that Abu Dharr said, "My Khalil (intimate friend, the Messenger) has commanded me to do seven deeds. He commanded me to love the poor and to be close to them. He commanded me to look at those who are less than me and not those who are above me. He commanded me to keep the relations of the womb, even if they cut it. He commanded me not to ask anyone for anything, to say the truth even if it was bitter, and to not fear the blame of anyone for the sake of Allah. He commanded me to often repeat, `La hawla wa la quwwata illa billah (There is no strength or power except from Allah)', for these words are from a treasure under the Throne (of Allah)." It is confirmed in the Sahih;

«مَا يَنْبَغِي لِلْمُؤْمِنِ أَنْ يُذِلَّ نَفْسَه»

(The believer is not required to humiliate himself.) He was asked; "How does one humiliate himself, O Messenger of Allah" So he replied;

«يَتَحَمَّلُ مِنَ الْبَلَاءِ مَا لَا يُطِيق»

(He takes on tests that he cannot bear.)

﴿ذلِكَ فَضْلُ اللهِ يُؤْتِيهِ مَن يَشَآءُ﴾

(That is the grace of Allah which He bestows on whom He wills.) meaning, those who have these qualities, acquired it by Allah's bounty and favor and because He granted them these qualities.

﴿وَاللهُ وَسِعٌ عَلِيمٌ﴾

(And Allah is All-Sufficient for His creatures' needs, All-Knower,) His favor is ever extending, and He has perfect knowledge of those who deserve or do not deserve His favor and bounty.

Here the consequences of not strictly adhering to the prophetic religion is declared in that Allah will replace the lackadaisical with those whom he loves who will adhere strictly to all aspects of the faith. For whatever reason it is that one falls short if one persists then it is a promise from God that just as prior nations were replaced then there is no guarantee the current claimants to the prophetic faith will not be replaced by others who will uphold the banner spreading the light of God worldwide. This happens daily as many revert to Islam who were once its enemies while others born into Muslim families become innovators which in reality are enemies in the clothes of Muslims. Basically if you dislike the command of snitching in Islam then that's okay, God will just abandon you and replace you with others who do like it and act accordingly without any harm done to Allah or his faith in the least. Servants are easily replaceable especially if they don't do what they are commanded.

Quran 5:62-63

وَتَرَىٰ كَثِيرًا مِّنْهُمْ يُسَٰرِعُونَ فِى ٱلْإِثْمِ وَٱلْعُدْوَٰنِ وَأَكْلِهِمُ ٱلسُّحْتَ ۚ لَبِئْسَ مَا كَانُواْ يَعْمَلُونَ (٦٢) لَوْلَا يَنْهَٰهُمُ ٱلرَّبَّٰنِيُّونَ وَٱلْأَحْبَارُ عَن قَوْلِهِمُ ٱلْإِثْمَ وَأَكْلِهِمُ ٱلسُّحْتَ ۚ لَبِئْسَ مَا كَانُواْ يَصْنَعُونَ (٦٣)

And you see many of them (Jews) hurrying towards sin and transgression, and eating illegal things [as bribes and Ribâ (usury), etc.]. Evil indeed is that which they have been doing (62) Why do not the rabbis and the religious learned men forbid them from uttering sinful words and from eating illegal things. Evil indeed is that which they have been performing. (63)

Allah's statement,

﴿وَتَرَى كَثِيراً مِّنْهُمْ يُسَٰرِعُونَ فِى الإِثْمِ وَالْعُدْوَانِ وَأَكْلِهِمُ السُّحْتَ﴾

(And you see many of them (Jews) hurrying for sin and transgression, and eating illegal things.) They hurry to devour prohibited and illegal things, all the while transgressing against people, unjustly consuming their property through bribes and Riba,

﴿لَبِئْسَ مَا كَانُواْ يَعْمَلُونَ﴾

(Evil indeed is that which they have been doing.) Indeed, horrible is that which they used to do and the transgression that they committed.

Allah said,

﴿لَوْلاَ يَنْهَـهُمُ الرَّبَّـنِيُّونَ وَالأُّحْبَارُ عَن قَوْلِهِمُ الإِثْمَ وَأَكْلِهِمُ السُّحْتَ لَبِئْسَ مَا كَانُواْ يَصْنَعُونَ ﴾

(Why do not the Rabbaniyyun and the Ahbar forbid them from uttering sinful words and from eating illegal things. Evil indeed is that which they have been performing.) meaning why don't the Rabbaniyyun and the Ahbar forbid them from this evil. The Rabbaniyyun are the scholars who are in positions of authority, while the Ahbar are the regular scholars.

﴿لَبِئْسَ مَا كَانُواْ يَصْنَعُونَ﴾

(Evil indeed is that which they have been performing.) referring to the Rabbaniyyun, as `Ali bin Abi Talhah reported from Ibn `Abbas, because they abandoned forbidding evil. Ibn Jarir recorded that Ibn `Abbas said, "There is no Ayah in the Qur'an that has more severe admonition than this Ayah,

﴿لَوْلاَ يَنْهَـهُمُ الرَّبَّـنِيُّونَ وَالأُّحْبَارُ عَن قَوْلِهِمُ الإِثْمَ وَأَكْلِهِمُ السُّحْتَ لَبِئْسَ مَا كَانُواْ يَصْنَعُونَ ﴾

(Why do not the Rabbaniyyun and the Ahbar forbid them from uttering sinful words and from eating illegal things. Evil indeed is that which they have been performing.)" Ibn Abi Hatim recorded that Yahya bin Ya`mar said, " `Ali bin Abi Talib once gave a speech, which he started by praising Allah and thanking Him. He then said, `O people! Those who were before you were destroyed because they committed sins and the Rabbaniyyun and Ahbar did not forbid them from evil. When they persisted in sin, they were overcome by punishment. Therefore, enjoin righteousness and forbid evil before what they suffered also strikes you. Know that enjoining righteousness and forbidding evil does not reduce the provision or shorten the term of life." Imam Ahmad recorded that Jarir said that the Messenger of Allah said,

«مَا مِنْ قَوْمٍ يَكُونُ بَيْنَ أَظْهُرِهِمْ مَنْ يَعْمَلُ بِالْمَعَاصِي هُمْ أَعَزُّ مِنْهُ وَأَمْنَعُ، وَلَمْ يُغَيِّرُوا إِلَّا أَصَابَهُمُ اللهُ مِنْهُ بِعَذَابٍ»

(There is no people among whom there are those who commit sins, while the rest are more powerful and mightier than the sinners, yet they do not stop them, but Allah will send a punishment upon them.) Ahmad was alone with this wording. Abu Dawud recorded it, but in his narration Jarir said, "I heard the Messenger of Allah saying,

«مَا مِنْ رَجُلٍ يَكُونُ فِي قَوْمٍ يُعْمَلُ فِيهِمْ بِالْمَعَاصِي، يَقْدِرُونَ أَنْ يُغَيِّرُوا عَلَيْهِ، فَلَا يُغَيِّرُوا إِلَّا أَصَابَهُمُ اللهُ بِعِقَابٍ قَبْلَ أَنْ يَمُوتُوا»

(There is no one who resides among people committing evil among them, and they do not stop him though they are able to do so, but Allah will punish them all before they die.)" Ibn Majah also recorded this Hadith.

Evil is not merely performing sin but evil is also failing to forbid sin. There is no such thing as a sinless bystander among sinful people. If the good is not enjoined and the evil is not forbidden then that is sufficient to be sinful regardless of whether other sins are actually committed. So these pious religious people if they aren't teaching and preaching in whatever form they are able to then they are perhaps just as sinful as the sinners who are known to be impious if not more sinful because the learned religious people have religious knowledge that the common sinner doesn't. Thus they owe God more and have extra responsibilities due to the prophetic wisdom they carry. Hence the attitude towards snitching is a tiny aspect of forbidding evil and enjoining good that has been neglected and misunderstood in this era but is so important that if implemented can turn the tide and contribute to the salvation of societies.

Quran 5:66-67

وَلَوْ أَنَّهُمْ أَقَامُوا ٱلتَّوْرَىٰةَ وَٱلْإِنجِيلَ وَمَآ أُنزِلَ إِلَيْهِم مِّن رَّبِّهِمْ لَأَكَلُوا۟ مِن فَوْقِهِمْ وَمِن تَحْتِ أَرْجُلِهِمْ مِّنْهُمْ أُمَّةٌ مُّقْتَصِدَةٌ وَكَثِيرٌ مِّنْهُمْ سَآءَ مَا يَعْمَلُونَ (٦٦) ۞ يَـٰٓأَيُّهَا ٱلرَّسُولُ بَلِّغْ مَآ أُنزِلَ إِلَيْكَ مِن رَّبِّكَ وَإِن لَّمْ تَفْعَلْ فَمَا بَلَّغْتَ رِسَالَتَهُ ۚ وَٱللَّهُ يَعْصِمُكَ مِنَ ٱلنَّاسِ إِنَّ ٱللَّهَ لَا يَهْدِى ٱلْقَوْمَ ٱلْكَـٰفِرِينَ (٦٧)

And if only they had acted according to the Taurât (Torah), the Injeel, and what has (now) been sent down to them from their Lord (the Qur'ân), they would surely have gotten provision from above them and from underneath their feet. There are from among them people who are on the right course (i.e. they act on the revelation and believe in Prophet Muhammad such as 'Abdullâh bin Salâm), but many of them do evil deeds. (66) O Messenger (Muhammad)! Proclaim (the Message) which has been sent down to you from your Lord. And if you do not, then you have not conveyed His Message. Allâh will protect you from mankind. Verily, Allâh guides not the people who disbelieve. (67)

Allah said,

﴿وَلَوْ أَنَّ أَهْلَ الْكِتَـبِ ءَامَنُواْ وَاتَّقَوْاْ﴾

(And if only the People of the Scripture had believed and had Taqwa...) Consequently, had the People of the Book believed in Allah and His Messenger and avoided the sins and prohibitions that they committed;

﴿لَكَفَّرْنَا عَنْهُمْ سَيِّئَـتِهِمْ وَلَأَدْخَلْنَـهُمْ جَنَّـتِ النَّعِيمِ﴾

(We would indeed have expiated for them their sins and admitted them to Gardens of pleasure (in Paradise).) meaning We would have removed the dangers from them and granted them their objectives.

﴿وَلَوْ أَنَّهُمْ أَقَامُواْ التَّوْرَاةَ وَالإِنجِيلَ وَمَآ أُنزِلَ إِلَيهِم مِّن رَّبِّهِمْ﴾

(And if only they had acted according to the Tawrah, the Injil, and what has (now) been sent down to them from their Lord,) meaning, the Qur'an, as Ibn `Abbas and others said.

﴿لأكَلُواْ مِن فَوْقِهِمْ وَمِن تَحْتِ أَرْجُلِهِمْ﴾

(they would surely have gotten provision from above them and from underneath their feet.) Had they adhered to the Books that they have with them which they inherited from the Prophets, without altering or changing these Books, these would have directed them to follow the truth and implement the revelation that Allah sent Muhammad with. These Books testify to the Prophet's truth and command that he must be followed. Allah's statement,

﴿لأَكَلُواْ مِن فَوْقِهِمْ وَمِن تَحْتِ أَرْجُلِهِم﴾

(they would surely have gotten provision from above them and from underneath their feet.) refers to the tremendous provision that would have descended to them from the sky and grown for them on the earth. Allah said in another Ayah,

﴿وَلَوْ أَنَّ أَهْلَ الْقُرَى ءَامَنُواْ وَاتَّقَوْاْ لَفَتَحْنَا عَلَيْهِم بَرَكَـتٍ مِّنَ السَّمَآءِ وَالأَرْضِ﴾

(And if the people of the towns had believed and had Taqwa, certainly, We should have opened for them blessings from the heaven and the earth.) Allah's statement,

﴿مِّنْهُمْ أُمَّةٌ مُّقْتَصِدَةٌ وَكَثِيرٌ مِّنْهُمْ سَآءَ مَا يَعْمَلُونَ﴾

(And among them is a Muqtasid Ummah, but for most of them; evil is their work.) is similar to Allah's statement,

﴿وَمِن قَوْمِ مُوسَى أُمَّةٌ يَهْدُونَ بِالْحَقِّ وَبِهِ يَعْدِلُونَ﴾

(And of the people of Musa there is a community who lead (the men) with truth and establish justice therewith.)

7:159 and His statement about the followers of `Isa, peace be upon him,

﴿فَآتَيْنَا الَّذِينَ ءَامَنُواْ مِنْهُمْ أَجْرَهُمْ﴾

(So We gave those among them who believed, their (due) reward.) Therefore, Allah gave them the highest grade of Iqtisad, which is the middle course, given to this Ummah. Above them there is the grade of Sabiqun, as Allah described in His statement;

﴿ثُمَّ أَوْرَثْنَا الْكِتَـبَ الَّذِينَ اصْطَفَيْنَا مِنْ عِبَادِنَا فَمِنْهُمْ ظَـلِمٌ لِنَفْسِهِ وَمِنْهُمْ مُّقْتَصِدٌ وَمِنْهُمْ سَابِقٌ بِالْخَيْرَتِ بِإِذْنِ اللهِ ذَلِكَ هُوَ الْفَضْلُ الْكَبِيرُ ـ جَنَّـتُ عَدْنٍ يَدْخُلُونَهَا يُحَلَّوْنَ فِيهَا مِنْ أَسَاوِرَ مِن ذَهَبٍ وَلُؤْلُؤاً وَلِبَاسُهُمْ فِيهَا حَرِيرٌ ﴾

(Then We gave the Book as inheritance to such of Our servants whom We chose. Then of them are some who wrong themselves, and of them are some who follow a middle course, and of them are some who, by Allah's permission, are Sabiq (foremost) in good deeds. That itself is indeed a great grace. `Adn (Eden) Paradise (everlasting Gardens) will they enter, therein will they be adorned with bracelets of gold and pearls, and their garments there will be of silk.

Allah addresses His servant and Messenger Muhammad by the title `Messenger' and commands him to convey all that He has sent him, a command that the Prophet has fulfilled in the best manner. Al-Bukhari recorded that `A'ishah said, "Whoever says to you that Muhammad hid any part of what Allah revealed to him, then he is uttering a lie. Allah said,

﴿يَـٰٓأَيُّهَا ٱلرَّسُولُ بَلِّغْ مَآ أُنزِلَ إِلَيْكَ مِن رَّبِّكَ﴾

(O Messenger! Convey what has been sent down to you from your Lord.)" Al-Bukhari collected the short form of this story here, but mentioned the full narration in another part of his book. Muslim in the Book of Iman, At-Tirmidhi, and An-Nasa'i in the Book of Tafsir of their Sunans also collected this Hadith. In is recorded in the Two Sahihs that `A'ishah said, "If Muhammad hid anything from the Qur'an, he would have hidden this Ayah,

﴿وَتُخْفِى فِى نِفْسِكَ مَا ٱللَّهُ مُبْدِيهِ وَتَخْشَى ٱلنَّاسَ وَٱللَّهُ أَحَقُّ أَن تَخْشَـٰهُ﴾

(But you did hide in yourself that which Allah will make manifest, you did fear the people while Allah had a better right that you should fear Him.)" Al-Bukhari recorded that Az-Zuhri said, "From Allah comes the Message, for the Messenger is its deliverance and for us is submission to it." The Ummah of Muhammad has testified that he has delivered the Message and fulfilled the trust, when he asked them during the biggest gathering in his speech during the Farewell Hajj. At that time, there were over forty thousand of his Companions. Muslim recorded that Jabir bin `Abdullah said that the Messenger of Allah said in his speech on that day,

«أَيُّهَا ٱلنَّاسُ إِنَّكُمْ مَسْؤُولُونَ عَنِّي، فَمَا أَنْتُمْ قَائِلُونَ؟»

(O people! You shall be asked about me, so what are you going to reply) They said, "We bear witness that you have conveyed (the Message), fulfilled (the trust) and offered sincere advice." The Prophet kept raising his finger towards the sky and then pointing at them, saying,

«اللَّهُمَّ هَلْ بَلَّغْتُ؟ اللَّهُمَّ هَلْ بَلَّغْتُ؟»

(O Allah! Did I convey O Allah! Did I convey) Allah's statement,

﴿وَإِن لَّمْ تَفْعَلْ فَمَا بَلَّغْتَ رِسَالَتَهُ﴾

(And if you do not, then you have not conveyed His Message.) meaning: If you do not convey to the people what I sent to you, then you have not conveyed My Message. Meaning, the Prophet knows the consequences of this failure. `Ali bin Abi Talhah reported that Ibn `Abbas commented on the Ayah,

﴿وَإِن لَّمْ تَفْعَلْ فَمَا بَلَّغْتَ رِسَالَتَهُ﴾

(And if you do not, then you have not conveyed His Message.) "It means, if you hide only one Ayah that was revealed to you from your Lord, then you have not conveyed His Message." Allah's statement,

﴿وَاللَّهُ يَعْصِمُكَ مِنَ النَّاسِ﴾

(Allah will protect you from mankind.) means, you convey My Message and I will protect, aid and support you over your enemies and will grant you victory over them. Therefore, do not have any fear or sadness, for none of them will be able to touch you with harm. Before this Ayah was revealed, the Prophet was being guarded, as Imam Ahmad recorded that `A'ishah said that the Prophet was vigilant one night when she was next to him;

she asked him, "What is the matter, O Allah's Messenger"
He said,

«لَيْتَ رَجُلًا صَالِحًا مِنْ أَصْحَابِي يَحْرُسُنِي اللَّيْلَة»

(Would that a pious man from my companions guard me
tonight!) She said, "Suddenly we heard the clatter of
arms. The Prophet said,

«مَنْ هَذَا؟»

(Who is that".) He (the new comer) replied, "I am Sa`d bin
Malik (Sa`d bin Abi Waqqas)." The Prophet asked,

«مَا جَاءَ بِكَ؟»

(What brought you here) He said, "I have come to guard
you, Allah's O Messenger." `A'ishah said, "So, the Prophet
slept (that night) and I heard the noise of sleep coming
from him.)" This Hadith is recorded in Two Sahihs.
Another narration for this Hadith reads, "The Messenger
of Allah was vigilant one night, after he came to Al-
Madinah...", meaning, after the Hijrah and after the
Prophet consummated his marriage to `A'ishah in the
second year of Hijrah. Ibn Abi Hatim recorded that
`A'ishah said, "The Prophet was being guarded until this
Ayah,

﴿وَاللَّهُ يَعْصِمُكَ مِنَ النَّاسِ﴾

(Allah will protect you from mankind) was revealed." She
added; "The Prophet raised his head from the room and
said;

«يَا أَيُّهَا النَّاسُ انْصَرِفُوا فَقَدْ عَصَمَنِي اللهُ عَزَّ وَجَل»

(O people! Go away, for Allah will protect me.)'" At-Tirmidhi recorded it and said, "This Hadith is Gharib." It was also recorded by Ibn Jarir, and Al-Hakim in his Mustadrak, where he said, "Its chain is Sahih, but they did not record it." Allah's statement,

﴿إِنَّ اللَّهَ لاَ يَهْدِى الْقَوْمَ الْكَـفِرِينَ﴾

(Verily, Allah guides not those who disbelieve.) means, O Muhammad, you convey, and Allah guides whom He wills, and misguides whom He wills. In other Ayat, Allah said,

﴿لَّيْسَ عَلَيْكَ هُدَاهُمْ وَلَـكِنَّ اللَّهَ يَهْدِى مَن يَشَآءُ﴾

(Not upon you is their guidance, but Allah guides whom He wills,) and,

﴿فَإِنَّمَا عَلَيْكَ الْبَلَـغُ وَعَلَيْنَا الْحِسَابُ﴾

(Your duty is only to convey and on Us is the reckoning.)

To be straight to the point, fear of negative reactions from others is often the leading cause of failure to adhere to prophetic guidance. Yet Allah promises if people act according to instructions they will achieve security in this life and the next. All we have to do is do our part and Allah will do his part to protect us from what is feared. A snitch should not fear consequences from the evil creatures they are snitching on because even if harm were to befall them they would find it to be expiation for their sins and a raising of their rank with God which is exactly what we want anyways. Most people want to follow the prophets but without receiving the harm the prophets endured, though to truly follow the prophets entails getting the reaction they got since you are combatting devils amongst humans and jinn.

Quran 5:70

لَقَدْ أَخَذْنَا مِيثَاقَ بَنِىٓ إِسْرَآءِيلَ وَأَرْسَلْنَآ إِلَيْهِمْ رُسُلًا كُلَّمَا جَآءَهُمْ رَسُولٌ بِمَا لَا تَهْوَىٰٓ أَنفُسُهُمْ فَرِيقًا كَذَّبُواْ وَفَرِيقًا يَقْتُلُونَ (٧٠)

Verily, We took the covenant of the Children of Israel and sent Messengers to them. Whenever there came to them a Messenger with what they themselves desired not - a group of them they called liars, and others among them they killed. (70)

It is known prior prophets would be killed by the very people they were sent to simply because the people didn't like the message not conforming to their wickedness. Not every prophet people claimed to have killed was actually killed, such as Jesus who never died and went to paradise alive, but many others were killed such as the contemporaries of Jesus; prophets John and Zachariah. Here Allah snitches on this practice of the Jews who claimed to follow prophets who they belied and killed.

Quran 5:78-79

لُعِنَ ٱلَّذِينَ كَفَرُواْ مِنْ بَنِىٓ إِسْرَآءِيلَ عَلَىٰ لِسَانِ دَاوُۥدَ وَعِيسَى ٱبْنِ مَرْيَمَ ذَٰلِكَ بِمَا عَصَواْ وَّكَانُواْ يَعْتَدُونَ (٧٨) كَانُواْ لَا يَتَنَاهَوْنَ عَن مُّنكَرٍ فَعَلُوهُ لَبِئْسَ مَا كَانُواْ يَفْعَلُونَ (٧٩)

Those among the Children of Israel who disbelieved were cursed by the tongue of Dawûd (David) and 'Īsā (Jesus), son of Maryam (Mary). That was because they disobeyed (Allâh and the Messengers) and were ever transgressing beyond bounds.

(78) They used not to forbid one another from Al-Munkar (wrong, evil-doing, sins, polytheism, disbelief) which they committed. Vile indeed was what they used to do. (79)

Allah states that He has cursed the disbelievers among the Children of Israel long ago, and revealed this fact to His Prophets Dawud and `Isa, son of Maryam. He cursed them because they disobeyed Allah and transgressed against His creatures. Al-`Awfi reported that Ibn `Abbas said, "They were cursed in the Tawrah, the Injil, the Zabur (Psalms) and the Furqan (Qur'an)." Allah then states that during their time, their habit was that,

﴿كَانُواْ لاَ يَتَنَـهَوْنَ عَن مُّنكَرٍ فَعَلُوهُ﴾

(They used not to forbid one another from the evil they committed.) They did not forbid each other from committing sins and the prohibitions. Allah chastised them for this behavior, so that their behavior would not be imitated. Allah said,

﴿لَبِئْسَ مَا كَانُواْ يَفْعَلُونَ﴾

(Vile indeed was what they used to do.)

There are many Hadiths that order enjoining righteousness and forbidding evil. Imam Ahmad recorded that Hudhayfah bin Al-Yaman said that the Prophet said,

«وَالَّذِي نَفْسِي بِيَدِهِ، لَتَأْمُرُنَّ بِالْمَعْرُوفِ، وَلَتَنْهَوُنَّ عَنِ الْمُنْكَرِ، أَوْ لَيُوشِكَنَّ اللهُ أَنْ يَبْعَثَ عَلَيْكُمْ عِقَابًا مِنْ عِنْدِهِ، ثُمَّ لَتَدْعُنَّهُ فَلَا يَسْتَجِيبَ لَكُم»

(By He in Whose Hand is my soul! You will enjoin righteousness and forbid evil, or Allah will send a punishment on you from Him. Then, you will supplicate to Him, but He will not accept your supplication.) At-Tirmidhi also recorded it and said, "This Hadith is Hasan." Muslim recorded that Abu Sa`id Al-Khudri said that the Messenger of Allah said,

«مَنْ رَأَى مِنْكُمْ مُنْكَرًا فَلْيُغَيِّرْهُ بِيَدِهِ، فَإِنْ لَمْ يَسْتَطِعْ فَبِلِسَانِهِ، فَإِنْ لَمْ يَسْتَطِعْ فَبِقَلْبِهِ، وَذلِكَ أَضْعَفُ الْإِيمَانِ»

(He among you who witnesses an evil, let him change it with his hand, if he cannot do that, then by his tongue, if he cannot do even that, then with his heart, and this is the weakest faith.) Abu Dawud said that Al-`Urs, meaning Ibn `Amirah, said that the Prophet said,

«إِذَا عُمِلَتِ الْخَطِيئَةُ فِي الْأَرْضِ كَانَ مَنْ شَهِدَهَا فَكَرِهَهَا، وَقَالَ مَرَّةً فَأَنْكَرَهَا كَانَ كَمَنْ غَابَ عَنْهَا، وَمَنْ غَابَ عَنْهَا فَرَضِيَهَا كَانَ كَمَنْ شَهِدَهَا»

(When sin is committed on the earth, then whoever witnesses it and hates - (once he said): forbids it, will be like those who did not witness it. Whoever was absent from it, but agreed with it, will be like those who witness it.) Only Abu Dawud recorded this Hadith. Abu Dawud recorded that one of the Companions said that the Prophet said,

«لَنْ يَهْلِكَ النَّاسُ حَتَّى يَعْذِرُوا أَوْ يُعْذِرُوا مِنْ أَنْفُسِهِمْ»

(The people will not perish until they do not leave -or- have any excuse for themselves.) Ibn Majah recorded that Abu Sa`id Al-Khudri said that the Messenger of Allah gave a speech once and said,

«أَلَا لَا يَمْنَعَنَّ رَجُلًا هَيْبَةُ النَّاسِ أَنْ يَقُولَ الْحَقَّ إِذَا عَلِمَهُ»

(Behold! Fear from people should not prevent one from saying the truth if he knows it.) Abu Sa`id then cried and said, "By Allah! We have seen some errors, but we feared (the people)." Another Hadith that Abu Sa`id narrated states that the Messenger of Allah said,

«أَفْضَلُ الْجِهَادِ كَلِمَةُ حَقَ عِنْدَ سُلْطَانٍ جَائِرٍ»

(The best Jihad is a word of truth proclaimed before an unjust ruler.) Recorded by Abu Dawud, At-Tirmidhi, and Ibn Majah. At-Tirmidhi said, "Hasan Gharib from this route of narration." Imam Ahmad recorded that Hudhayfah said that the Prophet said,

«لَا يَنْبَغِي لِمُسْلِمٍ أَنْ يُذِلَّ نَفْسَه»

(It is not required of the Muslim that he humiliate himself.) They said, `How does one humiliate himself" he said;

«يَتَعَرَّضُ مِنَ الْبَلَاءِ لِمَا لَا يُطِيق»

(He takes on trials that he is not capable of enduring.) This was recorded by At-Tirmidhi and Ibn Majah, and At-Tirmidhi said, "This Hadith is Hasan Sahih Gharib."

Not only is it blameworthy to not forbid evil but it merits the curse of Allah and prophets and angels and all mankind and all creatures. As it's said: a silent witness to evil is nothing but a silent devil. Don't be confused about the obligation of forbidding evil with wisdom and the ruling of snitching. Allah labeled the witnessing of evil while not forbidding evil as vile. So if you can't stop the evil yourself then tell an authority figure who can do so.

Quran 5:104-108

وَإِذَا قِيلَ لَهُمْ تَعَالَوْاْ إِلَىٰ مَآ أَنزَلَ ٱللَّهُ وَإِلَى ٱلرَّسُولِ قَالُواْ حَسْبُنَا مَا وَجَدْنَا عَلَيْهِ ءَابَآءَنَآ
أَوَلَوْ كَانَ ءَابَآؤُهُمْ لَا يَعْلَمُونَ شَيْـًٔا وَلَا يَهْتَدُونَ (١٠٤) يَـٰٓأَيُّهَا ٱلَّذِينَ ءَامَنُواْ عَلَيْكُمْ
أَنفُسَكُمْ لَا يَضُرُّكُم مَّن ضَلَّ إِذَا ٱهْتَدَيْتُمْ إِلَى ٱللَّهِ مَرْجِعُكُمْ جَمِيعًا فَيُنَبِّئُكُم بِمَا كُنتُمْ
تَعْمَلُونَ (١٠٥) يَـٰٓأَيُّهَا ٱلَّذِينَ ءَامَنُواْ شَهَٰدَةُ بَيْنِكُمْ إِذَا حَضَرَ أَحَدَكُمُ ٱلْمَوْتُ حِينَ
ٱلْوَصِيَّةِ ٱثْنَانِ ذَوَا عَدْلٍ مِّنكُمْ أَوْ ءَاخَرَانِ مِنْ غَيْرِكُمْ إِنْ أَنتُمْ ضَرَبْتُمْ فِى ٱلْأَرْضِ
فَأَصَٰبَتْكُم مُّصِيبَةُ ٱلْمَوْتِ تَحْبِسُونَهُمَا مِنۢ بَعْدِ ٱلصَّلَوٰةِ فَيُقْسِمَانِ بِٱللَّهِ إِنِ ٱرْتَبْتُمْ لَا
نَشْتَرِى بِهِۦ ثَمَنًا وَلَوْ كَانَ ذَا قُرْبَىٰ وَلَا نَكْتُمُ شَهَٰدَةَ ٱللَّهِ إِنَّآ إِذًا لَّمِنَ ٱلْءَاثِمِينَ
(١٠٦) فَإِنْ عُثِرَ عَلَىٰٓ أَنَّهُمَا ٱسْتَحَقَّآ إِثْمًا فَـَٔاخَرَانِ يَقُومَانِ مَقَامَهُمَا مِنَ ٱلَّذِينَ ٱسْتَحَقَّ
عَلَيْهِمُ ٱلْأَوْلَيَٰنِ فَيُقْسِمَانِ بِٱللَّهِ لَشَهَٰدَتُنَآ أَحَقُّ مِن شَهَٰدَتِهِمَا وَمَا ٱعْتَدَيْنَآ إِنَّآ إِذًا لَّمِنَ
ٱلظَّٰلِمِينَ (١٠٧) ذَٰلِكَ أَدْنَىٰٓ أَن يَأْتُواْ بِٱلشَّهَٰدَةِ عَلَىٰ وَجْهِهَآ أَوْ يَخَافُوٓاْ أَن تُرَدَّ أَيْمَٰنُۢ
بَعْدَ أَيْمَٰنِهِمْ وَٱتَّقُواْ ٱللَّهَ وَٱسْمَعُواْ وَٱللَّهُ لَا يَهْدِى ٱلْقَوْمَ ٱلْفَٰسِقِينَ (١٠٨)

And when it is said to them: "Come to what Allâh has revealed and unto the Messenger (Muhammad for the verdict of that which you have made unlawful)." They say: "Enough for us is that which we found our fathers following," even though their fathers had no knowledge whatsoever and nor guidance. (104) O you who believe! Take care of your ownselves, If you follow the (right) guidance (and enjoin what is right Islâmic Monotheism and all that Islâm orders one to do) and forbid what is wrong (polytheism, disbelief and all that Islâm has forbidden) no hurt can come to you from those who are in error. The return of you all is to Allâh, then He will inform you about (all) that which you used to do. (105) O you who believe! When death approaches any of you, and you make a bequest, (then take) the testimony of two just men of your own folk or two others from outside, While you are travelling through the land and death befalls you. Detain them both after As-Salât (the prayer), (then) if you are in doubt (about their truthfulness), let them both swear by Allâh (saying): "We wish not for any worldly gain in this, even though he (the beneficiary) be our near relative. We shall not hide Testimony of Allâh, for then indeed we should be of the sinful." (106) If then it gets known that these two had been guilty of sin, let two others stand forth in their places, nearest in kin from among those who claim a lawful right. Let them swear by Allâh (saying): "We affirm that our testimony is truer than that of both of them, and that we have not trespassed (the truth), for then indeed we should be of the wrong¬doers." (107) That should make it closer (to the fact) that their testimony would be in its true shape (and thus accepted), or else they would fear that (other) oaths would be admitted after their oaths. And fear Allâh and listen (with obedience to Him). And Allâh guides not the people who are Al-Fâsiqûn (the rebellious and disobedient). (108)

﴿وَإِذَا قِيلَ لَهُمْ تَعَالَوْاْ إِلَى مَآ أَنزَلَ اللَّهُ وَإِلَى الرَّسُولِ قَالُواْ حَسْبُنَا مَا وَجَدْنَا عَلَيْهِ ءَابَاءَنَآ﴾

(And when it is said to them: "Come to what Allah has revealed and to the Messenger." They say: "Enough for us is that which we found our fathers following,") meaning, if they are called to Allah's religion, Law and commandments and to avoiding what He prohibited, they say, `The ways and practices that we found our fathers and forefathers following are good enough for us. ` Allah said,

﴿أَوَلَوْ كَانَ ءَابَاؤُهُمْ لاَ يَعْلَمُونَ شَيْئاً﴾

(even though their fathers had no knowledge whatsoever...) That is, even though their fathers did not understand or recognize the truth or find its way.

Therefore, who would follow their forefathers, except those who are even more ignorant and misguided than they were.

Allah commands His believing servants to reform themselves and to do as many righteous deeds as possible. He also informs them that whoever reforms himself, he would not be affected by the wickedness of the wicked, whether they were his relatives or otherwise. Imam Ahmad recorded that Qays said, "Abu Bakr As-Siddiq stood up, thanked Allah and praised Him and then said, `O people! You read this Ayah,

﴿يَـأَيُّهَا الَّذِينَ ءَامَنُواْ عَلَيْكُمْ أَنْفُسَكُمْ لاَ يَضُرُّكُم مَّن ضَلَّ إِذَا اهْتَدَيْتُمْ﴾

(O you who believe! Take care of yourselves. If you follow the right guidance, no hurt can come to you from those who are in error.) You explain it the wrong way. I heard the Messenger of Allah say,

«إِنَّ النَّاسَ إِذَا رَأَوُا الْمُنْكَرَ وَلَا يُغَيِّرُونَهُ، يُوشِكُ اللهُ عَزَّ وَجَلَّ أَنْ يَعُمَّهُمْ بِعِقَابِه»

(If the people witness evil and do not change it, then Allah is about to send His punishment to encompass them.) I (Qays) also heard Abu Bakr say, `O people! Beware of lying, for lying contradicts faith.'"

This honorable Ayah contains a glorious ruling from Allah. Allah's statement,

﴿يِـأَيُّهَا الَّذِينَ ءَامَنُواْ شَهَـدَةُ بَيْنِكُمْ إِذَا حَضَرَ أَحَدَكُمُ الْمَوْتُ حِينَ الْوَصِيَّةِ اثْنَانِ﴾

(O you who believe! When death approaches any of you, and you make a bequest, then take the testimony of two...) meaning that there should be two witnesses in such cases,

﴿ذَوَا عَدْلٍ﴾

(just men...) thus, describing them as just,

﴿مِّنكُمْ﴾

(of your own folk) Muslims.

﴿أَوْ ءَاخَرَانِ مِنْ غَيْرِكُمْ﴾

(or two others from outside) non-Muslims, meaning the People of the Book, according to Ibn `Abbas as Ibn Abi Hatim recorded. Allah said next,

﴿إِنْ أَنتُمْ ضَرَبْتُمْ فِى الْأَرْضِ﴾

(if you are traveling through the land) on a journey,

﴿فَأَصَابَتْكُم مُّصِيبَةُ الْمَوْتِ﴾

(and the calamity of death befalls you.) These are two conditions that permit using non-Muslims from among the Dhimmis for witnesses when there are no Muslims present: When one is traveling and needs to write a will, as Sharih Al-Qadi said. Ibn Jarir recorded that Sharih said, "The witness of the Jews and Christians is not allowed except while traveling, and even then only to witness the dictation of the will." Allah's statement,

﴿تَحْبِسُونَهُمَا مِن بَعْدِ الصَّلَوةِ﴾

(Detain them both after the Salah (the prayer),) refers to the `Asr prayer, according to Al-`Awfi who reported it from Ibn `Abbas. This is the same explanation reported from Sa`id bin Jubayr, Ibrahim An-Nakha`i, Qatadah, `Ikrimah and Muhammad bin Sirin. As for Az-Zuhri, he said that they are detained after Muslim prayer (i.e., in congregation). Therefore, these two witnesses will be detained after a congregational prayer,

﴿فَيُقْسِمَانِ بِاللَّهِ إِنِ ارْتَبْتُمْ﴾

(let them both swear by Allah if you are in doubt.) meaning, if you are in doubt that they might have committed treachery or theft, then they should swear by Allah,

﴿لاَ نَشْتَرِى بِهِ﴾

(We wish not in this) in our vows, according to Muqatil bin Hayyan,

﴿ثَمَناً﴾

(for any worldly gain) of this soon to end life,

﴿وَلَوْ كَانَ ذَا قُرْبَى﴾

(even though he be our near relative.) meaning, if the beneficiary be our near relative, we will still not compromise on the truth.

﴿وَلاَ نَكْتُمُ شَهَدَةَ اللَّهِ﴾

(We shall not hide the testimony of Allah,) thus stating that the testimony is Allah's, as a way of respecting it and valuing its significance,

﴿إِنَّا إِذاً لَّمِنَ الأَّثِمِينَ﴾

(for then indeed we should be of the sinful.) if we distort the testimony, change, alter or hide it entirely. Allah said next,

﴿فَإِنْ عُثِرَ عَلَى أَنَّهُمَا اسْتَحَقَّا إِثْماً﴾

(If it then becomes known that these two had been guilty of sin...) if the two witnesses were found to have cheated or stolen from the money that the will is being written about,

﴿فَيَقُومَانُ مَقَامَهُمَا مِنَ الَّذِينَ اسْتَحَقَّ عَلَيْهِمُ الأَوْلَيَانِ﴾

(let two others stand forth in their places, nearest in kin from among those who claim a lawful right.) This Ayah indicates that if the two witnesses were found to have committed treachery, then two of the nearest rightful inheritors should stand for witness in their place,

﴿فَيُقْسِمَانِ بِاللَّهِ لَشَهَدَتُنَا أَحَقُّ مِن شَهَدَتِهِمَا﴾

(Let them swear by Allah (saying): "We affirm that our testimony is truer than that of both of them...") Meaning, our testimony that they have cheated is more truthful than the testimony that they have offered,

﴿وَمَا اعْتَدَيْنَآ﴾

(and that we have not trespassed (the truth),) when we accused them of treachery,

﴿إِنَّا إِذاً لَّمِنَ الظَّـلِمِينَ﴾

(for then indeed we should be of the wrongdoers.) if we had lied about them. This is the oath of the heirs, and preference is to be given to their saying. Just as in the case with the oath of relative of a murdered person if he attempts to tarnish the case of the murdered person. So his family takes an oath in defense of his honor. This is discussed in the studies of the oaths in the books of Ahkam. Allah's statement,

﴿ذلِكَ أَدْنَى أَن يَأْتُواْ بِالشَّهَدَةِ عَلَى وَجْهِهَآ﴾

(That should make it closer (to the fact) that their testimony would be in its true nature and shape (and thus accepted),) means, the ruling requiring the two Dhimmi witnesses to swear, if there is a doubt that they were not truthful, might compel them to admit to the testimony in its true form. Allah's statement,

﴿أَوْ يَخَـٰفُواْ أَن تُرَدَّ أَيْمَـٰنٌ بَعْدَ أَيْمَـٰنِهِمْ﴾

(or else they would fear that (other) oaths would be admitted after their oaths.) means, requiring them to swear by Allah might encourage them to admit to the true testimony because they respect swearing by Allah and they glorify and revere Him. They also fear exposure if the heirs of the deceased are required to swear instead of them. In this case, the heirs would swear and earn the rightful inheritance that the two witnesses failed to declare. This is why Allah said,

﴿أَوْ يَخَـٰفُواْ أَن تُرَدَّ أَيْمَنٌ بَعْدَ أَيْمَـٰنِهِمْ﴾

(or else they would fear that (other) oaths would be admitted after their oaths.), then,

﴿وَاتَّقُواْ اللَّهَ﴾

(And have Taqwa of Allah) in all of your affairs,

﴿وَاسْمَعُواْ﴾

(and listen.) and obey,

﴿وَاللَّهُ لاَ يَهْدِى الْقَوْمَ الْفَـسِقِينَ﴾

(And Allah guides not the rebellious people.) who do not obey Him or follow His Law.

Another reason people disobey Allah's laws is due to following tribalism aka family religion and due to their love for kin they prioritize their family's instructions over the faithful prophets. Allah chose prophets for us to follow we don't just follow our family, regardless of our feelings for them. If your love for family is greater than love for prophetic commands and prohibitions then that is tantamount to disbelief in the prophets and the one whom the prophets sent. Prophets should be the most beloved people to you, not your family members and oftentimes you have to side with prophetic teachings against your own family because family members can be stupid and stubborn set in their ways thinking religion is a heirloom or that relatives with good intentions can't possibly have taught them wrong. The strictness with which testimony regarding wills and other than that is also mentioned in these verses which again demonstrates how serious it is to bear false testimony and how it is incumbent to be truthful and report lies and crimes.

Quran 6:130

يَٰمَعْشَرَ ٱلْجِنِّ وَٱلْإِنسِ أَلَمْ يَأْتِكُمْ رُسُلٌ مِّنكُمْ يَقُصُّونَ عَلَيْكُمْ ءَايَٰتِى وَيُنذِرُونَكُمْ لِقَآءَ
يَوْمِكُمْ هَٰذَا قَالُوٓا۟ شَهِدْنَا عَلَىٰٓ أَنفُسِنَا وَغَرَّتْهُمُ ٱلْحَيَوٰةُ ٱلدُّنْيَا وَشَهِدُوا۟ عَلَىٰٓ أَنفُسِهِمْ أَنَّهُمْ
كَانُوا۟ كَٰفِرِينَ (١٣٠)

O you assembly of jinn and mankind! "Did not there come to you Messengers from amongst you, reciting unto you My Verses and warning you of the meeting of this Day of yours?" They will say: "We bear witness against ourselves." It was the life of this world that deceived them. And they will bear witness against themselves that they were disbelievers (130)

Allah will chastise the disbelieving Jinns and humans on the Day of Resurrection, when He asks them, while having better knowledge, if the Messengers delivered His Messages to them,

﴿يَٰمَعْشَرَ الْجِنِّ وَالإِنْسِ أَلَمْ يَأْتِكُمْ رُسُلٌ مِّنْكُمْ﴾

("O you assembly of Jinn and humans! Did not there come to you Messengers from among you") We should note here that the Messengers are from among mankind only, not vice versa, as Mujahid, Ibn Jurayj and others from the Imams of Salaf and later generations have stated.

Allah said in this honorable Ayah,

﴿يَٰمَعْشَرَ الْجِنِّ وَالإِنْسِ أَلَمْ يَأْتِكُمْ رُسُلٌ مِّنْكُمْ يَقُصُّونَ عَلَيْكُمْ آيَٰتِي وَيُنذِرُونَكُمْ لِقَآءَ
يَوْمِكُمْ هَذَا قَالُوا۟ شَهِدْنَا عَلَى أَنْفُسِنَا﴾

(O you assembly of Jinn and humans! "Did not there come to you Messengers from amongst you, reciting unto you My verses and warning you of the meeting of this Day of yours" They will say: "We bear witness against ourselves.") meaning, we affirm that the Messengers have conveyed Your Messages to us and warned us about the meeting with You, and that this Day will certainly occur. Allah said next,

﴿وَغَرَّتْهُمُ الْحَيَوةُ الدُّنْيَا﴾

(It was the life of this world that deceived them.) and they wasted their lives and brought destruction to themselves by rejecting the Messengers and denying their miracles. This is because they were deceived by the beauty, adornment and lusts of this life.

﴿وَشَهِدُواْ عَلَى أَنفُسِهِمْ﴾

(And they will bear witness against themselves) on the Day of Resurrection,

﴿أَنَّهُمْ كَانُواْ كَفِرِينَ﴾

(that they were disbelievers...) in this worldly life, rejecting what the Messengers, may Allah's peace and blessings be on them, brought them.

As part of their punishment Allah will end up getting the disbelievers to snitch on themselves via their own testimony that messengers were sent to them from Allah whom they disbelieved in.

Quran 7:38-39

قَالَ ٱدْخُلُواْ فِى أُمَمٍ قَدْ خَلَتْ مِن قَبْلِكُم مِّنَ ٱلْجِنِّ وَٱلْإِنسِ فِى ٱلنَّارِ كُلَّمَا دَخَلَتْ أُمَّةٌ لَّعَنَتْ أُخْتَهَا حَتَّىٰ إِذَا ٱدَّارَكُواْ فِيهَا جَمِيعًا قَالَتْ أُخْرَىٰهُمْ لِأُولَىٰهُمْ رَبَّنَا هَٰؤُلَآءِ أَضَلُّونَا فَـَٔاتِهِمْ عَذَابًا ضِعْفًا مِّنَ ٱلنَّارِ قَالَ لِكُلٍّ ضِعْفٌ وَلَٰكِن لَّا تَعْلَمُونَ (٣٨) وَقَالَتْ أُولَىٰهُمْ لِأُخْرَىٰهُمْ فَمَا كَانَ لَكُمْ عَلَيْنَا مِن فَضْلٍ فَذُوقُواْ ٱلْعَذَابَ بِمَا كُنتُمْ تَكْسِبُونَ (٣٩)

(Allâh) will say: "Enter you in the company of nations who passed away before you, of men and jinn, into the Fire." Every time a new nation enters, it curses its sister nation (that went before), until they will be gathered all together in the Fire. The last of them will say to the first of them: "Our Lord! These misled us, so give them a double torment of the Fire." He will say: "For each one there is double (torment), but you know not." (38) The first of them will say to the last of them: "You were not better than us, so taste the torment for what you used to earn." (39)

People of the Fire will dispute and curse Each Other Allah mentioned what He will say to those who associate others with Him, invent lies about Him, and reject His Ayat,

﴿ادْخُلُواْ فِى أُمَمٍ﴾

(Enter you in the company of nations), who are your likes and similar to you in conduct,

﴿قَدْ خَلَتْ مِن قَبْلِكُمْ﴾

(Who passed away before you) from the earlier disbelieving nations,

﴿مِّن الْجِنّ وَالإنْسِ فِى النَّارِ﴾

(Of men and Jinn, into the Fire.) Allah said next,

﴿كُلَّمَا دَخَلَتْ أُمَّةٌ لَّعَنَتْ أُخْتَهَا﴾

(Every time a new nation enters, it curses its sister nation (that went before)) Al-Khalil (Prophet Ibrahim), peace be upon him, said,

﴿ثُمَّ يَوْمَ الْقِيَمَةِ يَكْفُرُ بَعْضُكُم بِبَعْضٍ﴾

("But on the Day of Resurrection, you shall deny each other) 29:25. Also, Allah said,

﴿إِذْ تَبَرَّأَ الَّذِينَ اتُّبِعُواْ مِنَ الَّذِينَ اتَّبَعُواْ وَرَأَوُاْ الْعَذَابَ وَتَقَطَّعَتْ بِهِمُ الأُسْبَابُ ـ وَقَالَ الَّذِينَ اتَّبَعُواْ لَوْ أَنَّ لَنَا كَرَّةً فَنَتَبَرَّأَ مِنْهُمْ كَمَا تَبَرَّءُواْ مِنَّا كَذَلِكَ يُرِيهِمُ اللَّهُ أَعْمَـلَهُمْ حَسَرَتٍ عَلَيْهِمْ وَمَا هُم بِخَـرِجِينَ مِنَ النَّارِ﴾

(When those who were followed declare themselves innocent of those who followed (them), and they see the torment, then all their relations will be cut off from them. And those who followed will say: "If only we had one more chance to return (to the worldly life), we would declare ourselves as innocent from them as they have declared themselves as innocent from us." Thus Allah will show them their deeds as regrets for them. And they will never get out of the Fire) 2:166-167. Allah's statement,

﴿حَتَّى إِذَا ادَّارَكُواْ فِيهَا جَمِيعًا﴾

(until they are all together in the Fire) means, they are all gathered in the Fire,

﴿قَالَتْ أُخْرَاهُمْ لأُولَـهُمْ﴾

(The last of them will say to the first of them) that is, the nation of followers that enter last will say this to the first nations to enter. This is because the earlier nations were worse criminals than those who followed them, and this is why they entered the Fire first. For this reason, their followers will complain against them to Allah, because they were the ones who misguided them from the correct path, saying,

﴿رَبَّنَا هَؤُلاءِ أَضَلُّونَا فَآتِهِمْ عَذَابًا ضِعْفًا مِّنَ النَّارِ﴾

("Our Lord! These misled us, so give them a double torment of the Fire.") multiply their share of the torment. Allah said in another instance,

﴿يَوْمَ تُقَلَّبُ وُجُوهُهُمْ فِى النَّارِ يَقُولُونَ يَلَيْتَنَآ أَطَعْنَا اللَّهَ وَأَطَعْنَا الرَّسُولاَ ـ وَقَالُواْ رَبَّنَآ إِنَّآ أَطَعْنَا سَادَتَنَا وَكُبَرَآءَنَا فَأَضَلُّونَا السَّبِيلاْ رَبَّنَآ ءَاتِهِمْ ضِعْفَيْنِ مِنَ الْعَذَابِ﴾

(On the Day when their faces will be turned over in the Fire, they will say: "Oh! Would that we had obeyed Allah and obeyed the Messenger." And they will say: "Our Lord! Verily, we obeyed our chiefs and our great ones, and they misled us from the (right) way. Our Lord! Give them a double torment.") 33:66-68. Allah said in reply,

﴿قَالَ لِكُلٍّ ضِعْفٌ﴾

(He will say: "For each one there is double (torment)..."), We did what you asked, and recompensed each according to their deeds.' Allah said in another Ayah,

﴿الَّذِينَ كَفَرُواْ وَصَدُّواْ عَن سَبِيلِ اللَّهِ زِدْنَـهُمْ عَذَابًا﴾

(Those who disbelieved and hinder (men) from the path of Allah, for them We will add torment)16: 88 Furthermore, Allah said,

﴿وَلَيَحْمِلُنَّ أَثْقَالَهُمْ وَأَثْقَالاً مَّعَ أَثْقَالِهِمْ﴾

(And verily, they shall bear their own loads, and other loads besides their own) 29:13and,

﴿وَمِنْ أَوْزَارِ الَّذِينَ يُضِلُّونَهُمْ بِغَيْرِ عِلْمٍ﴾

(And also (some thing) of the burdens of those whom they misled without knowledge) 16:25.

﴾وَقَالَتْ أُولَـٰهُمْ لِأُخْرَاهُمْ﴿

(The first of them will say to the last of them) meaning, the followed will say to the followers,

﴾فَمَا كَانَ لَكُمْ عَلَيْنَا مِن فَضْلٍ﴿

("You were not better than us. ..") meaning, you were led astray as we were led astray, according to As-Suddi.

﴾فَذُوقُواْ الْعَذَابَ بِمَا كُنتُمْ تَكْسِبُونَ﴿

("So taste the torment for what you used to earn.") Allah again described the condition of the idolators during the gathering (of Resurrection), when He said;

﴾قَالَ الَّذِينَ اسْتَكْبَرُواْ لِلَّذِينَ اسْتُضْعِفُواْ أَنَحْنُ صَدَدنَـٰكُمْ عَنِ الْهُدَى بَعْدَ إِذْ جَآءَكُمْ بَلْ كُنتُمْ مُّجْرِمِينَ ـ وَقَالَ الَّذِينَ اسْتُضْعِفُواْ لِلَّذِينَ اسْتَكْبَرُواْ بَلْ مَكْرُ الَّيْلِ وَالنَّهَارِ إِذْ تَأْمُرُونَنَآ أَن نَّكْفُرَ بِاللَّهِ وَنَجْعَلَ لَهُ أَندَاداً وَأَسَرُّواْ النَّدَامَةَ لَمَّا رَأَوُاْ الْعَذَابَ وَجَعَلْنَا الْأَغْلَلَ فِى أَعْنَاقِ الَّذِينَ كَفَرُواْ هَلْ يُجْزَوْنَ إِلاَّ مَا كَانُواْ يَعْمَلُونَ﴿

(And those who were arrogant will say to those who were deemed weak: "Did we keep you back from guidance after it come to you Nay, but you were criminals." Those who were deemed weak will say to those who were arrogant: "Nay, but it was your plotting by night and day, when you ordered us to disbelieve in Allah and set up rivals to Him!" And each of them (parties) will conceal their own regrets, when they behold the torment. And We shall put iron collars round the necks of those who disbelieved. Are they requited aught except what they used to do) 34:32-33

Almost comically the kuffar will mutually snitch on each other in the hellfire cursing their co-religionists for their crimes which they are all partners in committing.

Quran 10:21

وَإِذَآ أَذَقْنَا ٱلنَّاسَ رَحْمَةً مِّن بَعْدِ ضَرَّآءَ مَسَّتْهُمْ إِذَا لَهُم مَّكْرٌ فِى ءَايَاتِنَا ۚ قُلِ ٱللَّهُ أَسْرَعُ مَكْرًا ۚ إِنَّ رُسُلَنَا يَكْتُبُونَ مَا تَمْكُرُونَ (٢١)

And when We let mankind taste mercy after some adversity has afflicted them, behold! they take to plotting against Our Ayât (proofs, evidences, verses, lessons, signs, revelations, etc.)! Say: "Allâh is more Swift in planning!" Certainly, Our Messengers (angels) record all of that which you plot. (21)

Quran 12:51

قَالَ مَا خَطْبُكُنَّ إِذْ رَاوَدتُّنَّ يُوسُفَ عَن نَّفْسِهِ ۚ قُلْنَ حَاشَ لِلَّهِ مَا عَلِمْنَا عَلَيْهِ مِن سُوٓءٍ ۚ قَالَتِ ٱمْرَأَتُ ٱلْعَزِيزِ ٱلْـَٰٔنَ حَصْحَصَ ٱلْحَقُّ أَنَا۠ رَاوَدتُّهُ ۥ عَن نَّفْسِهِ ۦ وَإِنَّهُ ۥ لَمِنَ ٱلصَّـٰدِقِينَ (٥١)

(The King) said (to the women): "What was your affair when you did seek to seduce Yûsuf (Joseph)?" The women said: "Allâh forbid! No evil know we against him!" The wife of Al-'Azîz said: "Now the truth is manifest (to all), it was I who sought to seduce him, and he is surely of the truthful." (51)

When the king's emissary came to Yusuf and conveyed the news of his imminent release, Yusuf refused to leave the prison until the king and his subjects declare his innocence and the integrity of his honor, denouncing the false accusation that the wife of the `Aziz made against him. He wanted them to know that sending him to prison was an act of injustice and aggression, not that he committed an offense that warranted it. He said,

﴿ارْجِعْ إِلَى رَبِّكَ﴾

(Return to your lord (i.e. king...) The Sunnah of our Prophet praised Prophet Yusuf and asserted his virtues, honor, elevated rank and patience, may Allah's peace and blessings be on him.

In a narration collected by Ahmad from Abu Hurayrah, the Prophet said about Yusuf's statement,

﴿فَاسْأَلْهُ مَا بَالُ النِّسْوَةِ الَّتِى قَطَّعْنَ أَيْدِيَهُنَّ إِنَّ رَبِّى بِكَيْدِهِنَّ عَلِيمٌ﴾

("...and ask him, `What happened to the women who cut their hands Surely, my Lord (Allah) is Well-Aware of their plot.'")

«لَوْ كُنْتُ أَنَا، لَأَسْرَعْتُ الْإِجَابَةَ وَمَا ابْتَغَيْتُ الْعُذْرَ»

(If it was me, I would have accepted the offer rather than await my exoneration first.) Allah said (that the king asked),

﴿قَالَ مَا خَطْبُكُنَّ إِذْ رَاوَدتُّنَّ يُوسُفَ عَن نَّفْسِهِ﴾

(He said, "What was your affair when you did seek to seduce Yusuf") The king gathered those women who cut their hands, while being hosted at the house of the wife of the `Aziz. He asked them all, even though he was directing his speech at the wife of his minister, the `Aziz in particular. He asked the women who cut their hands,

﴿مَا خَطْبُكُنَّ﴾

(What was your affair...), what was your story with regards to,

$$﴿إِذْ رَاوَدتُنَّ يُوسُفَ عَن نَفْسِهِ﴾$$

(when you did seek to seduce Yusuf) on the day of the banquet

$$﴿قُلْنَ حَاشَ للَّهِ مَا عَلِمْنَا عَلَيْهِ مِن سُوءٍ﴾$$

(The women said: "Allah forbid! No evil know we against him!") The women answered the king, `Allah forbid that Yusuf be guilty of this, for by Allah, we never knew him to do evil.' This is when,

$$﴿قَالَتِ امْرَأَتُ الْعَزِيزِ الَنَ حَصْحَصَ الْحَقُّ﴾$$

(The wife of the `Aziz said: "Now the truth has Hashasa...") or the truth is manifest to all, according to Ibn `Abbas, Mujahid and others. Hashasa also means, `became clear and plain'

This story of Yusuf shows the importance of truth and exoneration from false accusations related to crime. The man was imprisoned for protecting his chastity for years yet after being allowed to go he insisted upon just inquiry that led to the guilty women snitching on themselves or confessing to the reality prior to Yusuf's release from prison which was delayed due to the inquiry. How many of us would rather be falsely imprisoned for a little longer while an investigation is concluded if given the option to leave prior to the investigation starting or finishing?

Quran 12:53

۞ وَمَآ أُبَرِّئُ نَفْسِىٓ إِنَّ ٱلنَّفْسَ لَأَمَّارَةٌۢ بِٱلسُّوٓءِ إِلَّا مَا رَحِمَ رَبِّىٓ إِنَّ رَبِّى غَفُورٌ رَّحِيمٌ (٥٣)

"And I free not myself (from the blame). Verily, the (human) self is inclined to evil, except when my Lord bestows His Mercy (upon whom He wills). Verily, my Lord is Oft-Forgiving, Most Merciful." (53)

Furthermore Yusuf snitches on his hidden desires/temptations. After being declared legally innocent of sexual sin, he admits that he was not free from desire in order to teach that even with human desires it is possible to win the struggle against sin.

Quran 12:81

ٱرْجِعُوٓا۟ إِلَىٰٓ أَبِيكُمْ فَقُولُوا۟ يَٰٓأَبَانَآ إِنَّ ٱبْنَكَ سَرَقَ وَمَا شَهِدْنَآ إِلَّا بِمَا عَلِمْنَا وَمَا كُنَّا لِلْغَيْبِ حَٰفِظِينَ (٨١)

"Return to your father and say, 'O our father! Verily, your son (Benjamin) has stolen, and we testify not except according to what we know, and we could not know the unseen! (81)

Benjamin's brothers are advised to snitch on Benjamin for his alleged crime and this was the noble thing to do in their understanding of the situation.

Quran 18:94

قَالُوا۟ يَٰذَا ٱلْقَرْنَيْنِ إِنَّ يَأْجُوجَ وَمَأْجُوجَ مُفْسِدُونَ فِى ٱلْأَرْضِ فَهَلْ نَجْعَلُ لَكَ خَرْجًا عَلَىٰٓ أَن تَجْعَلَ بَيْنَنَا وَبَيْنَهُمْ سَدًّا (٩٤)

They said: "O Dhul-Qarnain! Verily! Ya'jûj and Ma'jûj (Gog and Magog) are doing great mischief in the land. Shall we then pay you a tribute in order that you might erect a barrier between us and them?" (94)

The victims of Yajuj and Majuj snitched on them for their mischief. This led Dhul-Qarnain to erect a wall as a ongoing charity to protect them and it has done its job so well that people today sadly disbelieve in the mischievous yajuj and majuj nations doubting their very existence because snitching led to such a thorough solution to the problems being snitched about. Thus correct snitching to proper authority figures can lead to problems being solved so much that people deny the problems even existed.

Quran 20:85-87

قَالَ فَإِنَّا قَدْ فَتَنَّا قَوْمَكَ مِن بَعْدِكَ وَأَضَلَّهُمُ ٱلسَّامِرِىُّ (٨٥) فَرَجَعَ مُوسَىٰ إِلَىٰ قَوْمِهِۦ غَضْبَٰنَ أَسِفًا ۚ قَالَ يَٰقَوْمِ أَلَمْ يَعِدْكُمْ رَبُّكُمْ وَعْدًا حَسَنًا ۚ أَفَطَالَ عَلَيْكُمُ ٱلْعَهْدُ أَمْ أَرَدتُّمْ أَن يَحِلَّ عَلَيْكُمْ غَضَبٌ مِّن رَّبِّكُمْ فَأَخْلَفْتُم مَّوْعِدِى (٨٦) قَالُوا۟ مَآ أَخْلَفْنَا مَوْعِدَكَ بِمَلْكِنَا وَلَٰكِنَّا حُمِّلْنَآ أَوْزَارًا مِّن زِينَةِ ٱلْقَوْمِ فَقَذَفْنَٰهَا فَكَذَٰلِكَ أَلْقَى ٱلسَّامِرِىُّ (٨٧)

(Allâh) said: "Verily! we have tried your people in your absence, and As-Samiri has led them astray." (85) Then Mûsa (Moses) returned to his people in a state of anger and sorrow. He said: "O my people! Did not your Lord promise you a fair promise? Did then the promise seem to you long in coming? Or did you desire that wrath should descend from your Lord on you, that you broke your promise to me (i.e disbelieving in Allâh and worshipping the calf)?" (86) They said: "We broke not the promise to you, of our own will, but we were made to carry the weight of the ornaments of the [Fir'aun's (Pharaoh)] people, then we cast them (into the fire), and that was what As-Samiri suggested." (87)

Allah informs His Prophet, Musa, of what happened to the Children of Israel after he left them, and their deification of the calf that As-Samiri had made for them. During this time period, Allah wrote for Musa the Tablets, which contained the Tawrah. Allah said,

﴿وَكَتَبْنَا لَهُ فِى الأَلْوَاحِ مِن كُلِّ شَىْءٍ مَّوْعِظَةً وَتَفْصِيلاً لِّكُلِّ شَىْءٍ فَخُذْهَا بِقُوَّةٍ وَأْمُرْ قَوْمَكَ يَأْخُذُواْ بِأَحْسَنِهَا سَأُوْرِيكُمْ دَارَ الْفَـسِقِينَ ﴾

(And We wrote for him on the Tablets the lesson to be drawn from all things and the explanation for all things (and said): "Hold unto these with firmness, and enjoin your people to take the better therein. I shall show you the home of evildoers.") 7:145 This means, "I will show you the final outcome of what will happen to those who abandon My obedience and oppose My command." Concerning Allah's statement,

﴿فَرَجَعَ مُوسَى إِلَى قَوْمِهِ غَضْبَـنَ أَسِفاً﴾

(Then Musa returned to his people in a state of anger and sorrow.) This means that after Allah informed him of what they were doing, he became extremely angry and upset with them. He was very worried for them. During this time he received the Tawrah, which contained their Shari`ah (Law), this was a great honor for them. For they were a people who used to worship other than Allah. Every person with sound reason and good sense could see that what they were doing was false and foolish. This is why Allah said that he (Musa) returned to them in a state of anger and sorrow. The word for sorrow used here is Asif, which is used to emphasize to the severity of his anger. Mujahid said, "In a state of anger and sorrow means worried." Qatadah and As-Suddi said, "Asif here means in a state of sadness because of what his people had done after him."

﴿قَالَ يَقَوْمِ أَلَمْ يَعِدْكُمْ رَبُّكُمْ وَعْداً حَسَناً﴾

(He (Musa) said: "O my people! Did not your Lord promise you a fair promise...") This means, "Did He not promise you in that which I have spoken to you, every good in this life and in the Hereafter, and the good end in the final outcome of things You have already witnessed how He helped you defeat your enemy (Fir`awn) and He made you victorious over him and He blessed you with other bounties as well through His help."

﴿أَفَطَالَ عَلَيْكُمُ الْعَهْدُ﴾

(Did then the promise seem to you long in coming) meaning, `in waiting for what Allah had promised you and forgetting His previous favors and the covenant that He made with you before.'

﴿أَمْ أَرَدتُّمْ أَن يَحِلَّ عَلَيْكُمْ غَضَبٌ مِّن رَّبِّكُمْ﴾

(Or did you desire that wrath should descend from your Lord on you,) The word `Or' here means `Nay, but.' It is used here to separate between a previous item and a coming item. It is as if it is saying, "Nay, but you want to make permissible the anger of your Lord upon you by what you have done. Therefore, you have broken your promise to me." The Children of Israel said in reply to Musa's blame and rebuke,

﴿مَآ أَخْلَفْنَا مَوْعِدَكَ بِمَلْكِنَا﴾

(We broke not our promise to you of our own will,) Meaning by our power and our choice. Then, they began making lame excuses and they told him how they got rid of that which they were carrying of Coptic jewelry that they had borrowed from them (the Egyptian Copts) when they left Egypt. Therefore they cast it, meaning that they threw it away. Thus, it became a calf that made a moaning sound that would gradually rise in pitch. This calf was an ordeal, a hindrance and test.

The first step to rectify the situation of Israelite idolatry was Allah telling Moses about it, thereby divinely snitching on the sinners to their prophet amounts to revelation. So a portion of the speech of God is a snitching testimonial. Thus whoever has a problem with the concept or practice of snitching must reevaluate and repent sincerely according to the prophetic instructions. Whereby the first step in the Israelite repentance was snitching on the culprit who suggested making the idol. Collectively they snitched on the criminal, had they not done so they'd have been in a even worser predicament.

Quran 24:4-9

وَٱلَّذِينَ يَرْمُونَ ٱلْمُحْصَنَـٰتِ ثُمَّ لَمْ يَأْتُوا۟ بِأَرْبَعَةِ شُهَدَآءَ فَٱجْلِدُوهُمْ ثَمَـٰنِينَ جَلْدَةً وَلَا تَقْبَلُوا۟ لَهُمْ شَهَـٰدَةً أَبَدًا ۚ وَأُو۟لَـٰٓئِكَ هُمُ ٱلْفَـٰسِقُونَ (٤) إِلَّا ٱلَّذِينَ تَابُوا۟ مِنۢ بَعْدِ ذَٰلِكَ وَأَصْلَحُوا۟ فَإِنَّ ٱللَّهَ غَفُورٌ رَّحِيمٌ (٥) وَٱلَّذِينَ يَرْمُونَ أَزْوَٰجَهُمْ وَلَمْ يَكُن لَّهُمْ شُهَدَآءُ إِلَّآ أَنفُسُهُمْ فَشَهَـٰدَةُ أَحَدِهِمْ أَرْبَعُ شَهَـٰدَٰتٍۭ بِٱللَّهِ ۙ إِنَّهُۥ لَمِنَ ٱلصَّـٰدِقِينَ (٦) وَٱلْخَـٰمِسَةُ أَنَّ لَعْنَتَ ٱللَّهِ عَلَيْهِ إِن كَانَ مِنَ ٱلْكَـٰذِبِينَ (٧) وَيَدْرَؤُا۟ عَنْهَا ٱلْعَذَابَ أَن تَشْهَدَ أَرْبَعَ شَهَـٰدَٰتٍۭ بِٱللَّهِ ۙ إِنَّهُۥ لَمِنَ ٱلْكَـٰذِبِينَ (٨) وَٱلْخَـٰمِسَةَ أَنَّ غَضَبَ ٱللَّهِ عَلَيْهَآ إِن كَانَ مِنَ ٱلصَّـٰدِقِينَ (٩)

And those who accuse chaste women, and produce not four witnesses, flog them with eighty stripes, and reject their testimony forever, They indeed are the Fâsiqûn (liars, rebellious, disobedient to Allâh). (4) Except those who repent thereafter and do righteous deeds, (for such) verily, Allâh is Oft-Forgiving, Most Merciful. (5) And for those who accuse their wives, but have no witnesses except themselves, let the testimony of one of them be four testimonies (i.e. testifies four times) by Allâh that he is one of those who speak the truth. (6) And the fifth (testimony should be) the invoking of the Curse of Allâh on him if he be of those who tell a lie (against her). (7) But it shall avert the punishment (of stoning to death) from her, if she bears witness four times by Allâh, that he (her husband) is telling a lie. (8) And the fifth (testimony) should be that the Wrath of Allâh be upon her if he (her husband) speaks the truth. (9)

This Ayah states the punishment for making false accusations against chaste women, i.e., those who are free, adult and chaste. If the person who is falsely accused is a man, the same punishment of flogging also applies. If the accuser produces evidence what he is saying is true, then the punishment does not apply. Allah said:

﴿نَّمْ لَمْ يَأْتُواْ بِأَرْبَعَةِ شُهَدَآءَ فَاجْلِدُوهُمْ ثَمَانِينَ جَلْدَةً وَلاَ تَقْبَلُواْ لَهُمْ شَهَادَةً أَبَداً وَأُوْلَـئِكَ هُمُ الْفَـسِقُونَ﴾

(and produce not four witnesses, flog them with eighty stripes, and reject their testimony forever. They indeed are the rebellious.) If the accuser cannot prove that what he is saying is true, then three rulings apply to him: (firstly) that he should be flogged with eighty stripes, (secondly) that his testimony should be rejected forever, and (thirdly) that he should be labelled as a rebellious who is not of good character, whether in the sight of Allah or of mankind.

Then Allah says:

﴿إِلاَّ الَّذِينَ تَابُواْ مِن بَعْدِ ذَلِكَ وَأَصْلَحُواْ فَإِنَّ اللَّه غَفُورٌ رَّحِيمٌ﴾

(Except those who repent thereafter and do righteous deeds; (for such) verily, Allah is Oft-Forgiving, Most Merciful.) This exception refers to the second and third rulings mentioned above. The flogging has been carried out regardless of whether he repents or persists, and after that there is no further punishment, as is agreed among the scholars. If he repents, then his testimony may be accepted, and he is no longer to be regarded as a rebellious. This was the view of Sa`id bin Al-Musayyib -- the leader of the Tabi`in -- and also a group among the Salaf. Ash-Sha`bi and Ad-Dahhak said, "His testimony cannot be accepted even if he does repent, unless he himself admits that he said something false, in which case his testimony may be accepted." And Allah knows best.

If a husband has accused his wife but cannot come up with proof, he can swear the Li`an (the oath of condemnation) as Allah commanded. This means that he brings her before the Imam and states what he is accusing her of. The ruler then asks him to swear four times by Allah in front of four witnesses

﴿إِنَّهُ لَمِنَ الصَّـدِقِينَ﴾

(that he is one of those who speak the truth) in his accusation of her adultery.

﴿وَالْخَامِسَةُ أَنَّ لَعْنَةَ اللَّهِ عَلَيْهِ إِن كَانَ مِنَ الْكَاذِبِينَ﴾

(And the fifth; the invoking of the curse of Allah on him if he be of those who tell a lie.) If he says that, then she is divorced from him by the very act of this Li`an; she is forever forbidden for him and he must give her Mahr to her. The punishment for Zina should be carried out on her, and nothing can prevent the punishment except if she also swears the oath of condemnation (Li`an) and swears by Allah four times that he is one of those who lied, i.e., in what he is accusing her of;

﴿وَالْخَامِسَةَ أَنَّ غَضَبَ اللَّهِ عَلَيْهَا إِن كَانَ مِنَ الصَّادِقِينَ﴾

(And the fifth; should be that the crath of Allah be upon her if he speaks the truth.) Allah says:

﴿وَيَدْرَؤُاْ عَنْهَا الْعَذَابَ﴾

(But she shall avert the punishment) meaning, the prescribed punishment.

﴿وَيَدْرَؤُاْ عَنْهَا الْعَذَابَ أَن تَشْهَدَ أَرْبَعَ شَهَادَاتٍ بِاللَّهِ إِنَّهُ لَمِنَ الْكَاذِبِينَ - وَالْخَامِسَةَ أَنَّ غَضَبَ اللَّهِ عَلَيْهَا إِن كَانَ مِنَ الصَّادِقِينَ﴾

(if she bears witness four times by Allah, that he is telling a lie. And the fifth; should be that the wrath of Allah be upon her if he speaks the truth.) The wrath of Allah is mentioned specially in the case of the woman, because usually a man would not go to the extent of exposing his wife and accusing her of Zina unless he is telling the truth and has good reason to do this, and she knows that what he is accusing her of is true. So in her case the fifth testimony calls for the wrath of Allah to be upon her, for the one upon whom is the wrath of Allah, is the one who knows the truth yet deviates from it. Then Allah mentions His grace and kindness to His creation in that He has prescribed for them a way out of their difficulties. Allah says:

$$﴿وَلَوْلاَ فَضْلُ اللَّهِ عَلَيْكُمْ وَرَحْمَتُهُ﴾$$

(And had it not been for the grace of Allah and His mercy on you!) meaning, many of your affairs would have been too difficult for you,

$$﴿وَأَنَّ اللَّهَ تَوَّابٌ﴾$$

(And that Allah is the One Who forgives and accepts repentance,) means, from His servants, even if that comes after they have sworn a confirmed oath.

$$﴿حَكِيمٌ﴾$$

(the All-Wise.) in what He prescribes and commands and forbids.

Imam Ahmad recorded that Ibn `Abbas said: "When the Ayah

$$﴿وَالَّذِينَ يَرْمُونَ الْمُحْصَنَـتِ ثُمَّ لَمْ يَأْتُواْ بِأَرْبَعَةِ شُهَدَآءَ فَاجْلِدُوهُمْ ثَمَانِينَ جَلْدَةً وَلاَ تَقْبَلُواْ لَهُمْ شَهَادَةً أَبَداً﴾$$

(And those who accuse chaste women, and produce not four witnesses, flog them with eighty stripes, and reject their testimony forever) 24:4 was revealed, Sa`d bin `Ubadah, may Allah be pleased with him, -- the leader of the Ansar -- said, `Is this how it was revealed, O Messenger of Allah' The Messenger of Allah said:

«يَا مَعْشَرَ الْأَنْصَارِ أَلَا تَسْمَعُونَ مَا يَقُولُ سَيِّدُكُمْ؟»

(O Ansar, did you hear what your leader said) They said, `O Messenger of Allah, do not blame him, for he is a jealous man. By Allah, he never married a woman who was not a virgin, and he never divorced a woman but none of us would dare to marry her because he is so jealous.' Sa`d said, `By Allah, O Messenger of Allah, I know that it (the Ayah) is true and is from Allah, but I am surprised. If I found some wicked man lying down with my wife, should I not disturb him until I have brought four witnesses By Allah, he would have finished what he was doing before I could bring them!' A little while later, Hilal bin Umayyah -- one of the three whose repentance had been accepted -- came back from his lands at night and found a man with his wife. He saw with his own eyes and heard with his own ears, but he did not disturb him until the morning. In the morning he went to the Messenger of Allah and said, `O Messenger of Allah, I came to my wife at night and found a man with her, and I saw with my own eyes and heard with my own ears.' The Messenger of Allah did not like what he had said and got very upset. The Ansar gathered around him and said, `We were being tested by what Sa`d bin Ubadah said, and now the Messenger of Allah will punish Hilal bin Umayyah and declare his testimony before people to be unacceptable.' Hilal said: `By Allah, I hope that Allah will make for me a way out from this problem.' Hilal said, `O

Messenger of Allah, I see how upset you are by what I have said, but Allah knows that I am telling the truth.' By Allah, the Messenger of Allah wanted to have him flogged, but then Allah sent revelation to His Messenger . When the revelation came upon him, they knew about it from the change in his face, so they would leave him alone until the revelation was finished. Allah revealed the Ayah:

﴿وَالَّذِينَ يَرْمُونَ أَزْوَجَهُمْ وَلَمْ يَكُنْ لَّهُمْ شُهَدَآءُ إِلاَّ أَنفُسُهُمْ فَشَهَدَةُ أَحَدِهِمْ أَرْبَعُ شَهَدَاتٍ بِاللَّهِ﴾

(And for those who accuse their wives, but have no witnesses except themselves, let the testimony of one of them be four testimonies by Allah...,) Then the revelation was finished and the Messenger of Allah said,

«أَبْشِرْ يَا هِلَالُ فَقَدْ جَعَلَ اللهُ لَكَ فَرَجًا وَمَخْرَجًا»

(Rejoice, O Hilal, for Allah has made a way out for you.) Hilal said, `I had been hoping for this from my Lord, may He be glorified.' The Messenger of Allah said:

«أَرْسِلُوا إِلَيْهَا»

(Send for her.) So they sent for her and she came. The Messenger of Allah recited this Ayah to them both, and reminded them that the punishment of the Hereafter is more severe than the punishment in this world. Hilal said, `By Allah, O Messenger of Allah, I have spoken the truth about her.' She said, `He is lying.' The Messenger of Allah said,

«لَاعِنُوا بَيْنَهُمَا»

(Make them both swear the Li`an.) So Hilal was told, `Testify.' So he testified four times by Allah that he was one of those who speak the truth. When he came to the fifth testimony, he was told, `O Hilal, have Taqwa of Allah, for the punishment of this world is easier than the punishment of the Hereafter, and this will mean that the punishment will be inevitable for you.' He said, `By Allah, Allah will not punish me for it, just as He has not caused me to be flogged for it.' So he testified for the fifth time that the curse of Allah would be upon him if he was telling a lie. Then it was said to his wife, `Testify four times by Allah that he is telling a lie.' And when his wife reached the fifth testimony, she was told, `Have Taqwa of Allah, for the punishment of this world is easier than the punishment of the Hereafter, and this will mean that the punishment will be inevitable for you.' She hesitated for a while, and was about to admit her guilt, then she said: `By Allah, I will not expose my people to shame, and she swore the fifth oath that the wrath of Allah would be upon her if he was telling the truth.' Then the Messenger of Allah separated them, and decreed that her child should not be attributed to any father, nor should the child be accused, and whoever accused her or her child, they would be subject to punishment. He also decreed that Hilal was not obliged to house her or feed her, because they had not been separated by divorce, nor had he died and left her a widow. He said,

«إِنْ جَاءَتْ بِهِ أُصَيْهِبَ (أُرَيْسِحَ) حَمْشَ السَّاقَيْنِ، فَهُوَ لِهِلَالٍ، وَإِنْ جَاءَتْ بِهِ أَوْرَقَ جَعْدًا جُمَالِيًّا خَدَلَّجَ السَّاقَيْنِ سَابِغَ الْأَلْيَتَيْنِ، فَهُوَ لِلَّذِي رُمِيَتْتِبِهِ»

(If she gives birth to a red-haired child (with skinny thighs) and thin legs, then he is Hilal's child, but if she gives birth to a curly-haired child with thick legs and plump buttocks, then this is what she is accused of.) She subsequently gave birth to a child who was curly-haired with thick legs and plump buttocks, and the Messenger of Allah said,

«لَوْلَا الْأَيْمَانُ لَكَانَ لِي وَلَهَا شَأْنٌ»

(Were it not for the oath that she swore, I would deal with her.)" `Ikrimah said, "The child grew up to become the governor of Egypt, and he was given his mother's name and was not attributed to any father." Abu Dawud recorded a similar but briefer report. This Hadith has corroborating reports in the books of Sahih and elsewhere, with many chains of narration, including the report narrated by Al-Bukhari from Ibn `Abbas, that Hilal bin Umayyah accused his wife before the Prophet with Sharik bin Sahma'. The Prophet said,

«الْبَيِّنَةَ أَوْ حَدٌّ فِي ظَهْرِكَ»

(Evidence or the punishment on your back.) He said, "O Messenger of Allah, if any one of us saw a man with his wife, how could he go and get evidence" The Prophet again said,

«الْبَيِّنَةَ وَإِلَّا حَدٌّ فِي ظَهْرِكَ»

(Evidence otherwise the punishment on your back.) Hilal said, "By the One Who sent you with the truth! I am telling the truth and Allah will reveal something that will protect my back from the punishment. " Then Jibril came down and brought the revelation,

﴾وَالَّذِينَ يَرْمُونَ أَزْوَجَهُمْ﴿

(And for those who accuse their wives,) Then he recited until he reached:

﴾إِن كَانَ مِنَ الصَّـٰدِقِينَ﴿

(that he is one of those who speak the truth) 24:6. When the revelation had finished, the Prophet sent for them both. Hilal came and gave his testimony, and the Prophet said,

«إِنَّ اللهَ يَعْلَمُ أَنَّ أَحَدَكُمَا كَاذِبٌ، فَهَلْ مِنْكُمَا تَائِبٌ؟»

(Allah knows that one of you is lying. Will one of you repent) Then she stood up and gave her testimony, and when she reached the fifth oath, they stopped her and said, "If you swear the fifth oath and you are lying, the curse of Allah will be inevitable." Ibn `Abbas said, "She hesitated and kept quiet until we thought that she had changed her mind, then she said, `I will not dishonor my people today', and she went ahead. Then the Messenger of Allah said,

«أَبْصِرُوهَا، فَإِنْ جَاءَتْ بِهِ أَكْحَلَ الْعَيْنَيْنِ سَابِغَ الْأَلْيَتَيْنِ خَدَلَّجَ السَّاقَيْنِ، فَهُوَ لِشَرِيكِ ابْنِ سَحْمَاءَ»

(Wait until she gives birth, and if she gives birth to a child whose eyes look as if they are ringed with kohl and who has plump buttocks and thick legs, then he is the child of Sharik bin Sahma'.) She gave birth to a child who matched this description, and the Prophet said,

«لَوْلاَ مَا مَضَى مِنْ كِتَابِ اللهِ لَكَانَ لِي وَ لَهَا شَأْنٌ»

(Were it not for the Book of Allah, I would deal with her.) This version was recorded only by Al-Bukhari, but the event has been narrated with additional chains of narration from Ibn `Abbas and others. Imam Ahmad recorded that Sa`id bin Jubayr said: During the governorship of Ibn Az-Zubayr I was asked about the couple who engage in Li`an, and whether they should be separated, and I did not know the answer. I got up and went to the house of Ibn `Umar, and said, "O Abu `Abdur-Rahman, should the couple who engage in Li`an be separated" He said, "Subhan Allah, the first one to ask about this was so-and-so the son of so-and-so. He said, `O Messenger of Allah, what do you think of a man who sees his wife committing an immoral sin If he speaks he will be speaking about something very serious, and if he keeps quiet he will be keeping quiet about something very serious.' The Prophet kept quiet and did not answer him. Later on, he came to him and said, `What I asked you about is something with which I myself being tested with.' Then Allah revealed the Ayat,

﴿وَالَّذِينَ يَرْمُونَ أَزْوَجَهُمْ﴾

(And for those who accuse their wives,) until he reached:

﴿أَنَّ غَضَبَ اللَّهِ عَلَيْهَآ إِن كَانَ مِنَ الصَّـدِقِينَ﴾

(That the wrath of Allah be upon her if he speaks the truth.) He started to advise the man and remind him about Allah, and told him that the punishment of this world is easier than the punishment of the Hereafter. The man said: `By the One Who sent you with the truth, I was not telling you a lie.' Then the Prophet turned to the woman and advised the woman and reminded her about Allah, and told her that the punishment of this world is easier than the punishment of the Hereafter. The woman said, `By the One Who sent you with the truth, he is lying.' So the Prophet started with the man, who swore four times by Allah that he was one of those who speak the truth, and swore the fifth oath that the curse of Allah would be upon him if he were lying. Then he turned to the woman, who swore four times by Allah that he was lying, and swore the fifth oath that the wrath of Allah would be upon her if he was telling the truth. Then he separated them." It was also recorded by An-Nasa'i in his Tafsir, and by Al-Bukhari and Muslim in the Two Sahihs.

This impactful revelation all came about due to snitching, first the punishment for false testimony which is a punishable crime via lashing and then the solution for mutually contradictory testimony regarding accusations of adultery. So if you falsely snitch you get punished but truthful snitching is so meritorious that Allah himself sent divine revelation to save all snitches who tell on their adulterous wives without the required 4 witnesses the Shariah stipulates is necessary. While even then should the accuser falsely snitch there is a way out for the accused but either way justice is served and the entire ruling came about due to a case of snitching. So as a result of people snitching on each other then core aspects of Allah's speech and Islam were made known. Thus if you ever remove snitching on sinners from Islam you are changing history and distorting the religion and revelation.

Quran 27:20-28

وَتَفَقَّدَ ٱلطَّيْرَ فَقَالَ مَا لِىَ لَا أَرَى ٱلْهُدْهُدَ أَمْ كَانَ مِنَ ٱلْغَآئِبِينَ (٢٠) لَأُعَذِّبَنَّهُۥ عَذَابًا شَدِيدًا أَوْ لَأَاْذْبَحَنَّهُۥ أَوْ لَيَأْتِيَنِّى بِسُلْطَـٰنٍ مُّبِينٍ (٢١) فَمَكَثَ غَيْرَ بَعِيدٍ فَقَالَ أَحَطتُ بِمَا لَمْ تُحِطْ بِهِۦ وَجِئْتُكَ مِن سَبَإٍ بِنَبَإٍ يَقِينٍ (٢٢) إِنِّى وَجَدتُّ ٱمْرَأَةً تَمْلِكُهُمْ وَأُوتِيَتْ مِن كُلِّ شَىْءٍ وَلَهَا عَرْشٌ عَظِيمٌ (٢٣) وَجَدتُّهَا وَقَوْمَهَا يَسْجُدُونَ لِلشَّمْسِ مِن دُونِ ٱللَّهِ وَزَيَّنَ لَهُمُ ٱلشَّيْطَـٰنُ أَعْمَـٰلَهُمْ فَصَدَّهُمْ عَنِ ٱلسَّبِيلِ فَهُمْ لَا يَهْتَدُونَ (٢٤) أَلَّا يَسْجُدُواْ لِلَّهِ ٱلَّذِى يُخْرِجُ ٱلْخَبْءَ فِى ٱلسَّمَـٰوَٰتِ وَٱلْأَرْضِ وَيَعْلَمُ مَا تُخْفُونَ وَمَا تُعْلِنُونَ (٢٥) ٱللَّهُ لَا إِلَـٰهَ إِلَّا هُوَ رَبُّ ٱلْعَرْشِ ٱلْعَظِيمِ ۩ (٢٦) ۞ قَالَ سَنَنظُرُ أَصَدَقْتَ أَمْ كُنتَ مِنَ ٱلْكَـٰذِبِينَ (٢٧) ٱذْهَب بِّكِتَـٰبِى هَـٰذَا فَأَلْقِهْ إِلَيْهِمْ ثُمَّ تَوَلَّ عَنْهُمْ فَٱنظُرْ مَاذَا يَرْجِعُونَ (٢٨)

He inspected the birds, and said: "What is the matter that I see not the hoopoe? Or is he among the absentees? (20) "I will surely punish him with a severe torment, or slaughter him, unless he brings me a clear reason." (21) But the hoopoe stayed not long, he (came up and) said: "I have grasped (the knowledge of a thing) which you have not grasped and I have come to you from Saba' (Sheba) with true news. (22) "I found a woman ruling over them", she has been given all things that could be possessed by any ruler of the earth, and she has a great throne. (23) "I found her and her people worshipping the sun instead of Allâh, and Shaitân (Satan) has made their deeds fair-seeming to them, and has barred them from (Allâh's) Way, so they have no guidance," (24) [As Shaitân (Satan) has barred them from Allâh's Way] so they do not worship (prostrate themselves before) Allâh, Who brings to light what is hidden in the heavens and the earth, and knows what you conceal and what you reveal. (25) Allâh, Lâ ilâha illa Huwa (none has the right to be

worshipped but He), the Lord of the Supreme Throne!
(26) [Sulaimân (Solomon)] said: "We shall see whether you
speak the truth or you are (one) of the liars (27) "Go you with
this letter of mine, and deliver it to them, then draw back from
them, and see what (answer) they return." (28)

Mujahid, Sa`id bin Jubayr and others narrated from Ibn
`Abbas and others that the hoopoe was an expert who
used to show Sulayman where water was if he was out in
open land and needed water. The hoopoe would look for
water for him in the various strata of the earth, just as a
man looks at things on the surface of the earth, and he
would know just how far below the surface the water
was. When the hoopoe showed him where the water was,
Sulayman would command the Jinn to dig in that place
until they brought water from the depths of the earth.
One day Sulayman went to some open land and checked
on the birds, but he could not see the hoopoe.

﴿فَقَالَ مَالِيَ لاَ أَرَى الْهُدْهُدَ أَمْ كَانَ مِنَ الْغَآئِبِينَ﴾

(and (Sulayman) said: "What is the matter that I see not
the hoopoe Or is he among the absentees") One day
`Abdullah bin `Abbas told a similar story, and among the
people was a man from the Khawarij whose name was
Nafi` bin Al-Azraq, who often used to raise objections to
Ibn `Abbas. He said to him, "Stop, O Ibn `Abbas; you will
be defeated (in argument) today!" Ibn `Abbas said: "Why"
Nafi` said: "You are telling us that the hoopoe can see
water beneath the ground, but any boy can put seed in a
trap and cover the trap with dirt, and the hoopoe will

come and take the seed, so the boy can catch him in the trap." Ibn `Abbas said, "If it was not for the fact that this man would go and tell others that he had defeated Ibn `Abbas in argument, I would not even answer." Then he said to Nafi`: "Woe to you! When the decree strikes a person, his eyes become blind and he loses all caution." Nafi` said: "By Allah I will never dispute with you concerning anything in the Qur'an. "

﴿لأُعَذِّبَنَّهُ عَذَاباً شَدِيداً﴾

(I will surely punish him with a severe torment) Al-A`mash said, narrating from Al-Minhal bin `Amr from Sa`id that Ibn `Abbas said: "He meant, by plucking his feathers." `Abdullah bin Shaddad said: "By plucking his feathers and exposing him to the sun." This was also the view of more than one of the Salaf, that it means plucking his feathers and leaving him exposed to be eaten by ants.

﴿أَوْ لأَذْبَحَنَّهُ﴾

(or slaughter him,) means, killing him.

﴿أَوْ لَيَأْتِيَنِّى بِسُلْطَـنٍ مُّبِينٍ﴾

(unless he brings me a clear reason.) i.e., a valid excuse. Sufyan bin `Uyaynah and `Abdullah bin Shaddad said: "When the hoopoe came back, the other birds said to him: "What kept you Sulayman has vowed to shed your blood." The hoopoe said: "Did he make any exception did he say `unless'" They said, "Yes, he said:

﴿لأُعَذِّبَنَّهُ عَذَاباً شَدِيداً أَوْ لأَذْبَحَنَّهُ أَوْ لَيَأْتِيَنِّى بِسُلْطَـنٍ مُّبِينٍ ﴾

(I will surely punish him with a severe torment or slaughter him, unless he brings me a clear reason.) The hoopoe said, "Then I am saved."

Allah says:

﴿فَمَكَثَ غَيْرَ بَعِيدٍ﴾

(But (the hoopoe) stayed not long,) meaning, he was absent for only a short time. Then he came and said to Sulayman:

﴿أَحَطتُ بِمَا لَمْ تُحِطْ بِهِ﴾

(I have grasped which you have not grasped) meaning, `I have come to know something that you and your troops do not know.'

﴿وَجِئْتُكَ مِن سَبَإٍ بِنَبَإٍ يَقِينٍ﴾

(and I have come to you from Saba' with true news.) meaning, with true and certain news. Saba' (Sheba) refers to Himyar, they were a dynasty in Yemen. Then the hoopoe said:

﴿إِنِّى وَجَدتُّ امْرَأَةً تَمْلِكُهُمْ﴾

(I found a woman ruling over them,) Al-Hasan Al-Basri said, "This is Bilqis bint Sharahil, the queen of Saba'." Allah's saying:

﴿وَأُوتِيَتْ مِن كُلِّ شَىْءٍ﴾

(she has been given all things,) means, all the conveniences of this world that a powerful monarch could need.

﴿وَلَهَا عَرْشٌ عَظِيمٌ﴾

(and she has a great throne.) meaning, a tremendous chair adorned with gold and different kinds of jewels and pearls. The historians said, "This throne was in a great, strong palace which was high and firmly constructed. In it there were three hundred and sixty windows on the east side, and a similar number on the west, and it was constructed in such a way that each day when the sun rose it would shine through one window, and when it set it would shine through the opposite window. And the people used to prostrate to the sun morning and evening. This is why the hoopoe said:

﴿وَجَدتُّهَا وَقَوْمَهَا يَسْجُدُونَ لِلشَّمْسِ مِن دُونِ اللَّهِ وَزَيَّنَ لَهُمُ الشَّيْطَـنُ أَعْمَـلَهُمْ فَصَدَّهُمْ عَنِ السَّبِيلِ﴾

(I found her and her people worshipping the sun instead of Allah, and Shaytan has made their deeds fair seeming to them, and has prevented them from the way,) meaning, from the way of truth,

﴿فَهُمْ لاَ يَهْتَدُونَ﴾

(so they have no guidance.) Allah's saying:

﴿وَزَيَّنَ لَهُمُ الشَّيْطَـنُ أَعْمَـلَهُمْ فَصَدَّهُمْ عَنِ السَّبِيلِ فَهُمْ لاَ يَهْتَدُونَأَلاَّ يَسْجُدُواْ للَّهِ﴾

(and Shaytan has made their deeds fair seeming to them, and has prevented them from the way, so they have no guidance, so they do not prostrate themselves before Allah.) They do not know the way of truth, prostrating only before Allah alone and not before anything that He has created, whether heavenly bodies or anything else. This is like the Ayah:

﴿وَمِنْ ءَايَـٰتِهِ الَّيْلُ وَالنَّهَارُ وَالشَّمْسُ وَالْقَمَرُ لاَ تَسْجُدُواْ لِلشَّمْسِ وَلاَ لِلْقَمَرِ وَاسْجُدُواْ لِلَّهِ الَّذِى خَلَقَهُنَّ إِن كُنتُمْ إِيَّاهُ تَعْبُدُونَ﴾

(And from among His signs are the night and the day, and the sun and the moon. Prostrate yourselves not to the sun nor to the moon, but prostrate yourselves to Allah Who created them, if you indeed worship Him.) (41:37)

﴿الَّذِى يُخْرِجُ الْخَبْءَ فِى السَّمَـوَتِ وَالأُرْضِ﴾

(Who brings to light what is hidden in the heavens and the earth,) `Ali bin Abi Talhah reported that Ibn `Abbas said: "He knows everything that is hidden in the heavens and on earth." This was also the view of `Ikrimah, Mujahid, Sa`id bin Jubayr, Qatadah and others. His saying:

﴿وَيَعْلَمُ مَا تُخْفُونَ وَمَا تُعْلِنُونَ﴾

(and knows what you conceal and what you reveal.) means, He knows what His servants say and do in secret, and what they say and do openly. This is like the Ayah:

﴿سَوَآءٌ مِّنْكُم مَّنْ أَسَرَّ الْقَوْلَ وَمَنْ جَهَرَ بِهِ وَمَنْ هُوَ مُسْتَخْفٍ بِالَّيْلِ وَسَارِبٌ بِالنَّهَارِ﴾

(It is the same whether any of you conceals his speech or declares it openly, whether he be hid by night or goes forth freely by day) (13:10). His saying:

﴿اللَّهُ لاَ إِلَـهَ إِلاَّ هُوَ رَبُّ الْعَرْشِ الْعَظِيمِ﴾

(Allah, La ilaha illa Huwa, the Lord of the Supreme Throne!) means, He is the One to be called upon, Allah,

He is the One other than Whom there is no god, the Lord of the Supreme Throne, and there is none greater than Him in all of creation. Since the hoopoe was calling to what is good, and for people to worship and prostrate to Allah alone, it would have been forbidden to kill him. Imam Ahmad, Abu Dawud and Ibn Majah recorded that Abu Hurayrah, may Allah be pleased with him, said that the Prophet forbade killing four kinds of animals: ants, bees, hoopoes and the sparrow hawks. Its chain of narration is Sahih.

Allah tells us what Sulayman said to the hoopoe when he told him about the people of Saba' and their queen:

﴿قَالَ سَنَنظُرُ أَصَدَقْتَ أَمْ كُنتَ مِنَ الْكَـذِبِينَ ﴾

((Sulayman) said: "We shall see whether you speak the truth or you are (one) of the liars.") meaning, `are you telling the truth'

﴿أَمْ كُنتَ مِنَ الْكَـذِبِينَ﴾

(or you are (one) of the liars.) meaning, `or are you telling a lie in order to save yourself from the threat I made against you'

﴿اذْهَب بِّكِتَابِى هَـذَا فَأَلْقِهْ إِلَيْهِمْ ثُمَّ تَوَلَّ عَنْهُمْ فَانْظُرْ مَاذَا يَرْجِعُونَ ﴾

(Go you with this letter of mine and deliver it to them then draw back from them and see what they return.) Sulayman wrote a letter to Bilqis and her people and gave it to the hoopoe to deliver. It was said that he carried it on his wings, as is the way with birds, or that he carried it in his beak. He went to their land and found the palace of

Bilqis, then he went to her private chambers and threw the letter through a small window, then he stepped to one side out of good manners. Bilqis was amazed and confused when she saw that, then she went and picked up the letter, opened its seal and read it.

The story of what happened next as a result of the letter the hoopoe delivered is known yet again we are met with another stark incident of snitching that led to goodness. Not only did the Hoopoe save his life due to snitching being the reason for its absence but it became a matter of international diplomacy that led to the eventual repentance of an entire nation from idolatry. May God bless the snitches for they truly do much goodness.

Quran 33:1-3

يَـٰٓأَيُّهَا ٱلنَّبِىُّ ٱتَّقِ ٱللَّهَ وَلَا تُطِعِ ٱلْكَـٰفِرِينَ وَٱلْمُنَـٰفِقِينَ إِنَّ ٱللَّهَ كَانَ عَلِيمًا حَكِيمًا (١) وَٱتَّبِعْ مَا يُوحَىٰ إِلَيْكَ مِن رَّبِّكَ إِنَّ ٱللَّهَ كَانَ بِمَا تَعْمَلُونَ خَبِيرًا (٢) وَتَوَكَّلْ عَلَى ٱللَّهِ وَكَفَىٰ بِٱللَّهِ وَكِيلًا (٣)

O Prophet! Keep your duty to Allâh, and obey not the disbelievers and the hypocrites (i.e., do not follow their advice). Verily, Allâh is Ever All¬Knower, All¬Wise. (1) And follow that which is revealed to you from your Lord. Verily, Allâh is Well¬Acquainted with what you do. (2) And put your trust in Allâh, and Sufficient is Allâh as a Wakîl (Trustee, or Disposer of affairs). (3)

Here Allah points out something lower by referring to something higher. When He commands His servant and Messenger to do this, He is also commanding those who are lower than him, and the command is addressed to them more so. Talq bin Habib said: "Taqwa means obeying Allah in the light of the guidance of Allah and in hope of earning the reward of Allah, and refraining from disobeying Allah in the light of the guidance of Allah and fearing the punishment of Allah."

﴿وَلاَ تُطِعِ الْكَـٰفِرِينَ وَالْمُنَـٰفِقِينَ﴾

(and obey not the disbelievers and the hypocrites.) means, do not listen to what they say and do not consult them.

﴿إِنَّ اللَّهَ كَانَ عَلِيماً حَكِيماً﴾

(Verily, Allah is Ever All-Knower, All-Wise) means, He is more deserving of your following His commandments and obeying Him, for He knows the consequences of all things and is Wise in all that He says and does. Allah says:

﴿وَاتَّبِعْ مَا يُوحَى إِلَيْكَ مِن رَّبِّكَ﴾

(And follow that which is revealed to you from your Lord.) meaning, of the Qur'an and Sunnah.

﴿إِنَّ اللَّهَ كَانَ بِمَا تَعْمَلُونَ خَبِيراً﴾

(Verily, Allah is Well-Acquainted with what you do.) means, nothing at all is hidden from Him, and put your trust in Allah, i.e., in all your affairs and situations.

﴿وَكَفَى بِاللَّهِ وَكِيلاً﴾

(and sufficient is Allah as a Wakil.) means, sufficient is He as a Trustee for the one who puts his trust in Him and turns to Him.

While this verse doesn't directly deal with snitching the principle of keeping one's duty to Allah despite what disbelievers and hypocrites may suggest does tie in because the rejectors deny the practice of snitching its due place in the religion and it is a prime duty to Allah to snitch sometimes in certain instances.

Quran 33:36

وَمَا كَانَ لِمُؤْمِنٍ وَلَا مُؤْمِنَةٍ إِذَا قَضَى ٱللَّهُ وَرَسُولُهُ ۥ أَمْرًا أَن يَكُونَ لَهُمُ ٱلْخِيَرَةُ مِنْ أَمْرِهِمْۗ وَمَن يَعْصِ ٱللَّهَ وَرَسُولَهُ ۥ فَقَدْ ضَلَّ ضَلَـٰلًا مُّبِينًا (٣٦)

It is not for a believer, man or woman, when Allâh and His Messenger have decreed a matter that they should have any option in their decision. And whoever disobeys Allâh and His Messenger, he has indeed strayed in to a plain error. (36)

Imam Ahmad recorded that Abu Barzah Al-Aslami said: "Julaybib was a man who used to enter upon women and joke with them. I said to my wife, `Do not let Julaybib enter upon you, for if he enters upon you I shall do such and such.' If any of the Ansar had a single female relative, they would not arrange a marriage for her until they found out whether the Prophet wanted to marry her or not. The Prophet said to one of the Ansar:

«زَوِّجْنِي ابْنَتَكَ»

(Give me your daughter for marriage.) He said, `Yes, O Messenger of Allah, it would be an honor and a blessing.' He said,

«إِنِّي لَسْتُ أُرِيدُهَا لِنَفْسِي»

(I do not want her for myself.) He said, `Then for whom,
O Messenger of Allah' He said,

«لِجُلَيْبِيب»

(For Julaybib.) He said, `O Messenger of Allah, let me
consult her mother.' So he went to the girl's mother and
said, `The Messenger of Allah is proposing marriage for
your daughter.' She said, `Yes, it would be a pleasure.' He
said, `He is not proposing to marry her himself, he is
proposing on behalf of Julaybib.' She said, `What!
Julaybib No, by Allah, we will not marry her to him.'
When he wanted to get up and go to the Messenger of
Allah to tell him what the girl's mother had said, the girl
asked, `Who is asking for my hand' So her mother told
her, and she said, `Are you refusing to follow the
command of the Messenger of Allah Follow his
command, for I will not come to any harm.' So her father
went to the Messenger of Allah and said, `Deal with her
as you wish.' So he married her to Julaybib. Then the
Messenger of Allah went out on one of his military
campaigns, and after Allah had granted him victory, he
said to his Companions, may Allah be pleased with them,

«هَلْ تَفْقِدُونَ مِنْ أَحَد»

(See whether there is anybody missing.) They said, `We
have lost so-and-so, and so-and-so.' He said,

«انْظُرُوا هَلْ تَفْقِدُونَ مِنْ أَحَد»

(See if there is anybody missing.) They said, `No one.' He
said:

«لَكِنَّنِي أَفْقِدُ جُلَيْبِيبًا»

(But I see that Julaybib is missing.) He said:

«فَاطْلُبُوهُ فِي الْقَتْلَى»

(Go and look for him among the dead.) So they looked for him, and found him beside seven of the enemy whom he had killed before he was himself killed. They said, `O Messenger of Allah, here he is, beside seven of the enemy whom he had killed before he was himself killed.' The Messenger of Allah came and stood beside him and said,

«قَتَلَ سَبْعَةً وَقَتَلُوهُ، هَذَا مِنِّي وَأَنَا مِنْه»

(He killed seven before he was himself killed. He belongs to me and I belong to him.) He said this two or three times, then the Messenger of Allah carried him in his arms and held him while his grave was dug, then he placed him in his grave. It was not mentioned that he washed him, may Allah be pleased with him." Thabit, may Allah be pleased with him, said: "There was no widow among the Ansar who was more sought after for marriage than that girl." Ishaq bin `Abdullah bin Abi Talhah asked Thabit, "Do you know how the Messenger of Allah prayed for that girl" He told him: "He said,

«اللَّهُمَّ صُبَّ عَلَيْهَا الْخَيْرَ صَبًّا وَلَا تَجْعَلْ عَيْشَهَا كَدًّا»

(O Allah, pour blessings upon her and do not make her life hard.) And this is how it was; there was no widow among the Ansar who was more sought after for marriage than her." This is how it was recorded by Imam Ahmad, in full. Muslim and An-Nasa'i recorded the story of his death in Al-Fada'il. Al-Hafiz Abu `Umar bin `Abd Al-Barr mentioned in Al-Isti`ab that when the girl said in her seclusion, `Are you refusing to follow the command of the Messenger of Allah ' -- This Ayah was revealed:

﴿وَمَا كَانَ لِمُؤْمِنٍ وَلاَ مُؤْمِنَةٍ إِذَا قَضَى اللَّهُ وَرَسُولُهُ أَمْراً أَن يَكُونَ لَهُمُ الْخِيَرَةُ مِنْ أَمْرِهِمْ﴾

(It is not for a believer, man or woman, when Allah and His Messenger have decreed a matter that they should have any option in their decision.) It was narrated that Tawus asked Ibn `Abbas about praying two Rak`ahs after `Asr and he told him not to do that. Ibn `Abbas recited:

﴿وَمَا كَانَ لِمُؤْمِنٍ وَلاَ مُؤْمِنَةٍ إِذَا قَضَى اللَّهُ وَرَسُولُهُ أَمْراً أَن يَكُونَ لَهُمُ الْخِيَرَةُ مِنْ أَمْرِهِمْ﴾

(It is not for a believer, man or woman, when Allah and His Messenger have decreed a matter that they should have any option in their decision.) This Ayah is general in meaning and applies to all matters, i.e., if Allah and His Messenger decreed a matter, no one has the right to go against that, and no one has any choice or room for personal opinion in this case. Allah says: o

﴿فَلاَ وَرَبِّكَ لاَ يُؤْمِنُونَ حَتَّى يُحَكِّمُوكَ فِيمَا شَجَرَ بَيْنَهُمْ ثُمَّ لاَ يَجِدُواْ فِى أَنفُسِهِمْ حَرَجاً مِّمَّا قَضَيْتَ وَيُسَلِّمُواْ تَسْلِيماً ﴾

(But no, by your Lord, they can have no faith, until they make you judge in all disputes between them, and find in themselves no resistance against your decisions, and accept (them) with full submission.) (4:65) Hence the issue of going against it is addressed in such strong terms, as Allah says:

﴿وَمَن يَعْصِ اللَّهَ وَرَسُولَهُ فَقَدْ ضَلَّ ضَلَلاً مُّبِيناً﴾

(And whoever disobeys Allah and His Messenger, he has indeed strayed into a plain error.) This is like the Ayah:

﴿فَلْيَحْذَرِ الَّذِينَ يُخَلِفُونَ عَنْ أَمْرِهِ أَن تُصِيبَهُمْ فِتْنَةٌ أَوْ يُصِيبَهُمْ عَذَابٌ أَلِيمٌ﴾

(And let those who oppose the Messenger's commandment, beware, lest some Fitnah should befall them or a painful torment be inflicted on them) (24:63).

It's a short simple concept that whatever Allah or his Messenger decree is what is to be implemented wholeheartedly by believers. If you understand that then you would understand how it applies to snitching on everything that is in opposition to Allah and his Messenger's rulings and that in reality there is no debate about snitching because the ruling is overwhelmingly clear, yet the evidence continues because the truth is a weapon against falsehood and overwhelms error.

Quran 33:65-68

خَٰلِدِينَ فِيهَآ أَبَدًا لَّا يَجِدُونَ وَلِيًّا وَلَا نَصِيرًا (٦٥) يَوْمَ تُقَلَّبُ وُجُوهُهُمْ فِى ٱلنَّارِ يَقُولُونَ يَٰلَيْتَنَآ أَطَعْنَا ٱللَّهَ وَأَطَعْنَا ٱلرَّسُولَا (٦٦) وَقَالُوا۟ رَبَّنَآ إِنَّآ أَطَعْنَا سَادَتَنَا وَكُبَرَآءَنَا فَأَضَلُّونَا ٱلسَّبِيلَا (٦٧) رَبَّنَآ ءَاتِهِمْ ضِعْفَيْنِ مِنَ ٱلْعَذَابِ وَٱلْعَنْهُمْ لَعْنًا كَبِيرًا (٦٨)

Wherein they will abide forever, and they will find neither a Walî (a protector) nor a helper. (65) On the Day when their faces will be turned over in the Fire, they will say: "Oh, would that we had obeyed Allâh and obeyed the Messenger (Muhammad)." (66) And they will say: "Our Lord! Verily, we obeyed our chiefs and our great ones, and they misled us from the (Right) Way. (67) Our Lord! Give them double torment and curse them with a mighty curse!" (68)

Allah says:

﴿يَوْمَ تُقَلَّبُ وُجُوهُهُمْ فِى النَّارِ يَقُولُونَ يٰلَيْتَنَا أَطَعْنَا اللَّهَ وَأَطَعْنَا الرَّسُولاَ﴾

(On the Day when their faces will be turned over in the Fire, they will say: "Oh, would that we had obeyed Allah and obeyed the Messenger.") means, they will be dragged into the Fire on their faces and their faces will be contorted in Hell, and in that state they will wish that they had been among those who had obeyed Allah and His Messenger in this world. Allah describes how they will be in the Hereafter:

﴿وَيَوْمَ يَعَضُّ الظَّـلِمُ عَلَى يَدَيْهِ يَقُولُ يٰلَيْتَنِى اتَّخَذْتُ مَعَ الرَّسُولِ سَبِيلاً - يٰوَيْلَتَا لَيْتَنِى لَمْ أَتَّخِذْ فُلاَناً خَلِيلاً﴾

﴿لَّقَدْ أَضَلَّنِى عَنِ الذِّكْرِ بَعْدَ إِذْ جَآءَنِى وَكَانَ الشَّيْطَـنُ لِلإِنْسَـنِ خَذُولاً﴾

(And the Day when the wrongdoer will bite at his hands, he will say: "Oh! Would that I had taken a path with the Messenger. Ah! Woe to me! Would that I had never taken so-and-so as an intimate friend! He indeed led me astray from the Reminder after it had come to me. And Shaytan is to man ever a deserter in the hour of need.") (25:27-29)

﴿رُّبَمَا يَوَدُّ الَّذِينَ كَفَرُواْ لَوْ كَانُواْ مُسْلِمِينَ﴾

(How much would those who disbelieved wish that they had been Muslims.) (15:2) And here too, Allah tells us that when they are in this state, they will wish that they had obeyed Allah and His Messenger in this world:

﴿وَقَالُوا رَبَّنَا إِنَّا أَطَعْنَا سَادَتَنَا وَكُبَرَاءَنَا فَأَضَلُّونَا السَّبِيلَا﴾

(And they will say: "Our Lord! Verily, we obeyed our chiefs and our great ones, and they misled us from the way.") Tawus said: " `Our chiefs' means their nobles and `our great ones' means their scholars."

﴿رَبَّنَا ءَاتِهِمْ ضِعْفَيْنِ مِنَ الْعَذَابِ﴾

(Our Lord! Give them double torment) means, `for their disbelief and because they mislead us.'

Regret is guaranteed for those who disobey Allah and die in a condition of disobedience instead of faith and repentance. After blaming their companions for their errors they will snitch on them then when it is too late to count instead of having done so in this life when they could have benefitted from obedience to Allah via obeying his Messengers.

Quran 50:21-28

وَجَاءَتْ كُلُّ نَفْسٍ مَّعَهَا سَائِقٌ وَشَهِيدٌ (٢١) لَّقَدْ كُنتَ فِى غَفْلَةٍ مِّنْ هَذَا فَكَشَفْنَا عَنكَ غِطَاءَكَ فَبَصَرُكَ ٱلْيَوْمَ حَدِيدٌ (٢٢) وَقَالَ قَرِينُهُ هَذَا مَا لَدَىَّ عَتِيدٌ (٢٣) أَلْقِيَا فِى جَهَنَّمَ كُلَّ كَفَّارٍ عَنِيدٍ (٢٤) مَّنَّاعٍ لِّلْخَيْرِ مُعْتَدٍ مُّرِيبٍ (٢٥) ٱلَّذِى جَعَلَ مَعَ ٱللَّهِ إِلَهًا ءَاخَرَ فَأَلْقِيَاهُ فِى ٱلْعَذَابِ ٱلشَّدِيدِ (٢٦) ۞ قَالَ قَرِينُهُ رَبَّنَا مَا أَطْغَيْتُهُ وَلَكِن كَانَ فِى ضَلَلٍ بَعِيدٍ (٢٧) قَالَ لَا تَخْتَصِمُوا لَدَىَّ وَقَدْ قَدَّمْتُ إِلَيْكُم بِٱلْوَعِيدِ (٢٨)

And every person will come forth along with an (angel) to drive (him), and an (angel) to bear witness. (21) (It will be said to the sinners): "Indeed you were heedless of this, now We have removed your covering, and sharp is your sight this Day!" (22) And his companion (angel) will say: "Here is (this Record) ready with me!" (23) (Allah will say to the angels): "Both of

you throw into Hell, every stubborn disbeliever (in the Oneness of Allâh, in His Messengers) — (24) "Hinderer of good, transgressor, doubter, (25) "Who set up another ilâh (god) with Allâh, Then both of you cast him in the severe torment."
(26) His companion (Satan — devil)] will say: "Our Lord! I did not push him to transgression, (in disbelief, oppression, and evil deeds) but he was himself in error far astray." (27) Allâh will say: "Dispute not in front of Me, I had already, in advance, sent you the threat. (28)

It was narrated from Yahya bin Rafi`, the freed servant of Thaqif, that he heard `Uthman bin `Affan, giving a speech in which he recited this Ayah,

﴿وَجَاءَتْ كُلُّ نَفْسٍ مَّعَهَا سَآئِقٌ وَشَهِيدٌ﴾

(And every person will come forth along with a Sa'iq and a Shahid.) and then said, "A Sa'iq to drive every person to Allah the Exalted, and a Shahid to witness against him what he has done." The statement of Allah the Exalted,

﴿لَّقَدْ كُنتَ فِى غَفْلَةٍ مِّنْ هَـذَا فَكَشَفْنَا عَنكَ غِطَآءَكَ فَبَصَرُكَ الْيَوْمَ حَدِيدٌ﴾

(Indeed you were heedless of this. Now We have removed from you, your covering, and sharp is your sight this Day!) is directed at humanity. Allah said,

﴿لَّقَدْ كُنتَ فِى غَفْلَةٍ مِّنْ هَذَا﴾

(Indeed you were heedless of this.), of this Day,

﴿فَكَشَفْنَا عَنكَ غِطَآءَكَ فَبَصَرُكَ الْيَوْمَ حَدِيدٌ﴾

(Now We have removed from you, your covering, and sharp is your sight this Day!) `your sight is now clear and strong.'

Allah the Exalted states that the scribe angel, who is entrusted with recording the deeds of mankind, will testify against him or her about the deeds he or she did on the Day of Resurrection. He will say,

﴿هَذَا مَا لَدَىَّ عَتِيدٌ﴾

("Here is (his record) ready with me!"), here it is prepared and completed without addition or deletion. This is when Allah the Exalted will judge the creation with fairness, saying,

﴿أَلْقِيَا فِى جَهَنَّمَ كُلَّ كَفَّارٍ عَنِيدٍ﴾

(Both of you throw into Hell every stubborn disbeliever.) It appears that Allah will say these words to the Sa'iq and Shahid angels; the Sa'iq drove him to the grounds where Reckoning is held and the Shahid testified. Allah the Exalted will order them to throw him in the fire of Jahannam, and worse it is as a destination,

﴿أَلْقِيَا فِى جَهَنَّمَ كُلَّ كَفَّارٍ عَنِيدٍ﴾

(Both of you throw into Hell every stubborn disbeliever.) meaning, whose disbelief and denial of truth was horrendous, who used to stubbornly reject the truth, knowingly contradicting it with falsehood,

﴿مَّنَّاعٍ لِّلْخَيْرِ﴾

(Hinderer of good,) meaning for he did not fulfill the duties he was ordered, nor was he dutiful, keeping ties to kith and kin nor giving charity,

﴿مُعْتَدٍ﴾

(transgressor,) meaning, he transgresses the limits in spending. Qatadah commented, "He is a transgressor in his speech, behavior and affairs." Allah said,

﴿مُّرِيبٍ﴾

(doubter,) meaning, he doubts and raises doubts in those who scrutinize his behavior,

﴿الَّذِى جَعَلَ مَعَ اللَّهِ إِلَـهاً ءَاخَرَ﴾

(who set up another god with Allah.) meaning, he associated others with Allah and worshipped others besides Him,

﴿فَأَلْقِيَـهُ فِى الْعَذَابِ الشَّدِيدِ﴾

(Then both of you cast him in the severe torment.) Imam Ahmad recorded that Abu Sa`id Al-Khudri said that the Prophet said,

«يَخْرُجُ عُنُقٌ مِنَ النَّارِ يَتَكَلَّمُ يَقُولُ: وُكِّلْتُ الْيَوْمَ بِثَلَاثَةٍ: بِكُلِّ جَبَّارٍ عَنِيدٍ، وَمَنْ جَعَلَ مَعَ اللهِ إِلَهًا آخَرَ، وَمَنْ قَتَلَ نَفْسًا بِغَيْرِ نَفْسٍ، فَتَنْطَوِي عَلَيْهِمْ فَتَقْذِفُهُمْ فِي غَمَرَاتِ جَهَنَّمَ»

(A neck from the Fire will appear and will speak saying, "Today, I have been entrusted with three: Every obstinate tyrant, everyone who ascribed another god with Allah, and he who took a life without right." The neck will then close in on them and throw them in the midst of Jahannam.)"

Allah's saying;

﴿قَالَ قَرِينُهُ﴾

(His companion will say), refers to the devil who is entrusted to every man, according to `Abdullah bin `Abbas, Mujahid, Qatadah and several othes. He will say,

﴿رَبَّنَا مَآ أَطْغَيْتُهُ﴾

(Our Lord! I did not push him to transgression,) meaning, the devil will say this about the human who came on the Day of Resurrection as a disbeliever. The devil will disown him, saying,

﴿رَبَّنَا مَآ أَطْغَيْتُهُ﴾

(Our Lord! I did not push him to transgression) meaning, "I did not lead him astray,"

﴿وَلَـكِن كَانَ فِى ضَلَلٍ بَعِيدٍ﴾

(but he was himself in error far astray.) meaning, he himself was misguided, accepting falsehood and stubborn to the truth. Allah the Exalted and Most Honored said in another Ayah,

﴿وَقَالَ الشَّيْطَنُ لَمَّا قُضِىَ الأَمْرُ إِنَّ اللَّه وَعَدَكُمْ وَعْدَ الْحَقِّ وَوَعَدتُّكُمْ فَأَخْلَفْتُكُمْ وَمَا كَانَ لِىَ عَلَيْكُمْ مِّن سُلْطَنٍ إِلاَّ أَن دَعَوْتُكُمْ فَاسْتَجَبْتُمْ لِى فَلاَ تَلُومُونِى وَلُومُواْ أَنفُسَكُمْ مَّا أَنَاْ بِمُصْرِخِكُمْ وَمَا أَنتُمْ بِمُصْرِخِىَّ إِنِّى كَفَرْتُ بِمَا أَشْرَكْتُمُونِ مِن قَبْلُ إِنَّ الظَّلِمِينَ لَهُمْ عَذَابٌ أَلِيمٌ﴾

(And Shaytan will say when the matter has been decided: "Verily, Allah promised you a promise of truth. And I too promised you, but I betrayed you. I had no authority over you except that I called you, and you responded to me. So blame me not, but blame yourselves. I cannot help you, nor can you help me. I deny your former act in associating me as a partner with Allah. Verily, there is a painful torment for the wrongdoers.") (14:22) Allah the Exalted said,

﴿قَالَ لاَ تَخْتَصِمُواْ لَدَىَّ﴾

((Allah) will say: "Dispute not in front of Me.") The Lord, the Exalted and Most Honored will say this to the man and his devil companion, who will be disputing before Him. The man will say, "O, Lord! This devil has misguided me away from the Remembrance after it came to me," while the devil will declare,

﴿رَبَّنَا مَآ أَطْغَيْتُهُ وَلَـكِن كَانَ فِى ضَلَلٍ بَعِيدٍ﴾

(Our Lord! I did not push him to transgression, but he was himself in error far astray.) from the path of truth. The Lord, the Exalted and Most Honored will say to them,

﴿لاَ تَخْتَصِمُواْ لَدَىَّ﴾

(Dispute not in front of Me,) or `before Me,'

﴿وَقَدْ قَدَّمْتُ إِلَيْكُم بِالْوَعِيدِ﴾

(I had already in advance sent you the threat.) `I have given you sufficient proof by the words of the

Messengers, and I have sent down the Divine Books; the evidences, signs and proofs have thus been established against you.'

Even the angels will honorably snitch on the day of judgement exposing the sinners in addition to their daily snitching of our good and bad deeds. This angelic testimony will be given more importance than the disputation and blaming of the humans versus devils.

Quran 58:1

قَدْ سَمِعَ ٱللَّهُ قَوْلَ ٱلَّتِى تُجَـٰدِلُكَ فِى زَوْجِهَا وَتَشْتَكِىٓ إِلَى ٱللَّهِ وَٱللَّهُ يَسْمَعُ تَحَاوُرَكُمَآ إِنَّ ٱللَّهَ سَمِيعُۢ بَصِيرٌ (١)

Indeed Allâh has heard the statement of her (Khaulah bint Tha'labah) that disputes with you (O Muhammad) concerning her husband (Aus bin As¬Sâmit), and complains to Allâh. And Allâh hears the argument between you both. Verily, Allâh is All-Hearer, All-Seer. (1)

Imam Ahmad recorded that `A'ishah said, "All praise be to Allah, Who hears all voices. "The woman who disputed" came to the Prophet and argued with him while I was in another part of the room, unable to hear what she said. Allah the Exalted and Most Honored revealed this Ayah,

﴿قَدْ سَمِعَ اللَّهُ قَوْلَ الَّتِى تُجَادِلُكَ فِى زَوْجِهَا﴾

(Indeed Allah has heard the statement of her that disputes with you concerning her husband.)" till the end of this Ayah. Al-Bukhari collected this Hadith without a chain of narration in the Book of Tawhid in his Sahih. An-

Nasa'i, Ibn Majah, Ibn Abi Hatim and Ibn Jarir also collected this Hadith. In the narration that Ibn Abi Hatim collected, `A'ishah said, "Blessed is He, Whose hearing has encompassed all things. I heard what Khawlah bint Tha`labah said while some of it I could not hear. She was complaining to Allah's Messenger about her husband. She said, `O Allah's Messenger! He spent my wealth, exhausted my youth and my womb bore abundantly for him. When I became old, unable to bear children, he pronounced the Ziharon me! O Allah! I complain to you.' Soon after, Jibril brought down this Ayah,

$$﴿قَدْ سَمِعَ اللَّهُ قَوْلَ الَّتِى تُجَادِلُكَ فِى زَوْجِهَا﴾$$

(Indeed Allah has heard the statement of her that disputes with you concerning her husband,)" She added, "Her husband was Aws bin As-Samit."

It is important to note that complaining is a form of snitching and they are synonymous, so when someone complains to God about someone they are snitching whether they realize or not. The value Allah places on family ties is great so we must be wary to avoid oppressing our kin or anyone else for that matter. This woman whose voice wasn't even audible to humans within the same room was heard and listened to by Allah which indicates that complaining or snitching to Allah is never done in vain. All arguments between creatures are observed so we should be cognizant of the King's commands regarding argument etiquette if we argue.

Quran 66:3-4

وَإِذْ أَسَرَّ ٱلنَّبِيُّ إِلَىٰ بَعْضِ أَزْوَٰجِهِۦ حَدِيثًا فَلَمَّا نَبَّأَتْ بِهِۦ وَأَظْهَرَهُ ٱللَّهُ عَلَيْهِ عَرَّفَ بَعْضَهُۥ وَأَعْرَضَ عَن بَعْضٍۖ فَلَمَّا نَبَّأَهَا بِهِۦ قَالَتْ مَنْ أَنبَأَكَ هَٰذَاۖ قَالَ نَبَّأَنِىَ ٱلْعَلِيمُ ٱلْخَبِيرُ (٣) إِن تَتُوبَآ إِلَى ٱللَّهِ فَقَدْ صَغَتْ قُلُوبُكُمَاۖ وَإِن تَظَٰهَرَا عَلَيْهِ فَإِنَّ ٱللَّهَ هُوَ مَوْلَٰهُ وَجِبْرِيلُ وَصَٰلِحُ ٱلْمُؤْمِنِينَۖ وَٱلْمَلَٰٓئِكَةُ بَعْدَ ذَٰلِكَ ظَهِيرٌ (٤)

And (remember) when the Prophet disclosed a matter in confidence to one of his wives (Hafsah), then she told it (to another i.e. 'Aishah), and Allâh made it known to him, he informed part thereof and left a part. Then when he told her (Hafsah) thereof, she said: "Who told you this?" He said: "The All-Knower, the All-Aware (Allâh) has told me". (3) If you two (wives of the Prophet, 'Aishah and Hafsah) turn in repentance to Allâh, (it will be better for you), your hearts are indeed so inclined (to oppose what the Prophet likes); but if you help one another against him (Muhammad), then verily, Allâh is his Maula (Lord, or Master, or Protector), and Jibril (Gabriel), and the righteous among the believers, and furthermore, the angels are his helpers. (4)

Al-Bukhari recorded that `Ubayd bin `Umayr said that he heard `A'ishah claiming that Allah's Messenger used to stay for a period in the house of Zaynab bint Jahsh and drink honey in her house. (She said) "Hafsah and I decided that when the Prophet entered upon either of us, we would say, `I smell Maghafir on you. Have you eaten Maghafir' When he entered upon one of us, she said that to him. He replied (to her),

«لَا، بَلْ شَرِبْتُ عَسَلًا عِنْدَ زَيْنَبَ بِنْتِ جَحْشٍ وَلَنْ أَعُودَ لَهُ»

(No, but I drank honey in the house of Zaynab bint Jahsh, and I will never drink it again.)" Then the following was revealed;

﴿يَأَيُّهَا النَّبِيُّ لِمَ تُحَرِّمُ مَآ أَحَلَّ اللَّهُ لَكَ﴾

(O Prophet! Why do you forbid that which Allah has allowed to you) up to,

﴿إِن تَتُوبَآ إِلَى اللَّهِ فَقَدْ صَغَتْ قُلُوبُكُمَا﴾

(If you both turn in repentance to Allah, your hearts are indeed so inclined;) in reference to `A'ishah and Hafsah.

﴿وَإِذْ أَسَرَّ النَّبِيُّ إِلَى بَعْضِ أَزْوَجِهِ حَدِيثاً﴾

(And (remember) when the Prophet disclosed a matter in confidence to one of his wives,) which refers to this saying,

«بَلْ شَرِبْتُ عَسَلًا»

(But I have drunk honey.) Ibrahim bin Musa said that Hisham said that it also meant his saying,

«وَلَنْ أَعُودَ لَهُ وَقَدْ حَلَفْتُ فَلَا تُخْبِرِي بِذَلِكِ أَحَدًا»

(I will not drink it anymore, I have taken an oath to that. Therefore, do not inform anybody about it.) Al-Bukhari also recorded this Hadith in the Book of Divorce; then he said, "Al-Maghafir is a type of sap, and in Ar-Rimth (a type of citrus) its taste is sweet..." Al-Jawhari said, "The `Urfut is a tree of the shrub variety, which secretes Maghfur." Muslim collected this Hadith from `A'ishah in the Book of Divorce in his Sahih, and his wording is the same as Al-Bukhari in the Book of Vows. In the Book of Divorce, Al-Bukhari recorded that `A'ishah said, "Allah's Messenger liked sweets and honey. After performing the `Asr prayer, he used to visit his wives, going close to them. So he went to Hafsah, daughter of `Umar, and stayed with her more than his usual stay. I (`A'ishah) became jealous and asked about that. It was said to me, `A woman of her family sent her a small vessel of honey as a gift, and she gave a drink to Allah's Messenger made from it.' I said, `By Allah, we will contrive a plot against him.' I said to Sawdah bint Zam`ah, `When the Messenger visits you and draws close to you, say to him, `Have you eaten Maghafir' And when he says to you, `No', then ask him, `What is this odor' He will say to you, `Hafsah has given me a drink of honey.' Then you should say to him, `The honeybees might have eaten from Urfut, and I will also say the same to him. Safiyyah, you should also say this.' Sawdah later said, `It was under compulsion that I had decided to state that which you told me; soon, by Allah, he was standing at my door.' So when Allah's Messenger came near her, she said, `O Messenger of Allah! Did you eat Maghafir' He said, `No.' She again said, `Then what is this odor' He said,

«سَقَتْنِي حَفْصَةُ شَرْبَةَ عَسَل»

(Hafsah gave me honey to drink.) She said, `The honeybees might have eaten from `Urfut.')" `A'ishah continued, "When he came to me I said the same to him. He then visited Safiyyah and she also said similar to him. When he again visited Hafsah, she said, `O Messenger of Allah, should I not give you that (drink)' He said,

«لَا حَاجَةَ لِي فِيهِ»

(I do not need it.) Sawdah said, `By Allah! We have prevented him from drinking honey.' I said to her, `Keep quiet!'" Muslim also recorded this Hadith, but this wording is from Al-Bukhari. In the narration of Muslim, `A'ishah said, "The Messenger of Allah used to hate to have a bad odor coming from him" This is why they suggested to him that he ate Maghafir, because it causes a bad odor. When he said,

«بَلْ شَرِبْتُ عَسَلًا»

(No, I had some honey.) They said that the bees ate from a tree that is called Al-`Urfut, which has Maghafir gum, suggesting that this is the reason behind the bad odor they claimed was coming from him. The latter narration, collected through `Urwah from `A'ishah, mentions that it was Hafsah who gave the Prophet the honey. In another narration collected from `Ubayd bin `Umayr, from `A'ishah, it was Zaynab bint Jahsh who gave the honey to the Prophet , while `A'ishah and Hafsah were the plotters. Allah knows best. Some might say that they were two separate incidents. However, it is not likely that the Ayat were revealed about both incidents, if indeed they were two separate incidents. A Hadith that Imam Ahmad collected in the Musnad mentions that `A'ishah and Hafsah were the plotters. Allah knows best.

The point of the story as it pertains to our topic is that once again we have an example of revelation being a type of snitching from Allah to a prophet with the act of snitching being the cause that kickstarted the chain-reaction of repentance. We must always remember the goal of snitching is for the repentance and reformation of those being snitched on, the goal is not necessarily for them to be punished for their crimes as many presume.

Quran 75:13-15

يُنَبَّؤُاْ ٱلْإِنسَٰنُ يَوْمَئِذٍ بِمَا قَدَّمَ وَأَخَّرَ (١٣) بَلِ ٱلْإِنسَٰنُ عَلَىٰ نَفْسِهِۦ بَصِيرَةٌ (١٤) وَلَوْ أَلْقَىٰ مَعَاذِيرَهُۥ (١٥)

On that Day man will be informed of what he sent forward (of his evil or good deeds), and what he left behind (of his good or evil traditions). (13) Nay! Man will be a witness against himself [as his body parts (skin, hands, legs, etc.) will speak about his deeds]. (14) Though he may put forth his excuses (to cover his evil deeds). (15)

Allah says,

﴿يُنَبَّأُ الإِنسَٰنُ يَوْمَئِذٍ بِمَا قَدَّمَ وَأَخَّرَ﴾

(On that Day man will be informed of what he sent forward, and what he left behind.) meaning, he will be informed of all of his deeds, the old of them and the recent of them, the first of them and the last of them, the small of them and the large of them. This is as Allah says,

﴿وَوَجَدُواْ مَا عَمِلُواْ حَاضِرًا وَلاَ يَظْلِمُ رَبُّكَ أَحَدًا﴾

(And they will find all that they did, placed before them, and your Lord treats no one with injustice.) (18:49) Likewise, Allah says here,

﴿ بَلِ الإِنسَنُ عَلَى نَفْسِهِ بَصِيرَةٌ - وَلَوْ أَلْقَى مَعَاذِيرَهُ ﴾

(Nay! Man will be well informed about himself, though he may put forth his excuses.) meaning, he will be a witness against himself, knowing full well what he did, even though he will try to make excuses and deny it. This is as Allah says,

﴿ اقْرَأْ كَتَبَكَ كَفَى بِنَفْسِكَ الْيَوْمَ عَلَيْكَ حَسِيبًا ﴾

((It will be said to him): "Read your book. You are sufficient as a reckoner against yourself this Day.") `Ali bin Abi Talhah reported that Ibn `Abbas said,

﴿ بَلِ الإِنسَنُ عَلَى نَفْسِهِ بَصِيرَةٌ ﴾

(Nay! Man will be well informed about himself.) "His hearing, his sight, his two hands, his two legs and his limbs." Qatadah said, "This means he is a witness against himself." In another narration from Qatadah he said, "By Allah! If you wish to see him, you would see him as someone who sees the shortcomings of the people and their sins, yet he is heedless of his own sins." It used to be said, "Verily, it is written in the Injil: `O Son of Adam, do you see the small splinters in the eye of your brother and disregard the tree stump that is in your eye, so you do not see it'" Mujahid said,

﴿ وَلَوْ أَلْقَى مَعَاذِيرَهُ ﴾

(Though he may put forth his excuses.) "This means, even though he argues in defense of it, he is a witness against it." Qatadah said,

﴿وَلَوْ أَلْقَى مَعَاذِيرَهُ﴾

(Though he may put forth his excuses.) "Even though he will try to make false excuses on that Day, they will not be accepted from him." As-Suddi said,

﴿وَلَوْ أَلْقَى مَعَاذِيرَهُ﴾

(Though he may put forth his excuses.) "This means his argument."

These verses expose how we will all expose ourselves in that our own body parts will snitch on us as to what we did of good and evil when in the court of Allah. Our own tongues will even refute our speech we may try to contrive to save ourselves. So do good and avoid evil because soon you will snitch on yourself whether you like it or not to the Judge who is most severe in punishment.

Quran 80:1-2

عَبَسَ وَتَوَلَّىٰ (١) أَن جَآءَهُ ٱلْأَعْمَىٰ (٢)

(The Prophet) frowned and turned away, (1) Because there came to him the blind man (i.e. 'Abdullâh bin Umm-Maktûm, who came to the Prophet while he was preaching to one or some of the Quraish chiefs) (2)

More than one of the scholars of Tafsir mentioned that one day the Messenger of Allah was addressing one of the great leaders of the Quraysh while hoping that he would accept Islam. While he was speaking in direct conversation with him, Ibn Umm Maktum came to him, and he was of those who had accepted Islam in its earliest days. He (Ibn Umm Maktum) then began asking the

Messenger of Allah about something, urgently beseeching him. The Prophet hoped that the man would be guided, so he asked Ibn Umm Maktum to wait for a moment so he could complete his conversation. He frowned in the face of Ibn Umm Maktum and turned away from him in order to face the other man. Here Allah commands His Messenger to not single anyone out with the warning. Rather, he should equally warn the noble and the weak, the poor and the rich, the master and the slave, the men and the women, the young and the old. Then Allah will guide whomever He chooses to a path that is straight. He has the profound wisdom and the decisive proof.

Another example of Allah snitching this time on his prophet to all who learn of these verses providing numerous lessons and motivating repentance.

Quran 82:10-12

وَإِنَّ عَلَيْكُمْ لَحَافِظِينَ (١٠) كِرَامًا كَاتِبِينَ (١١) يَعْلَمُونَ مَا تَفْعَلُونَ (١٢)

But verily, over you (are appointed angels in charge of mankind) to watch you , (10) Kirâman (Honourable) Kâtibîn writing down (your deeds), (11) They know all that you do. (12)

Concerning Allah's statement,

﴿وَإِنَّ عَلَيْكُمْ لَحَافِظِينَ ـ كِرَاماً كَاتِبِينَ ـ يَعْلَمُونَ مَا تَفْعَلُونَ﴾

(But verily, over you to watch you (are) Kiraman Katibin, they know all that you do.) (82:10-12) meaning, `indeed there are noble guardian angels over you, so do not meet them with evil deeds, because they write down all that you do.'

Here we are warned of the angels who record all our deeds and report back to Allah to inform him daily as well as on Judgment day despite Allah not being in need of any reports. The angels are there as extra evidence because of the immense justice and lessons that can be had due to knowledge of being snitched on daily. The Angels snitch on you daily so if you got a problem with snitches you got a problem with angels who obey all orders Allah commands. They snitch on sinners when Allah orders them to do so, then why don't we snitch when commanded with the same?

Quran 86:4

إِن كُلُّ نَفْسٍ لَّمَّا عَلَيْهَا حَافِظٌ (٤)

There is no human being but has a protector over him (or her) (i.e. angels in charge of each human being guarding him, writing his good and bad deeds). (4)

Allah says,

﴿إِن كُلُّ نَفْسٍ لَّمَّا عَلَيْهَا حَافِظٌ﴾

(There is no human being but has a protector over him.) meaning, every soul has a guardian over it from Allah that protects it from the calamities.

As the previous section explains the label of guardian angels could just as easily being snitching angels but people have distorted the meaning thinking the angels merely act as servants to us rather than snitching on our deeds amongst their other acts of worshipping Allah.

Quran 99:1-8

إِذَا زُلْزِلَتِ ٱلْأَرْضُ زِلْزَالَهَا (١) وَأَخْرَجَتِ ٱلْأَرْضُ أَثْقَالَهَا (٢) وَقَالَ ٱلْإِنسَٰنُ مَا لَهَا (٣) يَوْمَئِذٍ تُحَدِّثُ أَخْبَارَهَا (٤) بِأَنَّ رَبَّكَ أَوْحَىٰ لَهَا (٥) يَوْمَئِذٍ يَصْدُرُ ٱلنَّاسُ أَشْتَاتًا لِّيُرَوْاْ أَعْمَٰلَهُمْ (٦) فَمَن يَعْمَلْ مِثْقَالَ ذَرَّةٍ خَيْرًا يَرَهُۥ (٧) وَمَن يَعْمَلْ مِثْقَالَ ذَرَّةٍ شَرًّا يَرَهُۥ (٨)

When the earth is shaken with its (final) earthquake. (1) And when the earth throws out its burdens, (2) And man will say: "What is the matter with it?" (3) That Day it will declare its information (about all that happened over it of good or evil). (4) Because your Lord will inspire it. (5) That Day mankind will proceed in scattered groups that they may be shown their deeds. (6) So whosoever does good equal to the weight of an atom (or a small ant), shall see it. (7) And whosoever does evil equal to the weight of an atom (or a small ant), shall see it. (8)

Ibn `Abbas said,

﴿إِذَا زُلْزِلَتِ الْأَرْضُ زِلْزَالَهَا﴾

(When the earth quakes with its Zilzal.) "This means that it will move from beneath it."

﴿وَأَخْرَجَتِ الْأَرْضُ أَثْقَالَهَا﴾

(And when the earth throws out its burdens.) meaning, it will throw forth that which is in it of the dead. More than one of the Salaf have said this and it is similar to Allah's statement,

﴿يَأَيُّهَا النَّاسُ اتَّقُوا رَبَّكُمْ إِنَّ زَلْزَلَةَ السَّاعَةِ شَيْءٌ عَظِيمٌ﴾

(O mankind! Have Taqwa of your Lord! Verily, the earthquake (Zalzalah) of the Hour is a terrible thing.) (22:1) This is also similar to His saying,

﴿وَإِذَا الْأَرْضُ مُدَّتْ ـ وَأَلْقَتْ مَا فِيهَا وَتَخَلَّتْ ﴾

(And when the earth is stretched forth, and has cast out all that was in it and became empty.) (84:3-4) Muslim recorded in his Sahih from Abu Hurayrah that the Messenger of Allah said,

«تُلْقِي الْأَرْضُ أَفْلَاذَ كَبِدِهَا أَمْثَالَ الْأُسْطُوَانِ مِنَ الذَّهَبِ وَالْفِضَّةِ، فَيَجِيءُ الْقَاتِلُ فَيَقُولُ فِي هَذَا قَتَلْتُ، وَيَجِيءُ الْقَاطِعُ فَيَقُولُ فِي هَذَا قَطَعْتُ رَحِمِي، وَيَجِيءُ السَّارِقُ فَيَقُولُ: فِي هَذَا قُطِعَتْ يَدِي، ثُمَّ يَدَعُونَهُ فَلَا يَأْخُذُونَ مِنْهُ شَيْئًا»

(The earth will throw out the pieces of its liver (its contents). Gold and silver will come out like columns. A murderer will come and say, `I killed for this' The one who broke the ties of kinship will say, `For this I severed the ties of kinship' The thief will say, `For this I got my hands amputated' Then they will leave it there and no one will take anything from it.)" Then Allah says,

﴿وَقَالَ الْإِنسَـنُ مَا لَهَا ﴾

(And man will say: "What is the matter with it") meaning, he will be baffled by its situation after it used to be stable, settled and firm, and he used to be settled upon its surface. This refers to the alteration of the state of things and the earth moving and shaking. There will come to it inescapable quaking that Allah prepared for it. Then it will throw out its dead people -- from the first to the last generations. At that time the people will be baffled by the events and the earth changing into other than the earth, and the heavens as well. Then they will be presented before Allah, the One, the Irresistible. Concerning Allah's statement,

﴿يَوْمَئِذٍ تُحَدِّثُ أَخْبَارَهَا ﴾

(That Day it will declare its information.) meaning, it will speak of what the people did upon its surface. Imam Ahmad, At-Tirmidhi and Abu `Abdur-Rahman An-Nasa'i all recorded a Hadith from Abu Hurayrah -- and in the wording of An-Nasa'i's version it states -- that he said, "The Messenger of Allah recited this Ayah,

﴿يَوْمَئِذٍ تُحَدِّثُ أَخْبَارَهَا ﴾

(That Day it will declare its information.) Then he said,

«أَتَدْرُونَ مَا أَخْبَارُهَا؟»

(Do you know what is its information) They said, `Allah and His Messenger know best.' He said,

«فَإِنَّ أَخْبَارَهَا أَنْ تَشْهَدَ عَلَى كُلِّ عَبْدٍ وَأَمَةٍ بِمَا عَمِلَ عَلَى ظَهْرِهَا أَنْ تَقُولَ: عَمِلَ كَذَا وَكَذَا يَوْمَ كَذَا وَكَذَا، فَهَذِهِ أَخْبَارُهَا»

(Verily, its information is that it will testify against every male and female servant, about what they did upon its surface. It will say that he did such and such on such and such day. So this is its information.)" Then At-Tirmidhi said, "This Hadith is Sahih Gharib." Concerning Allah's statement,

﴿بِأَنَّ رَبَّكَ أَوْحَى لَهَا ﴾

(Because your Lord will inspire it.) It is apparent that the implied meaning here is that He will permit it (the earth). Shabib bin Bishr narrated from `Ikrimah that Ibn `Abbas said,

﴿يَوْمَئِذٍ تُحَدِّثُ أَخْبَارَهَا﴾

(That Day it will declare its information.) "Its Lord will say to it, `Speak.' So it will speak." Mujahid commented (on "inspire it"), " He commands it (i.e., to speak). " Al-Qurazi said, "He will command it to separate from them." Then Allah says,

﴿يَوْمَئِذٍ يَصْدُرُ النَّاسُ أَشْتَاتاً﴾

(That Day mankind will proceed in scattered groups (Ashtat)) meaning, they will return from the station of the Judgement in separate groups. This means that they will be divided into types and categories: between those who are miserable and those who are happy, and those who are commanded to go to Paradise and those who are commanded to go to the Hellfire. As-Suddi said, "Ashtat means sects." Allah said,

﴿لِيُرَوْاْ أَعْمَـٰلَهُمْ﴾

(that they may be shown their deeds.) meaning, so that they may act and be rewarded for what they did in this life of good and evil.

Allah goes on to say,

﴿فَمَن يَعْمَلْ مِثْقَالَ ذَرَّةٍ خَيْراً يَرَهُ - وَمَن يَعْمَلْ مِثْقَالَ ذَرَّةٍ شَرّاً يَرَهُ﴾

(So whosoever does good equal to the weight of a speck of dust shall see it. And whosoever does evil equal to the weight of speck of dust shall see it.) Al-Bukhari recorded from Abu Hurayrah that the Messenger of Allah said,

«الْخَيْلُ لِثَلَاثَةٍ، لِرَجُلٍ أَجْرٌ، وَلِرَجُلٍ سِتْرٌ، وَعَلَى رَجُلٍ وِزْرٌ. فَأَمَّا الَّذِي لَهُ أَجْرٌ فَرَجُلٌ رَبَطَهَا فِي سَبِيلِ اللهِ فَأَطَالَ طِيَلَهَا فِي مَرْجٍ أَوْ رَوْضَةٍ، فَمَا أَصَابَتْ فِي طِيَلِهَا ذَلِكَ فِي الْمَرْجِ وَالرَّوْضَةِ كَانَ لَهُ حَسَنَاتٍ، وَلَوْ أَنَّهَا قَطَعَتْ طِيَلَهَا فَاسْتَنَّتْ شَرَفًا أَوْ شَرَفَيْنِ كَانَتْ آثَارُهَا وَأَرْوَاثُهَا حَسَنَاتٍ لَهُ، وَلَوْ أَنَّهَا مَرَّتْ بِنَهَرٍ فَشَرِبَتْ مِنْهُ وَلَمْ يُرِدْ أَنْ يَسْقِيَ بِهِ كَانَ ذَلِكَ حَسَنَاتٍ لَهُ، وَهِيَ لِذَلِكَ الرَّجُلِ أَجْرٌ. وَرَجُلٌ رَبَطَهَا تَغَنِّيًا وَتَعَفُّفًا وَلَمْ يَنْسَ حَقَّ اللهِ فِي رِقَابِهَا وَلَا ظُهُورِهَا فَهِيَ لَهُ سِتْرٌ، وَرَجُلٌ رَبَطَهَا فَخْرًا وَرِيَاءً وَنِوَاءً فَهِيَ عَلَى ذَلِكَ وِزْرٌ»

(The horses are for three. For one man they are a reward, for another man they are a shield, and for another man they are a burden. In reference to the man for whom they are a reward, he is the man who keeps them to be used in the way of Allah. Thus, they spend their entire life grazing in the pasture or garden (waiting in preparation for Jihad). So whatever afflicts them during that lengthy period in the pasture or garden, it will be counted as good deeds for him. Then, if their lengthy period is ended and they are used for a noble battle or two, their hoof prints and their dung are counted as good deeds for him.

When they passed through a stream from which they did drink, though he (their owner) does not intend to quench their thirst, yet, it would be counted as good deeds, Therefore, they are a reward for that man. A man who keeps them to maintain himself and to be independent of others (i.e., begging, etc.), and he does not forget the right of Allah upon their necks and their backs (i.e., their

Zakah), then they are a shield for him (from the Hellfire). A man who keeps them in order to boast, brag and show off, then they are a burden for him (on Judgement Day).) So the Messenger of Allah was then asked about the donkeys and he said,

»مَا أَنْزَلَ اللهُ فِيهَا شَيْئًا إِلَّا هَذِهِ الْآيَةَ الْفَاذَّةَ الْجَامِعَةَ

﴿فَمَن يَعْمَلْ مِثْقَالَ ذَرَّةٍ خَيْرًا يَرَهُ - وَمَن يَعْمَلْ مِثْقَالَ ذَرَّةٍ شَرًّا يَرَهُ ﴾

(Allah has not revealed anything concerning them except this single, comprehensive Ayah: (So whosoever does good equal to the weight of a speck of dust shall see it. And whosoever does evil equal to the weight of speck of dust shall see it.)) Muslim also recorded this Hadith.

Planet earth will also snitch on the sinners as Allah commands on the Day of Resurrection. So know that wherever you go on earth a mighty snitch is observing you everywhere waiting and compiling its report of good and evil which you've done. Since failing to snitch is an evil then make sure you snitch when required by Islamic law to do so lest the earth and angels and others snitch on you for failing to fulfill your duty.

Hadith regarding Snitching on Sinners

Abu Sa'id Al-Khudri reported:

Prophet of Allah (ﷺ) said: "There was a man from among a nation before you who killed ninety-nine people and then made an inquiry about the most learned person on the earth. He was directed to a monk. He came to him and told him that he had killed ninety-nine people and asked him if there was any chance for his repentance to be accepted. He replied in the negative and the man killed him also completing one hundred. He then asked about the most learned man in the earth. He was directed to a scholar. He told him that he had killed one hundred people and asked him if there was any chance for his repentance to be accepted. He replied in the affirmative and asked, 'Who stands between you and repentance? Go to such and such land; there (you will find) people devoted to prayer and worship of Allah, join them in worship, and do not come back to your land because it is an evil place.' So he went away and hardly had he covered half the distance when death overtook him; and there was a dispute between the angels of mercy and the angels of torment. The angels of mercy pleaded, 'This man has come with a repenting heart to Allah,' and the angels of punishment argued, 'He never did a virtuous deed in his life.' Then there appeared another angel in the form of a human being and the contending angels agreed to make him arbiter between them. He said, 'Measure the distance between the two lands. He will be considered belonging to the land to which he is nearer.' They measured and found him closer to the land (land of piety) where he intended to go, and so the angels of mercy collected his soul".

Source: Al-Bukhari and Muslim

Abdullah bin Ka'b, who served as the guide of Ka'b bin Malik when he became blind, narrated:

I heard Ka'b bin Malik narrating the story of his remaining behind instead of joining Messenger of Allah (ﷺ) when he left for the battle of Tabuk. Ka'b said: "I accompanied Messenger of Allah (ﷺ) in every expedition which he undertook excepting the battle of Tabuk and the battle of Badr. As for the battle of Badr, nobody was blamed for remaining behind as Messenger of Allah (ﷺ) and the Muslims, when they set out, had in mind only to intercept the caravan of the Quraish. Allah made them confront their enemies unexpectedly. I had the honour of being with Messenger of Allah (ﷺ) on the night of 'Aqabah when we pledged our allegiance to Islam and it was dearer to me than participating in the battle of Badr, although Badr was more well-known among the people than that. And this is the account of my staying behind from the battle of Tabuk. I never had better means and more favorable circumstances than at the time of this expedition. And by Allah, I had never before possessed two riding-camels as I did during the time of this expedition. Whenever Messenger of Allah (ﷺ) decided to go on a campaign, he would not disclose his real destination till the last moment (of departure). But on this expedition, he set out in extremely hot weather; the journey was long and the terrain was waterless desert; and he had to face a strong army, so he informed the Muslims about the actual position so that they should make full preparation for the campaign. And the Muslims who accompanied Messenger of Allah (ﷺ) at that time were in large number but no proper record of them was maintained." Ka'b (further) said: "Few were the persons who chose to remain absent believing that they could easily hide themselves (and thus remain undetected) unless Revelation from Allah, the Exalted, and Glorious (revealed relating to them). And Messenger of Allah (ﷺ) set out on this expedition when the fruit were ripe and their shade was sought. I had a weakness for them and it was during this season that Messenger of Allah (ﷺ) and the Muslims made preparations. I also would set out in the morning to make preparations along with them but would come back having done nothing and said to myself: 'I have means enough (to make preparations) as soon as I like'. And I went on doing this (postponing my preparations) till the time of departure came and it was in the morning that Messenger of Allah (ﷺ) set out along with the Muslims, but I had made no preparations. I would go early in the morning and come back, but with no decision. I went on doing so until they (the Muslims) hastened and covered a good deal of distance. Then I wished to march on and join them. Would that I had done that! But perhaps it was not destined for me. After the departure of Messenger of Allah (ﷺ) whenever I went out, I was grieved to find no good example to follow but confirmed hypocrites or weak people whom Allah had exempted (from marching forth for Jihad). Messenger of Allah (ﷺ) made no mention of me until he reached Tabuk. While he was sitting with the people in Tabuk, he said, 'What happened to Ka'b bin Malik?' A person from Banu Salimah said: "O Messenger of Allah, the (beauty) of his cloak and an appreciation of his finery have detained him.' Upon this Mu'adh bin Jabal admonished him and said to

Messenger of Allah (ﷺ): "By Allah, we know nothing about him but good.' Messenger of Allah (ﷺ), however, kept quiet. At that time he (the Prophet (ﷺ)) saw a person dressed in white and said, 'Be Abu Khaithamah.' And was Abu Khaithamah Al-Ansari was the person who had contributed a Sa' of dates and was ridiculed by the hypocrites." Ka'b bin Malik further said: "When the news reached me that Messenger of Allah (ﷺ) was on his way back from Tabuk, I was greatly distressed. I thought of fabricating an excuse and asked myself how I would save myself from his anger the next day. In this connection, I sought the counsels of every prudent member of my family. When I was told that Messenger of Allah (ﷺ) was about to arrive, all the wicked ideas vanished (from my mind) and I came to the conclusion that nothing but the truth could save me. So I decided to tell him the truth. It was in the morning that Messenger of Allah (ﷺ) arrived in Al-Madinah. It was his habit that whenever he came back from a journey, he would first go to the mosque and perform two Rak'ah (of optional prayer) and would then sit with the people. When he sat, those who had remained behind him began to put forward their excuses and take an oath before him. They were more than eighty in number. Messenger of Allah (ﷺ) accepted their excuses on the very face of them and accepted their allegiance and sought forgiveness for them and left their insights to Allah, until I appeared before him. I greeted him and he smiled and there was a tinge of anger in that. He then said to me, 'Come forward'. I went forward and I sat in front of him. He said to me, 'What kept you back? Could you not afford to go in for a ride?' I said, 'O Messenger of Allah, by Allah, if I were to sit before anybody else, a man of the world, I would have definitely saved myself from his anger *on one pretext or the other and I have a gifted skill in argumentation, but, by Allah, I am fully aware that if I were to put forward before you a lame excuse to please you, Allah would definitely provoke your wrath upon me. In case, I speak the truth, you may be angry with me, but I hope that Allah would be pleased with me (and accept my repentance). By Allah, there is no valid excuse for me. By Allah, I never possessed so good means, and I never had such favorable conditions for me as I had when I stayed behind.' Thereupon, Messenger of Allah (ﷺ) said, 'This man spoke the truth, so get up (and wait) until Allah gives a decision about you.' I left and some people of Banu Salimah followed me. They said to me, 'By Allah, we do not know that you committed a sin before. You, however, showed inability to put forward an excuse before Messenger of Allah (ﷺ) like those who stayed behind him. It would have been enough for the forgiveness of your sin that Messenger of Allah (ﷺ) would have sought forgiveness for you.' By Allah, they kept on reproaching me until I thought of going back to Messenger of Allah (ﷺ) and retract my confession. Then I said to them, 'Has anyone else met the same fate?' They said, 'Yes, two persons have met the same fate. They made the same statement as you did and the same verdict was delivered in their case.' I asked, 'Who are they?' They said, 'Murarah bin Ar-Rabi' Al-'Amri and Hilal bin Umaiyyah Al- Waqifi.' They mentioned these two pious men who had taken part in the battle of Badr and there was an example for me in them. I was confirmed in my original resolve. Messenger of Allah (ﷺ) prohibited the Muslims to talk to the three of us from amongst those who had stayed behind. The people began to avoid us and their attitude towards us changed and it seemed as if the whole* atmosphere had turned against us, and it was in fact the same atmosphere of which I was fully aware and in which I had lived (for a fairly long time). We spent fifty nights in this very state and my two friends confined themselves within their houses and spent (most of their) time weeping. As I was the youngest and the strongest, I would leave my house, attend the congregational Salat, move about in the bazaars, but none would speak to me. I would come to Messenger of Allah (ﷺ) as he sat amongst (people) after the Salat, greet him and would ask myself whether or not his lips moved in response to my greetings. Then I would perform Salat near him and look at him stealthily. When I finish my Salat, he would look at me and when I would cast a glance at him he would turn away his eyes from me. When the harsh treatment of the Muslims to me continued for a (considerable) length of time, I walked and I climbed upon the wall of the garden of Abu Qatadah, who was my cousin, and I had a great love for him. I greeted him but, by Allah, he did not answer to my greeting. I said to him, 'O Abu Qatadah, I adjure you in the Name of Allah, are you not aware that I love Allah and His Messenger (ﷺ)?' I asked him the same question again but he remained silent. I again adjured him, whereupon he said, 'Allah and His Messenger (ﷺ) know better.' My eyes were filled with tears, and I came back climbing down the wall.

As I was walking in the bazaars of Al-Madinah, a man from the Syrian peasants, who had come to sell food grains in Al-Madinah, asked people to direct him to Ka'b bin Malik. People pointed towards me. He came to me and delivered a letter from the King of Ghassan, and as I was a scribe, I read that letter whose purport was: 'It has been conveyed to us that your friend (the Prophet (ﷺ)) was treating you harshly. Allah has not created you for a place where you are to be degraded and where you cannot find your right place; so come to us and we shall receive you graciously.' As I read that letter I said: 'This too is a trial,' so I put it to fire in an oven. When forty days had elapsed and Messenger of Allah (ﷺ) received no Revelation, there came to me a messenger of the Messenger of Allah and said, 'Verily, Messenger of Allah (ﷺ) has commanded you to keep away from your wife.' I said, 'Should I divorce her or what else should I do?' He said, 'No, but only keep away from her and don't have sexual contact with her.' The same message was sent to my companions. So, I said to my wife: 'You better go to your parents and stay there with them until Allah gives the decision in my case.' The wife of Hilal bin Umaiyyah came to Messenger of Allah (ﷺ) and said: 'O Messenger of Allah, Hilal bin Umaiyyah is a senile person and has no servant. Do you disapprove if I serve him?' He said, 'No, but don't let him have any sexual contact with you.' She said, 'By Allah, he has no such desire left in him. By Allah, he has been in tears since (this calamity) struck him.' Members of my family said to me, 'You should have sought permission from Messenger of Allah (ﷺ) in regard to your wife. He has allowed the wife of Hilal bin Umaiyyah to serve him.' I said, 'I would not seek permission from Messenger of Allah (ﷺ) for I do not know what Messenger of Allah might say in response to that, as I am a young man'. It was in this state that I spent ten more nights and thus fifty days had passed since people boycotted us and gave up talking to us. After I had offered my Fajr prayer on the early morning of the fiftieth day of this boycott on the roof of one of our houses, and had sat in the very state which Allah described as: 'The earth seemed constrained for me despite its vastness', I heard the voice of a proclaimer from the peak of the hill Sal' shouting at the top of his voice: 'O Ka'b bin Malik, rejoice.' I fell down in prostration and came to know that there was (a message of) relief for me. Messenger of Allah (ﷺ) had informed the people about the acceptance of our repentance by Allah after he had offered the Fajr prayer. So the people went on to give us glad tidings and some of them went to my companions in order to give them the glad tidings. A man spurred his horse towards me (to give the good news), and another one from the tribe of Aslam came running for the same purpose and, as he approached the mount, I received the good news which reached me before the rider did. When the one whose voice I had heard came to me to congratulate me, I took off my garments and gave them to him for the good news he brought to me. By Allah, I possessed nothing else (in the form of clothes) except these garments, at that time. Then I borrowed two garments, dressed myself and came to Messenger of Allah (ﷺ) On my way, I met groups of people who greeted me for (the acceptance of) repentance and they said: 'Congratulations for acceptance of your repentance.' I reached the mosque where Messenger of Allah (ﷺ) was sitting amidst people. Talhah bin 'Ubaidullah got up and rushed towards me, shook hands with me and greeted me. By Allah, no person stood up (to greet me) from amongst the Muhajirun besides him." Ka'b said that he never forgot (this good gesture of) Talhah. Ka'b further said: "I greeted Messenger of Allah (ﷺ) with 'As-salamu 'alaikum' and his face was beaming with pleasure. He (ﷺ) said, 'Rejoice with the best day you have ever seen since your mother gave you birth. 'I said: 'O Messenger of Allah! Is this (good news) from you or from Allah?' He said, 'No, it is from Allah.' And it was common with Messenger of Allah (ﷺ) that when ever he was happy, his face would glow as if it were a part of the moon and it was from this that we recognized it (his delight). As I sat before him, I said, I have placed a condition upon myself that if Allah accepts my Taubah, I would give up all of my property in charity for the sake of Allah and His Messenger (ﷺ)!' Thereupon Messenger of Allah (ﷺ) said, 'Keep some property with you, as it is better for you.' I said, 'I shall keep with me that portion which is in Khaibar'. I added: 'O Messenger of Allah! Verily, Allah has granted me salvation because of my truthfulness, and therefore, repentance obliges me to speak nothing but the truth as long as I am alive." Ka'b added: "By Allah, I do not know anyone among the Muslims who has been granted truthfulness better than me since I said this to the Prophet (ﷺ). By Allah! Since the time I made a pledge of this to Messenger of Allah (ﷺ), I have never intended to tell a lie, and I hope that Allah would protect me (against telling lies) for the rest of my life. Allah, the Exalted, the Glorious, revealed these Verses:

'Allah has forgiven the Prophet (ﷺ), the Muhajirun (Muslim Emigrants who left their homes and came to Al-Madinah) and the Ansar (Muslims of Al- Madinah) who followed him (Muhammad (ﷺ)) in the time of distress (Tabuk expedition), after the hearts of a party of them had nearly deviated (from the Right Path), but He accepted their repentance. Certainly, He is unto them full of kindness, Most Merciful. And (He did forgive also) the three who did not join [the Tabuk expedition and *whose case was deferred (by the Prophet (☀)) for Allah's Decision] till for them the earth, vast as it is, was straitened and their ownselves were straitened to them, and they perceived that there is no fleeing from Allah, and no refuge but with Him. Then, He forgave them (accepted their repentance), that they might beg for His Pardon [repent (unto Him)]. Verily, Allah is the One Who forgives and accepts repentance, Most Merciful. O you who believe! Be afraid of Allah, and be with those who are true (in word and deeds)." (9:117,118).*

Ka'b said: "By Allah, since Allah guided me to Islam, there has been no blessing more significant for me than this truth of mine which I spoke to Messenger of Allah (☀), and if I were to tell a lie I would have been ruined as were ruined those who had told lies, for Allah described those who told lies with the worst description He ever attributed to anybody else, as He sent down the Revelation:

They will swear by Allah to you (Muslims) when you return to them, that you may turn away from them. So turn away from them. Surely, they are Rijsun [i.e., Najasun (impure) because of their evil deeds], and Hell is their dwelling place - a recompense for that which they used to earn. They (the hypocrites) swear to you (Muslims) that you may be pleased with them, but if you are pleased with them, certainly Allah is not pleased with the people who are Al- Fa'siqun (rebellious, disobedient to Allah)". (9:95,96)

Ka'b further added: "The matter of the three of us remained pending for decision apart from the case of those who had made excuses on oath before Messenger of Allah (ﷺ) and he accepted those, took fresh oaths of allegiance from them and supplicated for their forgiveness. The Prophet (ﷺ) kept our matter pending till Allah decided it. The three whose matter was deferred have been shown mercy. The reference here is not to our staying back from the expedition but to his delaying our matter and keeping it pending beyond the matter of those who made their excuses on oath which he accepted".

Source: Al- Bukhari and Muslim

Imran bin Al-Husain Al-Khuza'i reported:

A woman from the tribe Juhainah came to Messenger of Allah (ﷺ) while she was pregnant from (Zina) adultery and said to him: "O Messenger of Allah! I have committed an offense liable to Hadd (prescribed punishment), so exact the execution of the sentence." Messenger of Allah (ﷺ) called her guardian and said to him, "Treat her kindly. Bring her to me after the delivery of the child." That man complied with the orders. At last the Prophet (ﷺ) commanded to carry out the sentence. Her clothes were secured around her and she was stoned to death. The Prophet (ﷺ) led her funeral prayers. 'Umar submitted: "O Messenger of Allah! She committed Zina and you have performed funeral prayer for her?" He replied, "Verily, she made repentance which would suffice for seventy of the people of Al-Madinah if it is divided among them. Can there be any higher degree of repentance than that she sacrificed her life voluntarily to win the Pleasure of Allah, the Exalted?".

Source: Riyad As Salihin 22 Grade: Sahih

Ibn Mas'ud reported:

After the battle of Hunain, Messenger of Allah (ﷺ) favoured some people in the distribution of spoils (for consolation). He gave Al-Aqra' bin Habis and 'Uyainah bin Hisn a hundred camels each and showed favour also to some more honourable persons among the Arabs. Someone said: "This division is not based on justice and it was not intended to win the Pleasure of Allah." I said to myself: "By Allah! I will inform Messenger of Allah (ﷺ) of this." I went to him and informed him. His face became red and he said, "Who will do justice if Allah and His Messenger do not?" Then he said, "May Allah have mercy on (Prophet) Musa (Moses); he was caused more distress than this but he remained patient." Having heard this I said to myself: "I shall never convey anything of this kind to him in future".

Source: Al-Bukhari and Muslim

Anas reported:

One of the sons of Abu Talhah was ailing. Abu Talhah went out and the boy died in his absence. When he came back, he inquired, "How is the boy?". Umm Sulaim, the mother of the boy, replied, "Better than before". Then she placed his evening meal before him and he ate it; and thereafter slept with her. At last, she said to him: "Arrange for the burial of the boy". In the morning, Abu Talhah went to Messenger of Allah (ﷺ) and informed him of the event. He enquired, "Did you sleep together last night?" Abu Talhah replied in the affirmative, on which the Prophet (ﷺ) supplicated, "O Allah bless them." Thereafter, she gave birth to a boy. Abu Talhah said to me: "Take up the boy and carry him to the Prophet (ﷺ)"; and he sent some dates with him. The Prophet (ﷺ) enquired, "Is there anything with him?" He said; "Yes, some dates". The Prophet

(⌘) took a date, chewed it and put it in the mouth of the baby and rubbed the chewed date around the baby's gum and named him 'Abdullah.

Source: Al-Bukhari and Muslim

Though there was no sin in this report the fact is the couple was blessed by the Prophet as a result of the concern Abu Talhah had over potentially sinning and thereby self-snitching regarding the marital intimacy the night his son died.

Abu Hurairah said:

He heard the Prophet (⌘) said: "There were three men among the Banu Israel, one leper, one bald and one blind. Allah wanted to test them. He therefore, sent to them an angel who came to the leper and asked him what he would like best. He replied: "A good color, a good skin and to be rid of what makes me loathsome to people". He (the angel) rubbed him and his loathsomeness vanished and he was given a good colour and a good skin. He then asked him what type of property he would like best. The leper replied that he would like camels - [or perhaps he said cattle, for Ishaq (one of the subnarrator of the Hadith) was uncertain, either said: 'Camels,' or: 'Cattle']. He was given a pregnant she-camel. The angel invoked for Allah's Blessing on it. The angel then went to the bald man and asked him what he would like best and he replied: "Good hair and to be rid of what makes me loathsome to people". The angel ran his hand over him and he was given good hair. He then asked him what property he would like best. He replied that he would like cattle, so he was given a pregnant cow. The angel invoked

Allah's Blessing on it. The angel then went to the blind man and asked him what he would like best, and he replied: "I wish that Allah restore my sight to me so that I may see people." Thereupon the angel ran his hand over him and Allah restored his sight. The angel then asked what property he would like best. He replied that he would like sheep, so he was given a pregnant ewe. Flocks and herds were produced for the three men, the first having a valley full of camels, the second one, a valley full of cows and the third one full of sheep. Then the angel came in the form of a leper, to the one who had been a leper, and said: "I am a poor man and my resources have been exhausted in my journey, and my only means of reaching my destination are dependent on Allah and then on you, so I ask you by Him Who gave you the good color, the good skin and the property, for a camel by which I may get to my destination". He replied: "I have many dues to pay." The angel then said: "I think I recognize you. Were you not a leper whom people found loathsome and a poor man to whom Allah gave property?" He replied: "I inherited this property through generations". The angel said: "If you are telling a lie, may Allah return you to your former condition". The angel went in the form of a bald man to the one who had been bald, and said the same as he had said to the former and received a similar reply. So he said: "If you are telling a lie, may Allah return you to your former condition". The angel then went to the one who had been blind and said: "I am a poor traveller and my resources have been exhausted in my journey. My only means of reaching my destination are dependent on Allah and then on you, so I ask you by Him Who restored your eyesight for a sheep by which I may get to the end of my journey". He replied: "Yes, I was blind. Allah restored my eyesight, so take what you wish and leave what you wish. I swear by Allah that I shall not argue with you today to return anything you take, as I give it for Allah's sake". The angel said: "Keep your property. You have all simply been put to a test, and Allah is pleased with you and displeased with both of your companions".

Source: Al-Bukhari and Muslim

This report also doesn't involve a typical sin but shows us blessings result from telling the truth even if it is seemingly against oneself and that lying or giving false testimony removes blessings and causes Allah's anger.

Jabir reported:

I went in an expedition along with the Prophet (ﷺ) in the direction of Najd. When Messenger of Allah (ﷺ) returned, I also returned with him. Then the mid-day sleep overtook us in a valley full of prickly shrubs. Messenger of Allah (ﷺ) got down and the people scattered around seeking shade under the trees. Messenger of Allah (ﷺ) hang up his sword on the branch of a tree. We were enjoying a sleep when Messenger of Allah (ﷺ) called us, and lo! There was a desert Arab bedouin near him. He (ﷺ) said, "This man brandished my sword over me while I was asleep. I woke up and saw it in his hand unsheathed. He asked: `Who will protect you from me?' I replied: 'Allah' - thrice". He did not punish him and sat down.

Source: Al-Bukhari and Muslim

Anas reported:

Three men came to the houses of the wives of the Prophet (ﷺ) to inquire about the worship of the Prophet (ﷺ). When they were informed, they considered their worship insignificant and said: "Where are we in comparison with the Prophet (ﷺ) while Allah has forgiven his past sins and future sins". One of them said: "As for me, I shall offer Salat all night long." Another said: "I shall observe Saum (fasting) continuously and shall not break it". Another said: "I shall abstain from women and shall never marry". The Prophet (ﷺ) came to them and said, "Are you the people who said such and such things? By Allah, I fear Allah more than you do, and I am most obedient and dutiful among you to Him, but still I observe fast and break it; perform Salat and sleep at night and take wives. So whoever turns away from my Sunnah does not belong to me".

Source: Al-Bukhari and Muslim

By the wives of the Prophet snitching on these sincere innovators we came to learn what the Sunnah is in contradiction to sinful but sincere innovation.

Abu Juhaifah reported:

The Prophet (ﷺ) made a bond of brotherhood between Salman and Abud-Darda'. Salman paid a visit to Abud-Darda' and found Umm Darda' (his wife) dressed in shabby clothes and asked her why she was in that state. She replied: "Your brother Abud-Darda' is not interested in (the luxuries of) this world. In the meantime Abud-Darda' came in and prepared a meal for Salman. Salman requested Abud-Darda' to eat (with him) but Abud-Darda' said: "I am fasting." Salman said: "I am not going to eat unless you eat." So, Abud-Darda' ate (with Salman). When it was night and (a part of the night passed),

Abud-Darda' got up (to offer the night prayer) but Salman asked him to sleep and Abud-Darda' slept. After some time Abud-Darda' again got up but Salman asked him to sleep. When it was the last hours of the night, Salman asked him to get up and both of them offered (Tahajjud) prayer. Then Salman told Abud-Darda': "You owe a duty to your Lord, you owe a duty to your body; you owe a duty to your family; so you should give to every one his due. Abud-Darda' came to the Prophet (ﷺ) and reported the whole story. Prophet (ﷺ) said, "Salman is right".

Source: Riyad As-Salihin 149 Grade: Sahih

Abdullah bin 'Amr bin Al-'as reported:

The Prophet (ﷺ) was informed that I said that I would perform prayers the whole night and observe fasting every day as long as I live. Messenger of Allah (ﷺ) said, "Is it you who said this?" I said to him, "O Messenger of Allah! I ransom you with my parents, it is I who said that." Messenger of Allah (ﷺ) said, "You will not be able to do that. Observe fast and break it; sleep and get up for prayer, and observe fast for three days during the month; for every good is multiplied ten times and that will be equal to fasting the whole year." I said, "O Messenger of Allah! I can do more than that." He said, "Observe fast one day and leave off the next two days." I said, "O Messenger of Allah! I have strength to do more than that." Messenger of Allah (ﷺ) said, "Observe fast every other day, and that is the fasting of Dawud (ﷺ) and that is the most moderate fasting".

According to another narration: Messenger of Allah (ﷺ) said, "That is the best fasting." I said, "But I am capable of doing more than this". Thereupon, Messenger of Allah (ﷺ) said, "There is nothing better than this." 'Abdullah bin 'Amr (May Allah be pleased with them) said (when he grew old): "Had I accepted the three days (fasting during every month) as the Messenger of Allah had said, it would have been dearer to me than my family and my property".

In another narration 'Abdullah is reported to have said: Messenger of Allah (ﷺ) said to me, "O 'Abdullah! Have I not been informed that you observe fast during the day and offer prayer all the night." I replied, "Yes, O Messenger of Allah!" Messenger of Allah (ﷺ) said, "Don't do that. Observe fast for few days and then leave off for few days, perform prayers and also sleep at night, as your body has a right upon you, and your eyes have a right upon you; and your wife has a right upon you; your visitors have a right upon you. It is sufficient for you to observe fast three days in a month, as the reward of good deeds is multiplied ten times, so it will be like fasting the whole year." I insisted (on fasting) and so I was given a hard instruction. I said, "O Messenger of Allah! I have strength." Messenger of Allah (ﷺ) said, "Observe fast like the fasting of Prophet Dawud (ﷺ); and do not fast more than that." I said: "How was the fasting of Prophet Dawud?" He (ﷺ) said, "Half of the year (i.e., he used to fast on every alternate day)."

Afterwards when 'Abdullah grew old, he used to say: "Would that I had availed myself of the concession granted to me by Messenger of Allah."

Source: Riyad As-Salihin 150

Hanzalah Al-Usayyidi who was one of the scribes of Messenger of Allah (ﷺ), reported:

I met Abu Bakr he said: "How are you O Hanzalah?" I said, "Hanzalah has become a hypocrite". He said, "Far removed is Allah from every imperfection, what are you saying?" I said, "When we are in the company of Messenger of Allah (ﷺ) and he reminds us of Hell-fire and Jannah, we feel as if we are seeing them with our very eyes, and when we are away from Messenger of Allah (ﷺ), we attend to our wives, our children, our business, most of these things (pertaining to life hereafter) slip out of our minds." Abu Bakr said, "By Allah, I also experience the same thing". So Abu Bakr (May Allah be pleased with him) and I went to Messenger of Allah (ﷺ) and I said to him, "O Messenger of Allah (ﷺ), Hanzalah has turned hypocrite." Thereupon Messenger of Allah (ﷺ) said, "What has happened to you?" I said, "O Messenger of Allah, when we are in your company, and are reminded of Hell-fire and Jannah, we feel as if we are seeing them with our own eyes, but when we go away from you and attend to our wives, children and business, much of these things go out of our minds." Thereupon Messenger of Allah (ﷺ) said, "By Him in Whose Hand is my life if your state of mind remains the same as it is in my presence and you are always busy in remembrance (of Allah), the angels will shake hands with you in your beds and in your roads; but Hanzalah, time should be devoted (to the worldly affairs) and time should be devoted (to prayer)". He (the Prophet (ﷺ)) said this thrice.

Source: Riyad As-Salihin 151 Grade: Sahih

Ibn 'Abbas reported:

While the Prophet (ﷺ) was delivering Khutbah (religious talk), he noticed a man who was standing, so he asked about him and was told that he was Abu Israel who had taken a vow to remain standing and not sit, or go into the shade, or speak while observing fasting. Thereupon Messenger of Allah (ﷺ) said, "Tell him to speak, to go into the shade, to sit and to complete his fast".

Source: Riyad As-Salihin 152 Grade: Sahih

Abu Sa'id Al-Khudri reported:

Messenger of Allah (ﷺ) said, "Whoever amongst you sees an evil, he must change it with his hand; if he is unable to do so, then with his tongue; and if he is unable to do so, then with his heart; and that is the weakest form of Faith".

Source: Riyad As-Salihin 184 Grade: Sahih

Abdullah bin Mas'ud reported:

Messenger of Allah (ﷺ) said, "Never a Prophet had been sent before me by Allah to his people but he had, among his people, (his) disciples and companions, who followed his ways and obeyed his command. Then there came after them their successors who proclaimed what they did not practice, and practiced what they were not commanded to do. And (he) who strove against them with his hand is a believer; he who strove against them with his heart is a believer; and he who strove against them with his tongue is a believer; and beyond that there is no grain of Faith".

Source: Riyad As-Salihin 185 Grade: Sahih

Ubadah bin As-Samit reported:

We swore allegiance to Messenger of Allah (ﷺ) to hear and obey; in time of difficulty and in prosperity, in hardship and in ease, to endure being discriminated against and not to dispute about rule with those in power, except in case of evident infidelity regarding which there is a proof from Allah. We swore allegiance to Messenger of Allah (ﷺ) to say what was right wherever we were, and not to fear from anyone's reproach.

Source: Al-Bukhari and Muslim

Nu'man bin Bashir reported:

The Prophet (ﷺ) said, "The likeness of the man who observes the limits prescribed by Allah and that of the man who transgresses them is like the people who get on board a ship after casting lots. Some of them are in its lower deck and some of them in its upper (deck). Those who are in its lower (deck), when they require water, go to the occupants of the upper deck, and say to them : 'If we make a hole in the bottom of the ship, we shall not harm you.' If they (the occupants of the upper deck) leave them to carry out their design they all will be drowned. But if they do not let them go ahead (with their plan), all of them will remain safe".

Source: Riyad As-Salihin 187 Grade: Sahih

Hudhaifah reported:

The Prophet (ﷺ) said, "By Him in Whose Hand my life is, you either enjoin good and forbid evil, or Allah will certainly soon send His punishment to you. Then you will make supplication and it will not be accepted".

Source: Riyad As-Salihin 193 Grade: Hasan

Abu Sa'id Al-Khudri reported:

The Prophet (ﷺ) said, "Beware of sitting on roads (ways)." The people said: "We have but them as sitting places." Messenger of Allah (ﷺ) said, "If you have to sit there, then observe the rights of the way". They asked, "What are the rights of the way?" He (ﷺ) said, "To lower your gaze (on seeing what is illegal to look at), and removal of harmful objects, returning greetings, enjoining good and forbidding wrong".

Source: Al-Bukhari and Muslim

The previous report proves what true "Street Smarts" are and what the real prophetic "Code of the Road" is to be.

Abu Sa'id Al-Khudri reported:

The Prophet (ﷺ) said, "The best type of Jihad (striving in the way of Allah) is speaking a true word <u>in the presence of</u> a tyrant ruler."

Source: Riyad As-Salihin 194 Grade: Hasan

Many think this report is limited to telling a tyrant ruler to reform to their face, but it covers much more than that. For snitching on the tyrant's supporters who have wronged you although it is likely not going to result in justice also falls under this category, especially knowing that tyrants often act unjustly towards those who report their subordinates' sins to them.

Abdullah bin Mas'ud reported:

Messenger of Allah (ﷺ) said, "The first defect (in religion) which affected the Children of Israel in the way that man would meet another and say to him: 'Fear Allah and abstain from what you are doing, for this is not lawful for you.' Then he would meet him the next day and find no change in him, but this would not prevent him from eating with him, drinking with him and sitting in his assemblies. When it came to this, Allah led their hearts into evil ways on account of their association with others." Then he (ﷺ) recited, "Those among the Children of Israel who disbelieved were cursed by the tongue of Dawud (David) and 'Isa (Jesus), son of Maryam (Mary). That was because they disobeyed (Allah and the Messengers) and were ever transgressing beyond bounds. They used not to forbid one another from the Munkar (wrong, evildoing, sins, polytheism, disbelief) which they committed. Vile indeed was what they used to do. You see many of them taking the disbelievers as their Auliya' (protectors and helpers). Evil indeed is that which their own selves have sent forward before them; for that (reason) Allah's wrath fell upon them and in torment will they abide. And had they believed in Allah and in the Prophet (Muhammad (ﷺ)) and in what has been revealed to him, never would they have taken them (the disbelievers) as Auliya' (protectors and helpers); but many of them are the Fasiqun (rebellious, disobedient to Allah)." (5:78-81)

Then he (ﷺ) continued: "Nay, by Allah, you either enjoin good and forbid evil and catch hold of the hand of the oppressor and persuade him to act justly and stick to the truth, or, Allah will involve the hearts of some of you with the hearts of others and will curse you as He had cursed them".

Source: Riyad As-Salihin 196 Grade: Hasan

Abu Bakr As-Siddiq reported:

"O you people! You recite this Verse: 'O you who believe! Take care of your own selves. If you follow the (right) guidance [and enjoin what is right (Islamic Monotheism and all that Islam orders one to do) and forbid what is wrong (polytheism, disbelief and all that Islam has forbidden)] no hurt can come to you from those who are in error.' (5:105) But I have heard Messenger of Allah (ﷺ) saying: "When people see an oppressor but do not prevent him from (doing evil), it is likely that Allah will punish them all."

Source: Riyad As-Salihin 197 Grade: Sahih

Umar bin Al-Khattab reported:

On the day (of the battle) of Khaibar, some Companions of the Prophet (ﷺ) came and remarked: "So-and-so is a martyr and so-and-so is a martyr". When they came to a man about whom they said: "So-and-so is a martyr," the Prophet (ﷺ) declared, "No. I have seen him in Hell for a mantle (or cloak) which he has stolen".

Source: Riyad As-Salihin 216 Grade: Sahih

Ibn 'Umar reported:

I heard Messenger of Allah (ﷺ) saying, "A believer will be brought close to his Lord on the Day of Resurrection and enveloping him in His Mercy, He will make him confess his sins by saying: 'Do you remember (doing) this sin and this sin?' He will reply: 'My Lord, I remember.' Then He will say: 'I covered it up for you in the life of world, and I forgive it for you today.' Then the record of his good deeds will be handed to him".

Source: Al-Bukhari and Muslim

Abdullah bin Mas'ud reported:

A man kissed a woman and he came to the Prophet (ﷺ) and made a mention of that to him. It was (on this occasion) that this Ayah was revealed:

"And perform As-Salat (Iqamat-As-Salat), at the two ends of the day and in some hours of the night [i.e., the five compulsory Salat (prayers)]. Verily, the good deeds remove the evil deeds (i.e., small sins)". (11:114)

That person said, "O Messenger of Allah (ﷺ), does it concern me only?". He (Messenger of Allah (ﷺ)) said, "It concerns the whole of my Ummah".

Source: Al-Bukhari and Muslim

Anas bin Malik reported:

A man came to the Prophet (ﷺ) and said, "O Messenger of Allah, I have committed a sin liable of ordained punishment. So execute punishment on me". Messenger of Allah (ﷺ) did not ask him about it, and then came the (time for) Salat (prayers). So he performed Salat with Messenger of Allah (ﷺ). When Messenger of Allah (ﷺ) finished Salat, the man stood up and said: "O Messenger of Allah! I have committed a sin. So execute the Ordinance of Allah upon me". He (ﷺ) asked, "Have you performed Salat with us?" "Yes", he replied. Messenger of Allah (ﷺ) said, "Verily, Allah has forgiven you".

Source: Al-Bukhari and Muslim

Uqbah bin Al-Harith reported that he had married a daughter of Abu Ihab bin 'Aziz and a woman came to him and said she had suckled both 'Uqbah and the woman whom he had married, to which he replied:

"I am not aware that you suckled me, and you did not inform me." So he ('Uqbah) rode to Messenger of Allah (ﷺ) in Al-Madinah and put the matter before him. The Messenger of Allah (ﷺ) said, "How can you continue (to be her husband) after what you have been told?" 'Uqbah (May Allah be pleased with him) therefore divorced her and she married another man.

Source: Riyad As-Salihin 591 Grade: Sahih

Aishah reported:

Abu Bakr had a slave who brought him his earnings and Abu Bakr would eat from it. One day he brought him something and when Abu Bakr had eaten some of it, the slave asked him whether he knew where he had got that (food) from, Abu Bakr asked what it was, and he replied: I acted as a soothsayer for a man in the pre-Islamic period, and not being good at it, I deceived him; today he met me and he rewarded me for that soothsaying what you have eaten. Abu Bakr put his hand in his mouth and vomited up all that he had eaten.

Source: Riyad As-Salihin 593 Grade: Sahih

Abu Mas'ud 'Uqbah bin 'Amr Al- reported:

A man came to the Prophet (ﷺ) and said: "I join the morning Salat late because of so-and-so who leads it and prolongs it." (Abu Mas'ud said): I have never seen the Prophet (ﷺ) so angry while giving a speech as he was on that day. He (ﷺ) said,

"Some of you create hatred among the people against faith. Whoever leads Salat (the prayer), should make it brief because the congregation includes old men and youngsters and those who have some urgent work to do."

Source: Al-Bukhari and Muslim

Mu'awiyah bin Al-Hakam As-Sulami reported:

While I was in Salat with Messenger of Allah (☷), a man in the congregation sneezed and I responded with: 'Yarhamuk-Allah (Allah have mercy on you).' The people stared at me with disapproving looks. So I said: "May my mother lose me. Why are you staring at me?" Thereupon, they began to strike their thighs with their hands. When I saw them urging to me to remain silent, I became angry but restrained myself. When Messenger of Allah (☷) concluded his Salat. I have never before seen an instructor who gave better instruction than he, may my father and mother be sacrificed for him. He neither remonstrated me, nor beat me, nor abused me. He simply said,"It is not permissible to talk during Salat because it consists of glorifying Allah, declaring His Greatness as well as recitation of the Qur'an," or he said words to that effect." I said: "O Allah's Messenger, I have but recently accepted Islam, and Allah has favored us with Islam. There are still some people among us who go to consult soothsayers." He said, "Do not consult them." Then I said: "There are some of us who are guided by omens." He said, "These things which come to their minds. They should not be influenced by them."

Source: Riyad As-Salihin 700 Grade: Sahih

Imran bin Husain reported:

A woman belonging to the Juhainah tribe came to the Messenger of Allah (ﷺ) after having conceived from adultery. She submitted: "O Messenger of Allah! I am liable to Hadd (punishment ordained by Allah), so execute it." The Messenger of Allah (ﷺ) called her guardian and said, "Treat her well and bring her to me after delivery." He acted accordingly. Then the Messenger of Allah (ﷺ) commanded to tie her clothes firmly around her and then stoned her to death. He (ﷺ) then offered funeral prayer for her.

Source: Riyad As-Salihin 913 Grade: Sahih

Anas reported:

Some Companions happened to pass by a funeral procession (bier) and they praised him (the deceased). The Prophet (ﷺ) said, "He will certainly enter it." Then they passed by another funeral procession and they spoke ill of the deceased. The Prophet (ﷺ) said, "He will certainly enter it." `Umar bin Al-Khattab (May Allah be pleased with him) said: "(O Messenger of Allah,) what do you mean by `He will certainly enter it?" He (ﷺ) replied, "You praised the first person, so he will enter Jannah; and you spoke ill of the second person, so he will enter Hell. You are Allah's witnesses on earth."

Source: Al-Bukhari and Muslim

Abul-Aswad reported:

I came to Al- Madinah, and while I was sitting beside 'Umar bin Al-Khattab, a funeral procession passed by. The people praised the deceased, and 'Umar bin Al-Khattab said: "He will certainly enter it." Then another funeral procession passed by and the people praised the deceased. 'Umar bin Al-Khattab said:

"He will certainly enter it." A third funeral procession passed by and the people spoke ill of the deceased. He said: "He will certainly enter it." I (Abul-Aswad) asked: "O Amir Al-Mu'minin (i.e., Leader of the Believers)! What do you mean by 'He will certainly enter it'?" He replied: "I said the same as was said by the Prophet (ﷺ). He (ﷺ) said, 'If four persons testify the righteousness of a Muslim, Allah will grant him Jannah.' We asked: 'If three persons testify his righteousness?' He (ﷺ) replied, 'Even three'. Then we asked: 'If two?' He (ﷺ) replied, 'Even two.' We did not ask him (regarding the testimony) of one."

Source: Riyad As-Salihin 951 Grade: Sahih

Abd Allaah bin Jafar said:

"The Apostle of Allaah(ﷺ) seated me behind him(on his ride) one day, and told me secretly a thing asking me not to tell it to anyone. The place for easing dearer to the Apostle of Allaah(ﷺ) was a mound or host of palm trees by which he could conceal himself. He entered the garden of a man from the Ansar(Helpers). All of a sudden when a Camel saw the Prophet (ﷺ) it wept tenderly producing yearning sound and it eyes flowed. The Prophet (ﷺ) came to it and wiped the temple of its head. So it kept silence. He then said "Who is the master of this Camel? Whose Camel is this? A young man from the Ansar came and said "This is mine, Apostle of Allaah(ﷺ)." He said "Don't you fear Allaah about this beast which Allaah has given in your possession. It has complained to me that you keep it hungry and load it heavily which fatigues it."

Source: Sunan Abi Dawud 2549 Grade: Sahih

Abu Hurairah reported:

The Messenger of Allah (ﷺ) put me in charge of charity of Ramadan (Sadaqat-ul- Fitr). Somebody came to me and began to take away some food-stuff. I caught him and said, "I must take you to the Messenger of Allah (ﷺ)." He said, "I am a needy man with a large family, and so I have a pressing need." I let him go. When I saw the Messenger of Allah (ﷺ) next morning, he asked me, "O Abu Hurairah! What did your captive do last night?" I said, "O Messenger of Allah! He complained of a pressing need and a big family. I felt pity for him so I let him go." He (ﷺ) said, "He told you a lie and he will return." I was sure, according to the saying of the Messenger of Allah (ﷺ) that he would return. I waited for him. He sneaked up again and began to steal food-stuff from the Sadaqah. I caught him and said; "I must take you to the Messenger of Allah (ﷺ)." He said, "Let go of me, I am a needy man. I have to bear the expenses of a big family. I will not come back." So I took pity on him and let him go. I went at dawn to the Messenger of Allah (ﷺ) who asked me, "O Abu Hurairah! What did your captive do last night?" I replied, "O Messenger of Allah! He complained of a pressing want and the burden of a big family. I took pity on him and so I let him go." He (ﷺ) said, "He told you a lie and he will return." (That man) came again to steal the food-stuff. I arrested him and said, "I must take you to the Messenger of Allah (ﷺ), and this is the last of three times. You promised that you would not come again but you did." He said, "Let go of me, I shall teach you some words with which Allah may benefit you." I asked, "What are those words?" He replied, "When you go to bed, recite Ayat-ul- Kursi (2:255) for there will be a guardian appointed over you from Allah, and Satan will not be able to approach you till morning." So I let him go. Next morning the Messenger of Allah (ﷺ) asked me, "What did your prisoner do last night." I answered, "He promised to teach me some words which he claimed will benefit me before Allah. So I let him go." The Messenger of Allah (ﷺ) asked, "What are those words that he taught you?" I said, "He told me: 'When you go to bed, recite Ayat- ul-Kursi from the beginning to the end i.e., [Allah! None has the right to be worshipped but He, the Ever Living, the One Who sustains and protects all that exists. Neither slumber nor sleep overtakes Him. To Him belongs whatever is in the heavens and whatever is on the earth. Who is he that can intercede with Him except with His Permission? He knows what happens to them (His creatures) in this world, and what will happen to them in the Hereafter. And they will never compass anything of His Knowledge except that which He wills. His Kursi encompasses the heavens and the earth, and preserving them does not fatigue Him. And He is the Most High, the Most Great].' (2:255). He added: 'By reciting it, there will be a guardian appointed over you from Allah who will protect you during the night, and Satan will not be able to come near you until morning'." The Messenger of Allah (ﷺ) said, "Verily, he has told you the truth though he is a liar. O Abu Huruirah! Do you know with whom you were speaking for the last three nights?" I said, "No." He (ﷺ) said, "He was Shaitan (Satan)."

Source: Riyad As Salihin 1020 Grade: Sahih

Zaid bin Arqam said:

"We were participating in a battle along with the Messenger of Allah, and there were some people from the Bedouins with us.

So we all rushed toward some water and the Bedouins raced us to it. One of the Bedouins beat his companions to it and he (tried to obstruct) the pond, he placed rocks around it and he put a leather sheet over it until his companions came." He said: "A man among the Ansar reached the Bedouin and he dropped the reigns of his camel to drink, but the Bedouin would not allow him. So he started removing the barriers around the water, but the Bedouin raised a stick beating the Ansari man on the head, and smashed it. He went to Abdullah bin Ubayy, the head of the hypocrite, to inform him – he was in fact one of his companions. So Abdullah bin Ubayy became enraged, the he said: 'Do not spend anything on whoever is with Muhammad until they depart.' Meaning the Bedouins. They were preparing food for the Messenger of Allah. So Abdullah said: 'When they depart from Muhammad, then bring Muhammad some food, and let him and whoever is with him eat it.' Then he said to his companions: 'If we return to Al-Madinah, indeed the more honorable will expel therefrom the meaner.'" Zaid said: "And I was riding behind the Messenger of Allah, and I had heard Abdullah bin Ubayy, so I informed my uncle who went to tell the Messenger of Allah. He sent a message to him (Abdullah) but he took an oath and denied it." He said: "So the Messenger of Allah accepted what he said and did not believe me. So my uncle came to me and said: 'You only wanted the Messenger of Allah to hate you, and the Muslims to say that you lied.'" He said: "I suffered such worry as has not been suffered by anyone else." He said: "(Later) while I was on the move with the Messenger of Allah on a journey, my mind was relieved of worry, since the Messenger of Allah came to me and rubbed my ear and smiled in my face. I would never be happier than with that as long as the world remained. Then Abu Bakr caught up to me, and said: 'What did the Messenger of Allah say to you?' I said: 'He did not say anything to me, he only rubbed my ear and smiled in my face.' He said: 'Receive the good news!' Then Umar caught up with me and I said the same to him as I had said to Abu Bakr. In the morning the Messenger of Allah recited Surat Al-Munafiqin."

Source: Jami Tirmidhi 3313 Grade: Sahih

It has been narrated that Hisham bin Hakim bin Hizam happened to pass by some (non-Arab) farmers of Syria who had been made to stand in the sun, and olive oil was poured on their heads. He said:

"What is the matter?" He was told that they had been detained for the non-payment of Jizyah. (Another narration says that they were being tortured for not having paid Al-Kharaj). Thereupon Hisham said: "I bear testimony to the fact that I heard the Messenger of Allah (ﷺ) saying, 'Allah will torment those who torment people in the world."' Then he proceeded towards their Amir and reported this Hadith to him. The Amir then issued orders for their release.

Source: Riyad As-Salihin 1606 Grade: Sahih

Humaid bin Abdur-Rahman said:

I saw Mu'awiyah during the Hajj (pilgrimage) standing on the pulpit. He took from the guard a bunch of hair, and said: "O people of Al-Madinah! Where are your scholars? (Why do they do not prohibit you) I heard the Prophet (ﷺ) prohibiting from using this (false hair) and saying, 'The people of Bani Israel were ruined when their women wore such hair."'

Source: Al-Bukhari and Muslim

Narrated Abu Huraira.:

Once Allah's Messenger (ﷺ) offered two rak`at and finished his prayer. So Dhul-Yadain asked him, "Has the prayer been reduced or have you forgotten?" Allah's Messenger (ﷺ) said, "Has Dhul-Yadain spoken the truth?" The people replied in the affirmative. Then Allah's Messenger (ﷺ) stood up and offered the remaining two rak`at and performed Taslim, and then said Takbir and performed two prostrations like his usual prostrations, or a bit longer, and then got up.

Source: Sahih al-Bukhari 1228

Yahya related to me from Malik from Zayd ibn Aslam from Ata ibn Yasar that:

A certain man kissed his wife while he was fasting in Ramadan. This made him very anxious, and so he sent his wife to the Prophet, may Allah bless him and grant him peace, to ask him about that for him. She went in and saw Umm Salama, the wife of the Prophet, may Allah bless him and grant him peace, and mentioned the matter to her, and Umm Salama told her that the Messenger of Allah, may Allah bless him and grant him peace, used to kiss while he was fasting. So she went back and told her husband that, but it only made him find fault all the more and he said, "We are not like the Messenger of Allah, may Allah bless him and grant him peace. Allah makes permissible for the Messenger of Allah, may Allah bless him and grant him peace, whatever He wishes."

His wife then went back to Umm Sal"ma a'd found the Messenger of Allah, may Allah bless him and grant him peace, with her. The Messenger of Allah, may Allah bless him and grant him peace, said, "What's the matter with this woman?", and Umm Salama told him. The Messenger of Allah, may Allah bless him and grant him peace, said, "Didn't you tell her that I do that myself?" and she said, "I told her, and she went to her husband and told him, but it only made him find fault all the more and say, 'We are not like the Messenger of Allah, may Allah bless him and grant him peace. Allah makes permissible for His Messenger, may Allah bless him and grant him peace, whatever He wishes.' " The Messenger of Allah, may Allah bless him and grant him peace, got angry and said, "By Allah, I am the one with the most taqwa of Allah of you all, and of you all the one who best knows His limits."

Source: Muwatta Imam Malik

Yahya related to me from Malik from Ata ibn Abdullah al-Khurasani that Said ibn al-Musayyab said:

"A Bedouin came to the Messenger of Allah beating his breast and tearing out his hair and saying, 'I am destroyed.' The Messenger of Allah said, 'Why is that?', and he said, 'I had intercourse with my wife while fasting in Ramadan.' The Messenger of Allah asked him, 'Are you able to free a slave?', and the man said, 'No.' Then he asked him, 'Are you able to give away a camel?', and the man replied, 'No.' He said, 'Sit down,' and someone brought a large basket of dates to the Messenger of Allah and he said to the man, 'Take this and give it away as sadaqa.' The man said, 'There is no one more needy than me,' and (the Messenger of Allah), said, 'Eat them, and fast one day for the day when you had intercourse.' "

Malik said that Ata said that he had asked Said ibn al-Musayyab how many dates there were in that basket, and he said, "Between fifteen and twenty sas."

Source: Muwatta Imam Malik

Yahya related to me from Malik, from Yahya ibn Said, from Muhammad ibn Ibrahim ibn al-Harith at-Taymi, *that Rabia ibn Abdullah ibn al-Hudayr once saw a man in a state of ihram in Iraq. So he asked people about him and they said, "He has given directions for his sacrificial animal to be garlanded, and it is for that reason that he has put on ihram ."*

Rabia said, "I then met Abdullah ibn az- Zubayr and so I mentioned this to him and he said, 'By the Lord of the Kaba, an innovation.' "

Source: Muwatta Imam Malik

Yahya related to me from Malik from Abd al-Malik ibn Qurayr from Muhammad ibn Sirin that a man came to Umar ibn al-Khattab and said:

"I was racing a friend on horseback towards a narrow mountain trail and we killed a gazelle accidently and we were in ihram. What is your opinion?" Umar said to a man by his side, "Come, so that you and I may make an assessment." They decided on a female goat for him, and the man turned away saying, "This amir al-muminin cannot even make an assessment in the case of a gazelle until he calls a man to decide with him." Umar overheard the man's words and called him and asked him, "Do you recite surat al-Ma'ida?" and he said, "No." He said, "Then do you recognize this man who has taken the decision with me?" and he said, "No." He said, "If you had

told me that you did recite surat al-Ma'ida, I would have dealt you a blow." Then he said, "Allah the Blessed, the Exalted says in His Book, 'as shall be judged by two men of justice among you, a sacrificial animal to reach the Kaba' (Sura 5 ayat 95), and this is Abd ar-Rahman ibn Awf."

Source: Muwatta Imam Malik

Narrated Ibn 'Abbas:

While the Prophet (ﷺ) was preaching a man was standing in the sun. He asked about him. They said: He is Abu Isra'il who has taken a vow to stand and not to sit, or go into shade, or speak, but to fast. Thereupon he said: Command him to speak, to go into the shade, sit and complete his fast.

Source: Sunan Abi Dawud 3300 Grade: Sahih

Malik related to me from Hilal ibn Usama from Ata ibn Yasar that Umar ibn al-Hakam said:

"I went to the Messenger of Allah, may Allah bless him and grant him peace, and said, 'Messenger of Allah, a slave girl of mine was tending my sheep. I came to her and one of the sheep was lost. I asked her about it and she said that a wolf had eaten it, so I became angry and I am one of the children of Adam, so I struck her on the face. As it happens, I have to set a slave free, shall I free her?' The Messenger of Allah, may Allah bless him and grant him peace, questioned her, 'Where is Allah?' She said, 'In heaven.' He said, 'Who am I?' She said, 'You are the Messenger of Allah.' The Messenger of Allah said, 'Free her.' "

Source: Muwatta Imam Malik

Yahya related to me from Malik that he had heard that receipts were given to people in the time of Marwan ibn al-Hakam for the produce of the market at al-Jar. People bought and sold the receipts among themselves before they took delivery of the goods. Zayd Thabit and one of the Companions of the Messenger of Allah, went to Marwan ibn al-Hakam and said:

"Marwan! Do you make usury halal?" He said, "I seek refuge with Allah! What is that?" He said, "These receipts which people buy and sell before they take delivery of the goods." Marwan therefore sent a guard to follow them and to take them from people's hands and return them to their owners.

Source: Muwatta Imam Malik

Zaid bin Khalid Al-Juhani narrated that the Messenger of Allah said:

"The best of witnesses is the one who gives his testimony before being asked for it."

Source: Jami` at-Tirmidhi 2297 Grade: Sahih

It was narrated from Abu Laila bin 'Abdullah bin 'Abdur-Rahman bin Sahl, from Sahl bin Abi Hathmah, that:

he informed him, and some men among the elders of his people, that "Abdullah bin Sahl and Muhayysah set out for Khaibar because of some problem that had arisen. Someone came to Muhayysah, and he told him that 'Abdullah bin Sahl had been killed and thrown into a pit or well. He came to the Jews and said: "By Allah, you killed him." They said: "By Allah, we did not kill him." *Then he went back to his people and told them about that. Then he and his brother Huwayysah, who was older than him, and 'Abdur-Rahman bin Sahl, came (to the prophet). Muhayysah, who was the one who had been at Khaibar, bnegan to speak, but the Messenger of Allah said: "Let the elder speak first." So Huwayysah spoke, then Muhayysah spoke. The Messenger of Allah said: "Either (the Jews) will pay the Diyah for your companion, or war will be declared on them." The Messenger of Allah sent a letter to that effect (to the Jews) and they wrote back saying: "By Allah, we did not kill him." The Messenger of Allah and 'Abdur-Rahman: "Will you swear an oath establishing your claim to the blood money of your companion?" They said: "No." He said: "Should the Jews swear an oath for you?" They said: "They are not Muslims." So the Messenger of Allah paid it himself, and he sent one hundred she-camels to their abodes. Sahl said: "A red she-camel from among them kicked me."*

Source: Sunan an-Nasa'I 4711 Grade: Sahih

Malik related from Nafi that Abdullah ibn Umar said:

"The Jews came to the Messenger of Allah and mentioned to him that a man and woman from among them had committed adultery. The Messenger of Allah 'What do you find in the Torah about stoning?' They said, 'We make their wrong action known and flog them.' Abdullah ibn Salam said, 'You have lied! It has stoning for it, so bring the Torah.' They spread it out and one of them placed his hand over the ayat of stoning. Then he read what was before it and what was after it. Abdullah ibn Salam told him to lift his hand. He lifted his hand and there was the ayat of stoning. They said, 'He has spoken the truth,

Muhammad. The ayat of stoning is in it.' So the Messenger of Allah gave the order and they were stoned . "

Abdullah ibn Umar added, "I saw the man leaning over the woman to protect her from the stones."

Malik commented, "By leaning he meant throwing himself over her so that the stones fell on him."

Source: Muwatta Imam Malik

Malik related to me from Yahya ibn Said from Said ibn al-Musayyab that:

A man from the Aslam tribe came to Abu Bakr as-Siddiq and said to him, "I have committed adultery." Abu Bakr said to him, "Have you mentioned this to anyone else?" He said, "No." Abu Bakr said to him, "Then cover it up with the veil of Allah. Allah accepts repentance from his slaves." His self was still unsettled, so he went to Umar ibn al- Khattab. He told him the same as he had said to Abu Bakr, and Umar told him the same as Abu Bakr had said to him. His self was still not settled so he went to the Messenger of Allah and said to him, "I have committed adultery," insistently. The Messenger of Allah turned away from him three times. Each time the Messenger of Allah turned away from him until it became too much. The Messenger of Allah, questioned his family, "Does he have an illness which affects his mind, or is he mad?" They said, "Messenger of Allah, by Allah, he is well." The Messenger of Allah said, "Unmarried or married?" They said, "Married, Messenger of Allah." The Messenger of Allah gave the order and he was stoned.

Source: Muwatta Imam Malik

Malik related to me from Ibn Shihab from Ubaydullah ibn Abdullah ibn Utba ibn Masud that Abu Hurayra and Zayd ibn Khalid al-Juhani informed him that:

"Two men brought a dispute to the Messenger of Allah. One of them said, "Messenger of Allah! Judge between us by the Book of Allah!" The other said, and he was the wiser of the two, "Yes, Messenger of Allah. Judge between us by the Book of Allah and give me permission to speak." He said, "Speak." He said, "My son was hired by this person and he committed fornication with his wife. He told me that my son deserved stoning, and I ransomed him for one hundred sheep and a slave-girl. Then I asked the people of knowledge and they told me that my son deserved to be flogged with one hundred lashes and exiled for a year, and they informed me that the woman deserved to be stoned." The Messenger of Allah said, "By him in whose Hand myself is, I will judge between you by the Book of Allah. As for your sheep and slave girl, they should be returned to you. Your son should have one hundred lashes and be exiled for a year." He ordered Unays al-Aslami to go to the wife of the other man and to stone her if she confessed. She confessed and he stoned her."

Source: Muwatta Imam Malik

Narrated Al-Ma'rur bin Suwaid:

I saw Abu Dhar Al-Ghifari wearing a cloak, and his slave, too, was wearing a cloak. We asked him about that (i.e. how both were wearing similar cloaks). He replied, "Once I abused a man and he complained of me to the Prophet (ﷺ). The Prophet (ﷺ) asked me, 'Did you abuse him by slighting his mother?' He added, 'Your slaves are your brethren upon whom Allah has given you authority. So, if one has one's brethren under one's control, one should feed them with the like of what one eats and clothe them with the like of what one wears. You should not overburden them with what they cannot bear, and if you do so, help them (in their hard job).

Source: Sahih Bukhari 2545

Narrated Abu Qilaba:

Anas said:"Some people of `Ukl or `Uraina tribe came to Medina and its climate did not suit them. So the Prophet (ﷺ) ordered them to go to the herd of (Milch) camels and to drink their milk and urine (as a medicine). So they went as directed and after they became healthy, they killed the shepherd of the Prophet and drove away all the camels. The news reached the Prophet (ﷺ) early in the morning and he sent (men) in their pursuit and they were captured and brought at noon. He then ordered to cut their hands and feet (and it was done), and their eyes were branded with heated pieces of iron, They were put in 'Al-Harra' and when they asked for water, no water was given to them." Abu Qilaba said, "Those people committed theft and murder, became infidels after embracing Islam and fought against Allah and His Apostle ."

Source: Sahih Bukhari 233

Narrated `Aisha:

We set out with Allah's Messenger (ﷺ) on one of his journeys till we reached Al- Baida' or Dhatul-Jaish, a necklace of mine was broken (and lost). Allah's Messenger (ﷺ) stayed there to search for it, and so did the people along with him. There was no water at that place, so the people went to Abu- Bakr As-

Siddiq and said, "Don't you see what `Aisha has done? She has made Allah's Apostle and the people stay where there is no water and they have no water with them." Abu Bakr came while Allah's Messenger (ﷺ) was sleeping with his head on my thigh, He said, to me: "You have detained Allah's Messenger (ﷺ) and the people where there is no water and they have no water with them. So he admonished me and said what Allah wished him to say and hit me on my flank with his hand. Nothing prevented me from moving (because of pain) but the position of Allah's Messenger (ﷺ) on my thigh. Allah's Messenger (ﷺ) got up when dawn broke and there was no water. So Allah revealed the Divine Verses of Tayammum. So they all performed Tayammum. Usaid bin Hudair said, "O the family of Abu Bakr! This is not the first blessing of yours." Then the camel on which I was riding was caused to move from its place and the necklace was found beneath it.

Source: Sahih Bukhari 334

Narrated `Abdullah:

The Prophet (ﷺ) prayed (and the sub-narrator Ibrahim said, "I do not know whether he prayed more or less than usual"), and when he had finished the prayers he was asked, "O Allah's Messenger (ﷺ)! Has there been any change in the prayers?" He said, "What is it?' The people said, "You have prayed so much and so much." So the Prophet (ﷺ) bent his legs, faced the Qibla and performed two prostration's (of Sahu) and finished his prayers with Taslim (by turning his face to right and left saying: 'As-Salamu `Alaikum- Warahmat-ullah'). When he turned his face to us he said, "If there had been anything changed in the prayer, surely I would have informed you but I am a human being like you and liable to forget like you. So if I forget remind me and if anyone of you is doubtful about his prayer, he should follow what he thinks to be correct and complete his prayer accordingly and finish it and do two prostrations (of Sahu).

Source: Sahih Bukhari 401

Narrated Ibn Mas`ud:

A man kissed a woman (unlawfully) and then went to the Prophet (ﷺ) and informed him. Allah revealed: And offer prayers perfectly At the two ends of the day And in some hours of the night (i.e. the five compulsory prayers). Verily! Good deeds remove (annul) the evil deeds (small sins) (11.114). The man asked Allah's Messenger (ﷺ), "Is it for me?" He said, "It is for all my followers."

Source: Sahih Bukhari 526

Narrated Abu Huraira:

Allah's Messenger (ﷺ) said, "Angels come to you in succession by night and day and all of them get together at the time of the Fajr and `Asr prayers. Those who have passed the night with you (or stayed with you) ascend (to the Heaven) and Allah asks them, though He knows everything about you well, "In what state did you leave my slaves?" The angels reply: "When we left them they were praying and when we reached them, they were praying."

Source: Sahih Bukhari 555

Narrated `Amr:

Jabir bin `Abdullah said, "Mu`adh bin Jabal used to pray with the Prophet (ﷺ) and then go to lead his people in prayer Once he led the `Isha' prayer and recited Surat "Al-Baqara." Somebody left the prayer and Mu`adh criticized him. The news reached the Prophet (ﷺ) and he said to Mu`adh, 'You are putting the people to trial,' and repeated it thrice (or said something similar) and ordered him to recite two medium Suras of Mufassal." (`Amr said that he had forgotten the names of those Suras).

Source: Sahih Bukhari 701

Narrated Jabir bin `Abdullah Al-Ansari:

Once a man was driving two Nadihas (camels used for agricultural purposes) and night had fallen. He found Mu`adh praying so he made his camel kneel and joined Mu`adh in the prayer. The latter recited Surat 'Al-Baqara" or Surat "An-Nisa", (so) the man left the prayer and went away. When he came to know that Mu`adh had criticized him, he went to the Prophet, and complained against Mu`adh. The Prophet said thrice, "O Mu`adh ! Are you putting the people to trial?" It would have been better if you had recited "Sabbih Isma Rabbika-l-A`la (87)", Wash-shamsi wa duhaha (91)", or "Wal-laili idha yaghsha (92)", for the old, the weak and the needy pray behind you." Jabir said that Mu`adh recited Sura Al-Baqara in the `Isha' prayer.

Source: Sahih Bukhari 705

Narrated Abu Sa`id Al-Khudri:

The Prophet (ﷺ) used to proceed to the Musalla on the days of Id-ul-Fitr and Id-ul-Adha; the first thing to begin with was the *prayer and after that he would stand in front of the people and the people would keep sitting in their rows. Then he would preach to them, advise them and give them orders, (i.e. Khutba). And after that if he wished to send an army for an expedition, he would do so; or if he wanted to give and order, he would do so, and then depart. The people followed this tradition till I went out with Marwan, the Governor of Medina, for the prayer of Id-ul-Adha or Id-ul-Fitr. When we reached the Musalla, there was a pulpit made by Kathir bin As-Salt. Marwan wanted to get up on that pulpit before the prayer. I got hold of his clothes but he pulled them and ascended the pulpit and delivered the Khutba before the prayer. I said to him, "By Allah, you have changed (the Prophet's tradition)." He replied, "O Abu Sa`id! Gone is that which you know." I said, "By Allah! What I know is better than what I do not know." Marwan said, "People do not sit to listen to our Khutba after the prayer, so I delivered the Khutba before the prayer."*

Source: Sahih Bukhari 956

Narrated Sa`id bin Jubair:

I was with Ibn `Umar when a spear head pierced the sole of his foot and his foot stuck to the paddle of the saddle and I got down and pulled his foot out, and that happened in Mina. Al-Hajjaj got the news and came to inquire about his health and said, "Alas! If we could only know the man who wounded you!" Ibn `Umar said, "You are the one who wounded me." Al-Hajjaj said, "How is that?" Ibn `Umar said, "You have allowed the arms to be carried on a day on which nobody used to carry them and you allowed arms to be carried in the Haram even though it was not allowed before."

Source: Sahih Bukhari 966

Narrated `Umar bin Al-Khattab:

When `Abdullah bin Ubai bin Salul died, Allah's Messenger (ﷺ) was called upon to offer his funeral prayer. When Allah's Messenger (ﷺ) stood up to offer the prayer, I got up quickly and said, "O Allah's Apostle! Are you going to pray for Ibn Ubai and he said so and so on such and such occasions?" And started mentioning all that he had said. Allah's Messenger (ﷺ) smiled and said, "O `Umar! Go away from me." When I talked too much he said, "I have been given the choice and so I have chosen (to offer the prayer). Had I known that he would be forgiven by asking for Allah's forgiveness for more than seventy times, surely I would have done so." (`Umar added): Allah's Messenger (ﷺ) offered his funeral prayer and returned and after a short while the two verses of Surat Bara' were revealed: i.e. "And never (O Muhammad) pray for any of them who dies . . . (to the end of the verse) (9.84)" – (`Umar added), "Later I was astonished at my daring before Allah's Messenger (ﷺ) on that day. And Allah and His Apostle know better."

Source: Sahih Bukhari 1366

Narrated Aisha:

When the news of the martyrdom of Zaid bin Haritha, Ja`far and `Abdullah bin Rawaha came, the Prophet sat down looking sad, and I was looking through the chink of the door. A man came and said, "O Allah's Messenger (ﷺ)! The women of Ja`far," and then he mentioned their crying . The Prophet ordered him to stop them from crying. The man went and came back and said, "I tried to stop them but they disobeyed." The

Prophet ordered him for the second time to forbid them. He went again and came back and said, "They did not listen to me, (or "us": the sub-narrator Muhammad bin Haushab is in doubt as to which is right). " (`Aisha added: The Prophet (ﷺ) said, "Put dust in their mouths." I said (to that man), "May Allah stick your nose in the dust (i.e. humiliate you)." By Allah, you could not (stop the women from crying) to fulfill the order, besides you did not relieve Allah's Apostle from fatigue."

Source: Sahih Bukhari 1305

Narrated Ma'n bin Yazid:

My grandfather, my father and I gave the pledge of allegiance to Allah's Messenger (ﷺ). The Prophet (ﷺ) got me engaged and then got me married. One day I went to the Prophet (ﷺ) with a complaint. My father Yazid had taken some gold coins for charity and kept them with a man in the mosque (to give them to the poor) But I went and took them and brought them to him (my father). My father said, "By Allah! I did not intend to give them to you. " I took (the case) to Allah's Messenger (ﷺ) . On that Allah's Messenger (ﷺ) said, "O Yazid, you will be rewarded for what you intended. O Ma'n, whatever you have taken is yours."

Source: Sahih Bukhari 1422

Narrated `Ali:

We have nothing except the Book of Allah and this written paper from the Prophet (wherein is written Medina is a sanctuary from the 'Air Mountain to such and such a place, and whoever innovates in it an heresy or commits a sin, or gives shelter to such an innovator in it will incur the curse of

Allah, the angels, and all the people, none of his compulsory or optional good deeds of worship will be accepted. And the asylum (of protection) granted by any Muslim is to be secured (respected) by all the other Muslims; and whoever betrays a Muslim in this respect incurs the curse of Allah, the angels, and all the people, and none of his compulsory or optional good deeds of worship will be accepted, and whoever (freed slave) befriends (take as masters) other than his manumitters without their permission incurs the curse of Allah, the angels, and all the people, and none of his compulsory or optional good deeds of worship will be accepted.

Source: Sahih Bukhari 1870

Narrated `Amr:

Here (i.e. in Mecca) there was a man called Nawwas and he had camels suffering from the disease of excessive and unquenchable thirst. Ibn `Umar went to the partner of Nawwas and bought those camels. The man returned to Nawwas and told him that he had sold those camels. Nawwas asked him, "To whom have you sold them?" He replied, "To such and such Sheikh." Nawwas said, "Woe to you; By Allah, that Sheikh was Ibn `Umar." Nawwas then went to Ibn `Umar and said to him, "My partner sold you camels suffering from the disease of excessive thirst and he had not known you." Ibn `Umar told him to take them back. When Nawwas went to take them, Ibn `Umar said to him, "Leave them there as I am happy with the decision of Allah's Messenger (ﷺ) that there is no oppression. "

Source: Sahih Bukhari 2099

Narrated Ibn `Abbas:

Once `Umar was informed that a certain man sold alcohol. `Umar said, "May Allah curse him! Doesn't he know that Allah's Messenger (ﷺ) said, 'May Allah curse the Jews, for Allah had forbidden them to eat the fat of animals but they melted it and sold it."

Source: Sahih Bukhari 2223

Narrated Husain bin `Ali:

`Ali bin Abi Talib said: "I got a she-camel as my share of the war booty on the day (of the battle) of Badr, and Allah's Messenger (ﷺ) gave me another she-camel. I let both of them kneel at the door of one of the Ansar, intending to carry Idhkhir on them to sell it and use its price for my wedding banquet on marrying Fatima. A goldsmith from Bani Qainqa' was with me. Hamza bin `Abdul-Muttalib was in that house drinking wine and a lady singer was reciting: "O Hamza! (Kill) the (two) fat old she camels (and serve them to your guests). So Hamza took his sword and went towards the two she-camels and cut off their humps and opened their flanks and took a part of their livers." (I said to Ibn Shihab, "Did he take part of the humps?" He replied, "He cut off their humps and carried them away.") `Ali further said, "When I saw that dreadful sight, I went to the Prophet (ﷺ) and told him the news. The Prophet (ﷺ) came out in the company of Zaid bin Haritha who was with him then, and I too went with them. He went to Hamza and spoke harshly to him. Hamza looked up and said, 'Aren't you only the slaves of my forefathers?' The Prophet (ﷺ) retreated and went out. This incident happened before the prohibition of drinking (intoxicants)."

Source: Sahih Bukhari 2375

Narrated `Abdullah:

I heard a man reciting a verse (of the Qur'an) but I had heard the Prophet (ﷺ) reciting it differently. So, I caught hold of the man by the hand and took him to Allah's Messenger (ﷺ) who said, "Both of you are right." Shu`ba, the sub-narrator said, "I think he said to them, "Don't differ, for the nations before you differed and perished (because of their differences). "

Source: Sahih Bukhari 2410

Narrated Abu Huraira:

Once while a Jew was selling something, he was offered a price that he was not pleased with. So, he said, "No, by Him Who gave Moses superiority over all human beings!" Hearing him, an Ansari man got up and slapped him on the face and said, "You say: By Him Who Gave Moses superiority over all human beings although the Prophet (Muhammad) is present amongst us!" The Jew went to the Prophet and said, "O Abu-l-Qasim! I am under the assurance and contract of security, so what right does so-and-so have to slap me?" The Prophet (ﷺ) asked the other, "Why have you slapped?". He told him the whole story. The Prophet (ﷺ) became angry, till anger appeared on his face, and said, "Don't give superiority to any prophet amongst Allah's Prophets, for when the trumpet will be blown, everyone on the earth and in the heavens will become unconscious except those whom Allah will exempt. The trumpet will be blown for the second time and I will be the first to be resurrected to see Moses holding Allah's Throne. I will not know whether the unconsciousness which Moses received on the Day of Tur has been sufficient for him, or has he got up before me. And I do not say that there is anybody who is better than Jonah bin Matta."

Source: Sahih Bukhari 3414

Narrated Anas bin Malik:

During the lifetime of Allah's Messenger (ﷺ) a Jew attacked a girl and took some silver ornaments she was wearing and crushed her head. Her relative brought her to the Prophet (ﷺ) while she was in her last breaths, and she was unable to speak. Allah's Messenger (ﷺ) asked her, "Who has hit you? So-and so?", mentioning somebody other than her murderer. She moved her head, indicating denial. The Prophet (ﷺ) mentioned another person other than the murderer, and she again moved her head indicating denial. Then he asked, "Was it so-and-so?", mentioning the name of her killer. She nodded, agreeing. Then Allah's Messenger (ﷺ); ordered that the head of that Jew be crushed between two stones.

Source: Sahih Bukhari 5295

Narrated `Abdullah bin Mas`ud:

Allah's Messenger (ﷺ) said, "Whoever takes a false oath so as to take the property of a Muslim (illegally) will meet Allah while He will be angry with him." Al-Ash'ath said: By Allah, that saying concerned me. I had common land with a Jew, and the Jew later on denied my ownership, so I took him to the Prophet who asked me whether I had a proof of my ownership. When I replied in the negative, the Prophet asked the Jew to take an oath. I said, "O Allah's Messenger (ﷺ)! He will take an oath and deprive me of my property." So, Allah revealed the following verse: "Verily! Those who purchase a little gain at the cost of Allah's covenant and their oaths." (3.77)

Source: Sahih Bukhari 2416

Narrated `Abdullah bin Ka`b bin Malik:

Ka`b demanded his debt back from Ibn Abi Hadrad in the Mosque and their voices grew louder till Allah's Messenger (☺) heard them while he was in his house. He came out to them raising the curtain of his room and addressed Ka`b, "O Ka`b!" Ka`b replied, "Labaik, O Allah's Messenger (☺)." (He said to him), "Reduce your debt to one half," gesturing with his hand. Ka`b said, "I have done so, O Allah's Apostle!" On that the Prophet (☺) said to Ibn Abi Hadrad, "Get up and repay the debt, to him."

Source: Sahih Bukhari 2418

Narrated `Umar bin Al-Khattab:

I heard Hisham bin Hakim bin Hizam reciting Surat-al-Furqan in a way different to that of mine. Allah's Messenger (☺) had taught it to me (in a different way). So, I was about to quarrel with him (during the prayer) but I waited till he finished, then I tied his garment round his neck and seized him by it and brought him to Allah's Messenger (☺) and said, "I have heard him reciting Surat-al-Furqan in a way different to the way you taught it to me." The Prophet (☺) ordered me to release him and asked Hisham to recite it. When he recited it, Allah s Apostle said, "It was revealed in this way." He then asked me to recite it. When I recited It, he said, "It was revealed in this way. The Qur'an has been revealed in seven different ways, so recite it in the way that is easier for you."

Source: Sahih Bukhari 2419

Narrated Aisha:

Hind bint `Utba (Abu Sufyan's wife) came and said, "O Allah's Messenger (ﷺ)! Abu Sufyan is a miser. Is there any harm if I spend something from his property for our children?" He said, there is no harm for you if you feed them from it justly and reasonably (with no extravagance).

Source: Sahih Bukhari 2460

Narrated An-Nu`man bin Bashir:

The Prophet (ﷺ) said, "The example of the person abiding by Allah's order and restrictions in comparison to those who violate them is like the example of those persons who drew lots for their seats in a boat. Some of them got seats in the upper part, and the others in the lower. When the latter needed water, they had to go up to bring water (and that troubled the others), so they said, 'Let us make a hole in our share of the ship (and get water) saving those who are above us from troubling them. So, if the people in the upper part left the others do what they had suggested, all the people of the ship would be destroyed, but if they prevented them, both parties would be safe."

Source: Sahih Bukhari 2493

Narrated `Urwa bin Al-Musaiyab Alqama bin Waqqas and Ubaidullah bin `Abdullah:

About the story of `Aisha and their narrations were similar attesting each other, when the liars said what they invented about `Aisha, and the Divine Inspiration was delayed, Allah's Messenger (ﷺ) sent for `Ali and Usama to consult them in divorcing his wife (i.e. `Aisha). Usama said, "Keep your wife, as we know nothing about her except good." Barirah said, "I cannot accuse her of any defect except that she is still a young *girl who sleeps, neglecting her family's dough which the domestic goats come to eat (i.e. she was too simpleminded to deceive her husband)." Allah's Messenger (ﷺ) said, "Who can help me to take revenge over the man who has harmed me by defaming the reputation of my family? By Allah, I have not known about my family-anything except good, and they mentioned (i.e. accused) a man about whom I did not know anything except good."*

Source: Sahih Bukhari 2637

Narrated `Abdullah bin `Umar:

Allah's Messenger (ﷺ) and Ubai bin Ka`b Al-Ansari went to the garden where Ibn Saiyad used to live. When Allah's Messenger (ﷺ) entered (the garden), he (i.e. Allah's Messenger (ﷺ)) started hiding himself behind the date palms as he wanted to hear secretly the talk of Ibn Saiyad before the latter saw him. Ibn Saiyad wrapped with a soft decorated sheet was lying on his bed murmuring. Ibn Saiyad's mother saw the Prophet hiding behind the stems of the date-palms. She addressed Ibn Saiyad saying, "O Saf, this is Muhammad." Hearing that Ibn Saiyad stopped murmuring (or got cautious), the Prophet (ﷺ) said, "If she had left him undisturbed, he would have revealed his reality."

Source: Sahih Bukhari 2638

Narrated Ibn `Abbas:

Hilal bin Umaiya accused his wife before the Prophet (ﷺ) of committing illegal sexual intercourse with Sharik bin Sahma.' The Prophet (ﷺ) said, "Produce a proof, or else you would get the legal punishment (by being lashed) on your back." Hilal said, "O Allah's Messenger (ﷺ)! If anyone of us saw another man over his wife, would he go to search for a proof?" The Prophet (ﷺ) went on saying, "Produce a proof or else you would get the legal punishment (by being lashed) on your back." The Prophet (ﷺ) then mentioned the narration of Lian (as in the Book). (Surat-al-Nur: 24)

Source: Sahih Bukhari 2671

Narrated Sahl bin Sa`d:

Once the people of Quba fought with each other till they threw stones on each other. When Allah's Apostle was informed about it, he said, "Let us go to bring about a reconciliation between them."

Source: Sahih Bukhari 2693

Narrated Anas:

Ar-Rabi, the daughter of An-Nadr broke the tooth of a girl, and the relatives of Ar-Rabi` requested the girl's relatives to accept the Irsh (compensation for wounds etc.) and forgive (the offender), but they refused. So, they went to the Prophet (ﷺ) who ordered them to bring about retaliation. Anas bin An-Nadr asked, "O Allah"; Apostle! Will the tooth of Ar-Rabi` be broken? No, by Him Who has sent you with the Truth, her tooth will not be broken." The Prophet (ﷺ) said, "O Anas! Allah"; law ordains retaliation." Later the relatives of the girl agreed and forgave her. The Prophet (ﷺ) said, "There are some of Allah's slaves who, if they take an oath by Allah, are responded to by Allah i.e. their oath is fulfilled). Anas added, "The people agreed and accepted the Irsh."

Source: Sahih Bukhari 2703

Ibn 'Abbas said:

"A man from the tribe of Bani Sahm went out in the company of Tamim Ad-Dari and 'Adi bin Badda'. The man of Bani Sahm died in a land where there was no Muslim. When Tamim and 'Adi returned conveying the property of the deceased, they claimed that they had lost a silver bowl with gold engraving. Allah's Messenger (ﷺ) made them take an oath (to confirm their claim), and then the bowl was found in Makkah with some people who claimed that they had bought it from Tamim and 'Adu, Then two witnesses from the relatives of the deceased got up and swore that their witnesses were more valid than the witnesses of 'Adi and Tamim, and that the bowl belonged to their deceased fellow. So, this verse was revealed in connection with this case ; 'O you who believe! When death approached any of you ...'," (5:106)

Source: Sahih Bukhari 2780

Narrated Jabir:

The Prophet (ﷺ) said, "Who will bring me the information about the enemy on the day (of the battle) of Al-Ahzab (i.e. Clans)?" Az-Zubair said, "I will." The Prophet (ﷺ) said again, "Who will bring me the information about the enemy?" Az-Zubair said again, "I will." The Prophet (ﷺ) said, "Every prophet had a disciple and my disciple is Az-Zubair. "

Source: Sahih Bukhari 2846

Narrated `Abdullah bin Abi Qatada:

(from his father) Abu Qatada went out (on a journey) with Allah's Messenger (ﷺ) but he was left behind with some of his companions who were in the state of Ihram. He himself was not in the state of Ihram. They saw an opener before he could see it. When they saw the opener, they did not speak anything till Abu Qatada saw it. So, he rode over his horse called Al-Jarada and requested them to give him his lash, but they refused. So, he himself took it and then attacked the opener and slaughtered it. He ate of its meat and his companions ate, too, but they regretted their eating. When they met the Prophet (they asked him about it) and he asked, "Have you some of its meat (left) with you?" Abu Qatada replied, "Yes, we have its leg with us." So, the Prophet (ﷺ) took and ate it.

Source: Sahih Bukhari 2854

Narrated Abu Huraira:

Tufail bin `Amr Ad-Dausi and his companions came to the Prophet (ﷺ) and said, "O Allah's Messenger (ﷺ)! The people of the tribe of Daus disobeyed and refused to follow you; so invoke Allah against them." The people said, "The tribe of Daus is ruined." The Prophet (ﷺ) said, "O Allah! Give guidance to the people of Daus, and let them embrace Islam."

Source: Sahih Bukhari 2937

Narrated Yali:

I participated in the Ghazwa of Tabuk along with Allah's Messenger (ﷺ) and I gave a young camel to be ridden in Jihad and that was, to me, one of my best deeds. Then I employed a laborer who quarreled with another person. One of them bit the hand of the other and the latter drew his hand from the mouth of the former pulling out his front tooth. Then the former instituted a suit against the latter before the Prophet who rejected that suit saying, "Do you expect him to put out his hand for you to snap as a male camel snaps (vegetation)?"

Source: Sahih Bukhari 2973

Narrated Salama bin Al-Akwa`:

"An infidel spy came to the Prophet (ﷺ) while he was on a journey. The spy sat with the companions of the Prophet (ﷺ) and started talking and then went away. The Prophet (ﷺ) said (to his companions), 'Chase and kill him.' So, I killed him." The Prophet (ﷺ) then gave him the belongings of the killed spy (in addition to his share of the war booty).

Source: Sahih Bukhari 3051

Narrated Abu Huraira:

We were in the company of Allah's Messenger (ﷺ) in a Ghazwa, and he remarked about a man who claimed to be a Muslim, saying, "This (man) is from the people of the (Hell) Fire." When the battle started, the man fought violently till he got wounded. Somebody said, "O Allah's Messenger (ﷺ)! The man whom you described as being from the people of the (Hell) Fire fought violently today and died." The Prophet (ﷺ) said, "He will go to the (Hell) Fire." Some people were on the point of doubting (the truth of what the Prophet had said) while they were in this state, suddenly someone said that he was still alive but severely wounded. When night fell, he lost patience and committed suicide. The Prophet (ﷺ) was informed of that, and he said, "Allah Is Greater! I testify that I am Allah's Slave and His Apostle." Then he ordered Bilal to announce amongst the people: 'None will enter Paradise but a Muslim, and Allah may support this religion (i.e. Islam) even with a disobedient man.'

Source: Sahih Bukhari 3062

Narrated `Abdullah:

On the day (of the battle) of Hunain, Allah's Messenger (ﷺ) favored some people in the distribution of the booty (to the exclusion of others); he gave Al-Aqra' bin H`Abis one-hundred camels and he gave 'Uyaina the same amount, and also gave to some of the eminent Arabs, giving them preference in this regard. Then a person came and said, "By Allah, in this distribution justice has not been observed, nor has Allah's Pleasure been aimed at." I said (to him), "By Allah, I will inform the Prophet (of what you have said), "I went and informed him, and he said, "If Allah and His Apostle did not act justly, who else would act justly. May Allah be merciful to Moses, for he was harmed with more than this, yet he kept patient."

Source: Sahih Bukhari 3150

Narrated Abu Huraira:

When Khaibar was conquered, a roasted poisoned sheep was presented to the Prophet (ﷺ) as a gift (by the Jews). The Prophet (ﷺ) ordered, "Let all the Jews who have been here, be assembled before me." The Jews were collected and the Prophet (ﷺ) said (to them), "I am going to ask you a question. Will you tell the truth?" They said, "Yes." The Prophet (ﷺ) asked, "Who is your father?" They replied, "So-and-so." He said, "You have told a lie; your father is so-and-so." They said, "You are right." He said, "Will you now tell me the truth, if I ask you about something?" They replied, "Yes, O Abu Al-Qasim; and if we should tell a lie, you can realize our lie as you have done regarding our father." On that he asked, "Who are the people of the (Hell) Fire?" They said, "We shall remain in the (Hell) Fire for a short period, and after that you will replace us." The Prophet (ﷺ) said, "You may be cursed and humiliated in it! By Allah, we shall never replace you in it." Then he asked, "Will you now tell me the truth if I ask you a question?" They said, "Yes, O Abu Al-Qasim." He asked, "Have you poisoned this sheep?" They said, "Yes." He asked, "What made you do so?" They said, "We wanted to know if you were a liar in which case we would get rid of you, and if you are a prophet then the poison would not harm you."

Source: Sahih Bukhari 3169

Narrated Um Hani:

I went to Allah's Messenger (ﷺ) on the day of the conquest of Mecca and found him taking a bath, and his daughter Fatima was screening him. I greeted him and he asked, "Who is that?" I said, "I, Um Hani bint Abi Talib." He said, "Welcome, O Um Hani." When he had finished his bath, he stood up and offered eight rak`at while dressed in one garment. I said, "O Allah's Messenger (ﷺ)! My brother `Ali has declared that he will kill a man to whom I have granted asylum. The man is so and-so bin Hubaira." Allah's Messenger (ﷺ) said, "O Um Hani! We will grant asylum to the one whom you have granted asylum." (Um Hani said, "That (visit) took place in the Duha (i.e. forenoon)).

Source: Sahih Bukhari 3171

Narrated Masruq:

I asked Um Ruman, `Aisha's mother about the accusation forged against `Aisha. She said, "While I was sitting with `Aisha, an Ansari woman came to us and said, 'Let Allah condemn such-and-such person.' I asked her, 'Why do you say so?' She replied, 'For he has spread the (slanderous) story.' `Aisha said, 'What story?' The woman then told her the story. `Aisha asked, 'Have Abu Bakr and Allah's Messenger (صلى الله عليه وسلم) heard about it?' She said, 'Yes.' `Aisha fell down senseless (on hearing that), and when she came to her senses, she got fever and shaking of the body. The Prophet (صلى الله عليه وسلم) came and asked, 'What is wrong with her?' I said, 'She has got fever because of a story which has been rumored.' `Aisha got up and said, 'By Allah! Even if I took an oath, you would not believe me, and if I put forward an excuse, You would not excuse me. My example and your example is just like that example of Jacob and his sons. Against that which you assert, it is Allah (Alone) Whose Help can be sought.' (12.18) The Prophet (صلى الله عليه وسلم) left and then Allah revealed the Verses (concerning the matter), and on that `Aisha said, 'Thanks to Allah (only) and not to anybody else."

Source: Sahih Bukhari 3388

Narrated Jabir:

We were in the company of the Prophet (صلى الله عليه وسلم) in a Ghazwa. A large number of emigrants joined him and among the emigrants there was a person who used to play jokes (or play with spears); so he (jokingly) stroked an Ansari man on the hip. The Ans-ari got so angry that both of them called their people. The Ansari said, "Help, O Ansar!" And the emigrant said "Help, O emigrants!" The Prophet (صلى الله عليه وسلم) came out and said, "What is wrong with the people (as they are calling) this call of the period

of Ignorance? "Then he said, "What is the matter with them?"
So he was told about the stroke of the emigrant to the Ansari.
The Prophet (ﷺ) said, "Stop this (i.e. appeal for help) for it is an
evil call. "Abdullah bin Ubai bin Salul (a hypocrite) said, "The
emigrants have called and (gathered against us); so when we
return to Medina, surely, the more honorable people will expel
therefrom the meaner," Upon that `Umar said, "O Allah's
Prophet! Shall we not kill this evil person (i.e. `Abdullah bin
Ubai bin Salul) ?" The Prophet) said, "(No), lest the people
should say that Muhammad used to kill his companions."

Source: Sahih Bukhari 3518

Narrated Abu Ad-Darda:

While I was sitting with the Prophet, Abu Bakr came, lifting up
one corner of his garment uncovering his knee. The Prophet (ﷺ)
said, "Your companion has had a quarrel." Abu Bakr greeted
(the Prophet (ﷺ)) and said, "O Allah's Messenger (ﷺ)! There
was something (i.e. quarrel) between me and the Son of Al-
Khattab. I talked to him harshly and then regretted that, and
requested him to forgive me, but he refused. This is why I have
come to you." The Prophet (ﷺ) said thrice, "O Abu Bakr! May
Allah forgive you." In the meanwhile, `Umar regretted (his
refusal of Abu Bakr's excuse) and went to Abu Bakr's house
and asked if Abu Bakr was there. They replied in the negative.
So he came to the Prophet (ﷺ) and greeted him, but signs of
displeasure appeared on the face of the Prophet (ﷺ) till Abu
Bakr pitied (`Umar), so he knelt and said twice, "O Allah's
Messenger (ﷺ)! By Allah! I was more unjust to him (than he to
me)." The Prophet (ﷺ) said, "Allah sent me (as a Prophet) to
you (people) but you said (to me), 'You are telling a lie,' while

Abu Bakr said, 'He has said the truth,' and consoled me with himself and his money." He then said twice, "Won't you then give up harming my companion?" After that nobody harmed Abu Bakr.

Source: Sahih Bukhari 3661

Narrated 'Ubaidullah bin `Adi bin Al-Khiyar:

That Al-Miswar bin Makhrama and `Abdur-Rahman bin Al-Aswad bin 'Abu Yaghuth had said to him, "What prevents you from speaking to your uncle `Uthman regarding his brother Al-Walid bin `Uqba?" The people were speaking against the latter for what he had done. 'Ubaidullah said, "So I kept waiting for `Uthman, and when he went out for the prayer, I said to him, 'I have got something to say to you as a piece of advice.' `Uthman said, 'O man! I seek Refuge with Allah from you. So I went away. When I finished my prayer, I sat with Al-Miswar and Ibn 'Abu Yaghutb and talked to both of them of what I had said to `Uthman and what he had said to me. They said, 'You have done your duty.' So while I was sitting with them. `Uthman's Messenger came to me. They said, 'Allah has put you to trial." I set out and when I reached `Uthman, he said, 'What is your advice which you mentioned a while ago?' I recited Tashahhud and added, 'Allah has sent Muhammad and has revealed the Book (i.e. Qur'an) to him. You (O `Uthman!) were amongst those who responded to the call of Allah and His Apostle and had faith in him. And you took part in the first two migrations (to Ethiopia and to Medina), and you enjoyed the company of Allah's Messenger (ﷺ) and learned his traditions and advice. Now the people are talking much about Al-Walid bin `Uqba and so it is your duty to impose on him the legal punishment.'

`Uthman then said to me, 'O my nephew! Did you ever meet Allah's Messenger (ﷺ)?' I said, 'No, but his knowledge has reached me as it has reached the virgin in her seclusion.' `Uthman then recited Tashahhud and said, 'No doubt, Allah has sent Muhammad with the Truth and has revealed to him His Book (i.e. Qur'an) and I was amongst those who responded to the call of Allah and His Apostle and I had faith in Muhammad's Mission, and I had performed the first two migrations as you have said, and I enjoyed the company of Allah's Messenger (ﷺ) and gave the pledge of allegiance to him. By Allah, I never disobeyed him and never cheated him till Allah caused him to die. Then Allah made Abu Bakr Caliph, and by Allah, I was never disobedient to him, nor did I cheat him. Then `Umar became Caliph, and by Allah, I was never disobedient to him, nor did I cheat him. Then I became Caliph. Have I not then the same rights over you as they had over me?' I replied in the affirmative. `Uthman further said, 'Then what are these talks which are reaching me from you? As for what you have mentioned about Al-Walid bin 'Uqb; Allah willing, I shall give him the leg; punishment justly. Then `Uthman ordered that Al-Walid be flogged forty lashes. He ordered `Ali to flog him and he himself flogged him as well."

Source: Sahih Bukhari 3872

Narrated Abu Musa:

The news of the migration of the Prophet (from Mecca to Medina) reached us while we were in Yemen. So we set out as emigrants towards him. We were (three) I and my two brothers. I was the youngest of them, and one of the two was Abu Burda, and the other, Abu Ruhm, and our total number was either 53 or 52 men from my people. We got on board a boat and our boat took us to Negus in Ethiopia. There we met Ja`far bin Abi Talib and stayed with him. Then we all came (to Medina) and met the Prophet (ﷺ) at the time of the conquest of Khaibar. Some of the people used to say to us, namely the people of the ship, "We have migrated before you." Asma' bint 'Umais who was one of those who had come with us, came as a visitor to Hafsa, the wife the Prophet (ﷺ) . She had migrated along with those other Muslims who migrated to Negus. `Umar came to Hafsa while Asma' bint 'Umais was with her. `Umar, on seeing Asma,' said, "Who is this?" She said, "Asma' bint 'Umais," `Umar said, "Is she the Ethiopian? Is she the sea-faring lady?" Asma' replied, "Yes." `Umar said, "We have migrated before you (people of the boat), so we have got more right than you over Allah's Messenger (ﷺ) " On that Asma' became angry and said, "No, by Allah, while you were with Allah's Messenger (ﷺ) who was feeding the hungry ones amongst you, and advised the ignorant ones amongst you, we were in the far-off hated land of Ethiopia, and all that was for the sake of Allah's Messenger (ﷺ) . By Allah, I will neither eat any food nor drink anything till I inform Allah's Messenger (ﷺ) of all that you have said. There we were harmed and frightened. I will mention this to the Prophet (ﷺ) and will not tell a lie or curtail your saying or add something to it."

Source: Sahih Bukhari 4230

So when the Prophet (ﷺ) came, she said:

"O Allah's Prophet `Umar has said so-and-so." He said (to Asma'), "What did you say to him?" Asma said, "I told him so-and-so." The Prophet (ﷺ) said, "He (i.e. `Umar) has not got more right than you people over me, as he and his companions have (the reward of) only one migration, and you, the people of the boat, have (the reward of) two migrations." Asma' later on said, "I saw Abu Musa and the other people of the boat coming to me in successive groups, asking me about this narration, and to them nothing in the world was more cheerful and greater than what the Prophet (ﷺ) had said about them." Narrated Abu Burda:

Asma' said, "I saw Abu Musa requesting me to repeat this narration again and again."

Source: Sahih Bukhari 4231

Narrated Abu Huraira:

When we conquered Khaibar, we gained neither gold nor silver as booty, but we gained cows, camels, goods and gardens. Then we departed with Allah's Messenger (ﷺ) to the valley of Al-Qira, and at that time Allah's Messenger (ﷺ) had a slave called Mid`am who had been presented to him by one of Banu Ad-Dibbab. While the slave was dismounting the saddle of Allah's Messenger (ﷺ) an arrow the thrower of which was unknown, came and hit him. The people said, "Congratulations to him for the martyrdom." Allah's Apostle said, "No, by Him in Whose Hand my soul is, the sheet (of cloth) which he had taken (illegally) on the day of Khaibar from the booty before the distribution of the booty, has become a flame of Fire burning him." On hearing that, a man brought one or two leather straps of shoes to the Prophet and said, "These are things I took (illegally)." On that Allah's Messenger (ﷺ) said, "This is a strap, or these are two straps of Fire."

Source: Sahih Bukhari 4234

Narrated Hisham's father:

When Allah's Messenger (ﷺ) set out (towards Mecca) during the year of the Conquest (of Mecca) and this news reached (the infidels of Quraish), Abu Sufyan, Hakim bin Hizam and Budail bin Warqa came out to gather information about Allah's Messenger (ﷺ), They proceeded on their way till they reached a place called Marr-az-Zahran (which is near Mecca). Behold! There they saw many fires as if they were the fires of `Arafat. Abu Sufyan said, "What is this? It looked like the fires of `Arafat." Budail bin Warqa' said, "Banu `Amr are less in number than that." Some of the guards of Allah's Messenger (ﷺ) saw them and took them over, caught them and brought them to Allah's Messenger (ﷺ). Abu Sufyan embraced Islam. When the Prophet (ﷺ) proceeded, he said to Al-Abbas, "Keep Abu Sufyan standing at the top of the mountain so that he would look at the Muslims. So Al-`Abbas kept him standing (at that place) and the tribes with the Prophet (ﷺ) started passing in front of Abu Sufyan in military batches. A batch passed and Abu Sufyan said, "O `Abbas Who are these?" `Abbas said, "They are (Banu) Ghifar." Abu Sufyan said, I have got nothing to do with Ghifar." Then (a batch of the tribe of) Juhaina passed by and he said similarly as above. Then (a batch of the tribe of) Sa`d bin Huzaim passed by and he said similarly as above. Then (Banu) Sulaim passed by and he said similarly as above. Then came a batch, the like of which Abu Sufyan had not seen. He said, "Who are these?" `Abbas said, "They are the Ansar headed by Sa`d bin Ubada, the one holding the flag." Sa`d bin Ubada said, "O Abu Sufyan! Today is the day of a great battle

*and today (what is prohibited in) the Ka`ba will be permissible."
Abu Sufyan said., "O `Abbas! How excellent the day of
destruction is! "Then came another batch (of warriors) which
was the smallest of all the batches, and in it there was Allah's
Messenger (ﷺ) and his companions and the flag of the Prophet
(ﷺ) was carried by Az-Zubair bin Al Awwam. When Allah's
Messenger (ﷺ) passed by Abu Sufyan, the latter said, (to the
Prophet), "Do you know what Sa`d bin 'Ubada said?" The
Prophet (ﷺ) said, "What did he say?" Abu Sufyan said, "He
said so-and-so." The Prophet (ﷺ) said, "Sa`d told a lie, but
today Allah will give superiority to the Ka`ba and today the
Ka`ba will be covered with a (cloth) covering." Allah's
Messenger (ﷺ) ordered that his flag be fixed at Al-Hajun.
Narrated `Urwa: Nafi` bin Jubair bin Mut`im said, "I heard
Al-Abbas saying to Az-Zubair bin Al- `Awwam, 'O Abu
`Abdullah ! Did Allah's Messenger (ﷺ) order you to fix the flag
here?' " Allah's Messenger (ﷺ) ordered Khalid bin Al-Walid to
enter Mecca from its upper part from Ka'da while the Prophet
(ﷺ) himself entered from Kuda. Two men from the cavalry of
Khalid bin Al-Wahd named Hubaish bin Al-Ash'ar and Kurz
bin Jabir Al-Fihri were martyred on that day.*

Source: Sahih Bukhari 4280

Narrated Ibn Abu Mulaika:

*Two women were stitching shoes in a house or a room. Then
one of them came out with an awl driven into her hand, and she
sued the other for it. The case was brought before Ibn `Abbas,
Ibn `Abbas said, "Allah's Messenger (ﷺ) said, 'If people were to
be given what they claim (without proving their claim) the life
and property of the nation would be lost.' Will you remind her*

(i.e. the defendant), of Allah and recite before her:--" Verily! Those who purchase a small gain at the cost of Allah's Covenant and their oaths..."(3.77) So they reminded her and she confessed. Ibn `Abbas then said, "The Prophet (ﷺ) said, 'The oath is to be taken by the defendant (in the absence of any proof against him).

Source: Sahih Bukhari 4552

Narrated 'Alqama:

While we were in the city of Hims (in Syria), Ibn Mas`ud recited Surat Yusuf. A man said to him), "It was not revealed in this way." Then Ibn Mas`ud said, "I recited it in this way before Allah's Messenger (ﷺ) and he confirmed my recitation by saying, 'Well done!' " Ibn Mas`ud detected the smell of wine from the man's mouth, so he said to him, "Aren't you ashamed of telling a lie about Allah's Book and (along with this) you drink alcoholic liquors too?" Then he lashed him according to the law.

Source: Sahih Bukhari 5001

Narrated Abu Huraira:

A man from Bani Aslam came to Allah's Messenger (ﷺ) while he was in the mosque and called (the Prophet (ﷺ)) saying, "O Allah's Messenger (ﷺ)! I have committed illegal sexual intercourse." On that the Prophet (ﷺ) turned his face from him to the other side, whereupon the man moved to the side towards which the Prophet (ﷺ) had turned his face, and said, "O Allah's Messenger (ﷺ)! I have committed illegal sexual intercourse." The Prophet turned his face (from him) to the other side whereupon the man moved to the side towards which the

Prophet (ﷺ) had turned his face, and repeated his statement. The Prophet (ﷺ) turned his face (from him) to the other side again. The man moved again (and repeated his statement) for the fourth time. So when the man had given witness four times against himself, the Prophet (ﷺ) called him and said, "Are you insane?" He replied, "No." The Prophet (ﷺ) then said (to his companions), "Go and stone him to death." The man was a married one. Jabir bin `Abdullah Al-Ansari said: I was one of those who stoned him. We stoned him at the Musalla (`Id praying place) in Medina. When the stones hit him with their sharp edges, he fled, but we caught him at Al-Harra and stoned him till he died.

Source: Sahih Bukhari 5271

Narrated Sahl bin Sa`d As-Sa`idi:

'Uwaimir Al-Ajlani came to `Asim bin Ad Al-Ansari and said to him, "O `Asim! Suppose a man saw another man with his wife, would he kill him whereupon you would kill him; or what should he do? Please, O `Asim, ask about this on my behalf." `Asim asked Allah's Messenger (ﷺ) about it. Allah's Messenger (ﷺ), disliked that question and considered it disgraceful. What `Asim heard from Allah's Messenger (ﷺ) was hard on him. When `Asim returned to his family, 'Uwaimir came to him and said, "O `Asim! What did Allah's Messenger (ﷺ). Say to you?" `Asim said to 'Uwaimir, "You never bring me any good. Allah's Messenger (ﷺ) disliked the problem which I asked him about." 'Uwaimir said, "By Allah, I will not give up this matter until I ask the Prophet (ﷺ) about it." So 'Uwaimir proceeded till he came to Allah's Messenger (ﷺ) in the midst of people, and said, "O Allah's Messenger (ﷺ)! If a man sees *another man with his wife, would he kill him, whereupon you would kill him, or what should he do?" Allah's Messenger (ﷺ) said, "Allah has revealed some decree as regards you and your wives case. Go and bring her." So they carried out the process of Lian while I was present among the people with Allah's Messenger (ﷺ). When they had finished their Lian, 'Uwaimir said, "O Allah's Messenger (ﷺ)! If I should now keep her with me as a wife, then I have told a lie." So he divorced her thrice before Allah's Messenger (ﷺ) ordered him. (Ibn Shihab said: So divorce was the tradition for all those who were involved in a case of Lian.)*

Source: Sahih Bukhari 5308

Narrated Abu Huraira:

Allah's Messenger (ﷺ) gave his verdict about two ladies of the Hudhail tribe who had fought each other and one of them had hit the other with a stone. The stone hit her `Abdomen and as she was pregnant, the blow killed the child in her womb. They both filed their case with the Prophet (ﷺ) and he judged that the blood money for what was in her womb. Was a slave or a female slave. The guardian of the lady who was fined said, "O Allah's Messenger (ﷺ)! Shall I be fined for a creature that has neither drunk nor eaten, neither spoke nor cried? A case like that should be nullified." On that the Prophet (ﷺ) said, "This is one of the brothers of soothsayers.

Source: Sahih Bukhari 5758

Narrated Ibn `Abbas:

When Ma'iz bin Malik came to the Prophet (in order to confess), the Prophet (ﷺ) said to him, "Probably you have only kissed (the lady), or winked, or looked at her?" He said, "No, O Allah's Messenger (ﷺ)!" The Prophet said, using no euphemism, "Did you have sexual intercourse with her?" The narrator added: At that, (i.e. after his confession) the Prophet (ﷺ) ordered that he be stoned (to death).

Source: Sahih Bukhari 6824

Narrated Abu Wail:

Someone said to Usama, "Will you not talk to this (Uthman)?" Usama said, "I talked to him (secretly) without being the first man to open an evil door. I will never tell a ruler who rules over two men or more that he is good after I heard Allah's Messenger (ﷺ) saying, 'A man will be brought and put in Hell (Fire) and he will circumambulate (go around and round) in Hell (Fire) like a donkey of a (flour) grinding mill, and all the people of Hell (Fire) will gather around him and will say to him, O so-and-so! Didn't you use to order others for good and forbid them from evil?' That man will say, 'I used to order others to do good but I myself never used to do it, and I used to forbid others from evil while I myself used to do evil.' "

Source: Sahih Bukhari 7098

This hadith has numerous benefits in that you snitch on the ruler of the state to the ruler himself face to face in secret without telling others of his sins or flaws. Also the obligation of forbidding evil is known as a duty even if one is doing the evil they forbid. For neglecting to forbid evil is an additional evil. The concept of not being a hypocritical snitch is nonsense. If you do the crime and also fail to forbid it then you are twice as sinful as the one doing the crime while forbidding the same evil they themselves are guilty of. Doing crime doesn't relieve you of the duty of forbidding crime and snitching on sinners just because you happen to be a sinner yourself. Ideally you don't do any crime at all but if you do then still you have to forbid the evil regardless. Snitching, including self-snitching, is a sacred duty for saints and sinners alike.

Narrated `Ali:

The Prophet (ﷺ) sent a Sariya under the command of a man from the Ansar and ordered the soldiers to obey him. He (i.e. the commander) became angry and said "Didn't the Prophet (ﷺ) order you to obey me!" They replied, "Yes." He said, "Collect fire-wood for me." So they collected it. He said, "Make a fire." When they made it, he said, "Enter it (i.e. the fire)." So they intended to do that and started holding each other and saying, "We run towards (i.e. take refuge with) the Prophet (ﷺ) from the fire." They kept on saying that till the fire was extinguished and the anger of the commander abated. When that news reached the Prophet (ﷺ) he said, "If they had entered it (i.e. the fire), they would not have come out of it till the Day of Resurrection. Obedience (to somebody) is required when he enjoins what is good."

Source: Sahih Bukhari 4340

Narrated 'Ubaidullah bin Abi Rafi`:

I heard `Ali saying, "Allah's Messenger (ﷺ) sent me, Az-Zubair and Al-Miqdad somewhere saying, 'Proceed till you reach Rawdat Khakh. There you will find a lady with a letter. Take the letter from her.' " So, we set out and our horses ran at *full pace till we got at Ar-Rawda where we found the lady and said (to her). "Take out the letter." She replied, "I have no letter with me." We said, "Either you take out the letter or else we will take off your clothes." So, she took it out of her braid. We brought the letter to Allah's Messenger (ﷺ) and it contained a statement from Hatib bin Abi Balta a to some of the Meccan pagans informing them of some of the intentions of Allah's Messenger (ﷺ). Then Allah's Messenger (ﷺ) said, "O Hatib! What is this?" Hatib replied, "O Allah's Messenger (ﷺ)! Don't hasten to give your judgment about me. I was a man closely connected with the Quraish, but I did not belong to this tribe, while the other emigrants with you, had their relatives in Mecca who would protect their dependents and property . So, I wanted to recompense for my lacking blood relation to them by doing them a favor so that they might protect my dependents. I did this neither because of disbelief not apostasy nor out of preferring Kufr (disbelief) to Islam." Allah's Messenger (ﷺ), said, "Hatib has told you the truth." `Umar said, O Allah's Apostle! Allow me to chop off the head of this hypocrite." Allah's Messenger (ﷺ) said, "Hatib participated in the battle of Badr, and who knows, perhaps Allah has already looked at the Badr warriors and said, 'Do whatever you like, for I have forgiven you."*

Source: Sahih Bukhari 3007

Abu Bakr As-Siddiq said:

"O you people! You recite this Ayah: Take care of yourselves! If you follow the guidance no harm shall come to you. I indeed heard the Messenger of Allah saying: 'When the people see the

wrongdoer and they do not take him by the hand, then soon Allah shall envelope you in a punishment from him.'"

Source: Jami Tirmidhi 2168 Grade: Sahih

Hudhaifah bin Al-Yaman narrated the Prophet said:

"By the One in Whose Hand is my soul! Either you command good and forbid evil, or Allah will soon send upon you a punishment from Him, then you will call upon Him, but He will not respond to you. "

Source: Jami Tirmidhi 2169 Grade: Hasan

Zaid bin Khalid Al-Juhani narrated that the Messenger of Allah said:

"Shall l not inform you of the best of witnesses? The one who comes with his testimony before being asked for it."

Source: Jami Tirmidhi 2295 Grade: Sahih

Narrated Kathir bin 'Abdullah bin 'Amr bin 'Awf bin Zaid bin Milhah narrated from his father, from his grandfather:

that the Messenger of Allah (ﷺ) said: "Indeed the religion with creep into the Hijaz just like a snake creeps into its hole, and the religion will cling to the Hijaz just like the female mountain goat cling to the peak of a mountain. Indeed the religion began as something strange and it will return to being strange. So Tuba is for the strangers who correct what the people have corrupted from my Sunnah after me."

Source: Jami Tirmidhi 2630 Grade: Daif

Narrated Anas bin Malik:

"There was a man from the Ansar who led them (in Salat) at Masjid Quba. Every time he was to recite a Surah for them during Salat, he would begin by reciting Qul Huwa Allahu Ahad until he finished, then he would recite another Surah with it. He did that in each Rak'ah. His companions talked to him and said: 'You recite this Surah. You should either recite it or leave it and recite another Surah.'" He said: "I shall not leave it, if you would like me to lead you with it then I shall do so, and if you do not like it then I shall leave you." And they considered him the best among them, and they did not like the idea of someone else leading them. So when the Prophet (ﷺ) came to them they informed him about what had happened and he (ﷺ) said: "O so-and-so! What prevents you from doing what your companions told you to do, why do recite this Surah in every Rak'ah" He said: "O Messenger of Allah! Indeed I love it." So the Messenger of Allah (ﷺ) said: "Your love for it shall have you admitted into Paradise."

Source: Jami Tirmidhi 2901 Grade: Sahih

Narrated Anas:

"When the women among the Jews menstruated, they would not eat with them, nor drink with them, nor mingle with them in their homes. The Prophet (ﷺ) was asked about that, so Allah, Blessed and Most High, revealed: "They ask you about menstruation. Say It is a Adha (harmful matter) (2:222).' So the Messenger of Allah (ﷺ) told them to eat with them, drink with them and to remain in the house with them, and to do everything besides intercourse with them. The Jews said: 'He does not want to leave any matter of ours without opposing us

in it.'" He said: "Then 'Abbad bin Bishr and Usaid bin Hudair came to the Messenger of Allah (ﷺ) to inform him about that. They said: 'O Messenger of Allah! Should we not (then) have intercourse with them during their menstruation?' The face of the Messenger of Allah (ﷺ) changed color, until they thought that he was angry with them. So they left, and afterwards the Prophet (ﷺ) was given some milk as a gift, so he sent some of it to them to drink. Then they knew that he was not angry with them."

Source: Jami Tirmidhi 2977 Grade: Sahih

Narrated Anas:

"It reached Safiyyah that Hafsah said: 'The daughter of a Jew' so she wept. Then the Prophet (ﷺ) entered upon her while she was crying, so he said: 'What makes you cry?' She said: 'Hafsah said to me that I am the daughter of a Jew.' So the Prophet (ﷺ) said: 'And you are the daughter of a Prophet, and your uncle is a Prophet, and you are married to a Prophet, so what is she boasting to you about?' Then he said: 'Fear Allah, O Hafsah.'"

Source: Jami Tirmidhi 3894 Grade Sahih

Narrated Umm Waraqah daughter of Nawfal:

When the Prophet (ﷺ) proceeded for the Battle of Badr, I said to him: Messenger of Allah allow me to accompany you in the battle. I shall act as a nurse for patients. It is possible that Allah might bestow martyrdom upon me. He said: Stay at your home. Allah, the Almighty , will bestow martyrdom upon you.

The narrator said: Hence she was called martyr. She read the Qur'an. She sought permission from the Prophet (☀) to have a mu'adhdhin in her house. He, therefore, permitted her (to do).

She announced that her slave and slave-girl would be free after her death. One night they went to her and strangled her with a sheet of cloth until she died, and they ran away.

Next day Umar announced among the people, "Anyone who has knowledge about them, or has seen them, should bring them (to him)."

Umar (after their arrest) ordered (to crucify them) and they were crucified. This was the first crucifixion at Medina.

Source: Sunan Abi Dawood 591 Grade: Hasan

Narrated Abdullah ibn Mas'ud:

Harithah ibn Mudarrib said that he came to Abdullah ibn Mas'ud and said (to him): There is no enmity between me and any of the Arabs. I passed a mosque of Banu Hanifah. They (the people) believed in Musaylimah. Abdullah (ibn Mas'ud) sent for them. They were brought, and he asked them to repent, except Ibn an-Nawwahah. He said to him: I heard the Messenger of Allah (☀) say: Were it not that you were not a messenger, I would behead you. But today you are not a messenger. He then ordered Qarazah ibn Ka'b (to kill him). He beheaded him in the market. Anyone who wants to see Ibn an-Nawwahah slain in the market (he may see him).

Source: Sunan Abi Dawood 2762 Grade: Sahih

Narrated Jabir ibn Samurah:

A man fell ill and a cry was raised (for his death). So his neighbour came to the Messenger of Allah (ﷺ) and said to him: He has died. He asked: Who told you? He said: I have seen him. The Messenger of Allah (ﷺ) said: He has not died. He then returned.

A cry was again raised (for his death). He came to the Messenger of Allah (ﷺ) and said: He has died. The Prophet (ﷺ) said: He has not died. He then returned.

A cry was again raised over him. His wife said: Go to the Messenger of Allah (ﷺ) and inform him. The man said: O Allah, curse him.

He said: The man then went and saw that he had killed himself with an arrowhead. So he went to the Prophet (ﷺ) and informed him that he had died.

He asked: Who told you? He replied: I myself saw that he had killed himself with arrowheads. He asked: Have you seen him? He replied: Yes. He then said: Then I shall not pray over him.

Source: Sunan Abi Dawood 3185 Grade: Sahih

Narrated Al-Ash'ath ibn Qays:

A man of Kindah and a man of Hadramawt brought their dispute to the Prophet (ﷺ) about a land in the Yemen. Al-Hadrami said: Messenger of Allah, the father of this (man) usurped my land and it is in his possession.

The Prophet asked: Have you any evidence?

Al-Hadrami replied: No, but I make him swear (that he should say) that he does not know that it is my land which his father usurped from me.

Al-Kindi became ready to take the oath.

The Messenger of Allah (ﷺ) said: If anyone usurps the property by taking an oath, he will meet Allah while his hand is mutilated.

Al-Kindi then said: It is his land.

Source: Sunan Abi Dawood 3244 Grade: Sahih

Narrated Suwayd ibn Hanzalah:

We went out intending (to visit) the Messenger of Allah (ﷺ) and Wa'il ibn Hujr was with us. His enemy caught him. The people desisted from swearing an oath, but I took an oath that he was my brother. So he left him. We then came to the Messenger of Allah (ﷺ), and I informed him that the people desisted from taking the oath, but I swore that he was my brother. He said: You spoke the truth: A Muslim is a brother of a Muslim.

Source: Sunan Abi Dawood 3256 Grade: Sahih

Narrated Anas:

Allah's Messenger (ﷺ) said, "Help your brother, whether he is an oppressor or he is an oppressed one. People asked, "O Allah's Messenger (ﷺ)! It is all right to help him if he is oppressed, but how should we help him if he is an oppressor?" The Prophet (ﷺ) said, "By preventing him from oppressing others."

Source: Sahih Bukhari 2444

Narrated Khalid ibn al-Walid:

I went with the Messenger of Allah (ﷺ) to fight at the battle of Khaybar, and the Jews came and complained that the people had hastened to take their protected property (as a booty), so the Messenger of Allah (ﷺ) said: The property of those who have been given a mules, every fanged beast of prey, and every bird with a talon are forbidden for you.

Source: Sunan abi Dawood 3806 Grade: Daif

Khalid said:

Al-Miqdam ibn Ma'dikarib and a man of Banu Asad from the people of Qinnisrin went to Mu'awiyah ibn Abu Sufyan.

Mu'awiyah said to al-Miqdam: Do you know that al-Hasan ibn Ali has died? Al-Miqdam recited the Qur'anic verse "We belong to Allah and to Him we shall return."

A man asked him: Do you think it a calamity? He replied: Why should I not consider it a calamity when it is a fact that the Messenger of Allah (ﷺ) used to take him on his lap, saying: This belongs to me and Husayn belongs to Ali?

The man of Banu Asad said: (He was) a live coal which Allah has extinguished. Al-Miqdam said: Today I shall continue to make you angry and make you hear what you dislike. He then said: Mu'awiyah, if I speak the truth, declare me true, and if I tell a lie, declare me false.

He said: Do so. He said: I adjure you by Allah, did you hear the Messenger of Allah (ﷺ) forbidding use to wear gold?

He replied: Yes. He said: I adjure you by Allah, do you know that the Messenger of Allah (ﷺ) prohibited the wearing of silk?

He replied: Yes. He said: I adjure you by Allah, do you know that the Messenger of Allah (ﷺ) prohibited the wearing of the skins of beasts of prey and riding on them?

He said: Yes. He said: I swear by Allah, I saw all this in your house, O Mu'awiyah.

Mu'awiyah said: I know that I cannot be saved from you, O Miqdam.

Khalid said: Mu'awiyah then ordered to give him what he did not order to give to his two companions, and gave a stipend of two hundred (dirhams) to his son. Al-Miqdam then divided it among his companions, and the man of Banu Asad did not give anything to anyone from the property he received. When Mu'awiyah was informed about it, he said: Al-Miqdam is a generous man; he has an open hand (for generosity). The man of Banu Asad withholds his things in a good manner.

Source: Sunan abi Dawood 4131 Grade: Sahih

Narrated Abu Umayyah al-Makhzumi:

A thief who had accepted (having committed theft) was brought to the Prophet (ﷺ), but no goods were found with him. The Messenger of Allah (ﷺ), said to him: I do not think you have stolen. He said: Yes, I have. He repeated it twice or thrice. So he gave orders. His hand was cut off and he was then brought to him. He said: Ask Allah's pardon and turn to Him in repentance. He said: I ask Allah's pardon and turn to Him in repentance. He (the Prophet) then said: O Allah, accept his repentance.

Source: Sunan abi Dawood 4380 Grade: Daif

Narrated 'Amr bin Shu'aib:

On his father's authority, said that his grandfather told that a A man came to the Prophet (ﷺ) crying for help. He said: His slave-girl, Messenger of Allah! He said: Woe to you, what happened with you ? He said that it was an evil one. He saw the slave-girl of his master; he became jealous of him, and cut off his penis. The Messenger of Allah (ﷺ) said: Bring the man to me. The man was called, but people could not get control over him. The Messenger of Allah (ﷺ) then said: Go away, you are free. He asked: Messenger of Allah! upon whom does my help lie? He replied: On every believer, or he said: On every Muslim.

Abu Dawud said: The name of the man who was emancipated was Rawh bin Dinar

Abu Dawud said: The man who cut off the penis was Zinba'

Abu Dawud said: The Zinba' Abu Rawh was master of the slave.

Source: Sunan abi Dawood 4519 Grade: Hasan

Narrated Ibn 'Abbas:

'Umar asked about the decision of the Prophet (ﷺ) about that (i.e. abortion). Haml bin Malik bin al-Nabhigah got up and said: I was between two women. One of them struck another with a rolling-pin killing both her and what was in her womb. So the Messenger of Allah (ﷺ) gave judgement that the

bloodwit for the unborn child should be a male or a female slave of the best quality and then she should be killed.

Source: Sunan abi Dawood 4572 Grade: Sahih

Bilal ibn Sa'd al-Ash'ari related:

Mu'awiya wrote to Abu Dharr:

"Write down for me the deviants of Damascus."

Abu Dharr said, "What do I have to do with the deviants of Damascus and how would I know them?"

His son Bilal said, "I will write them," so he wrote them.

Abu Dharr said, "How do you know? You would only know that they are deviants if you were one of them. Begin with yourself and do not send their names."

Source: Adab al Mufrad 1290

It was narrated from Abu Sa'eed Al-Khudri that:

he was praying and a son of Marwan wanted to pass in front of him. He tried to stop him but he did not go back, so he hit him. The boy went out crying and went to Marwan and told him (what had happened). Marwan said to Abu Sa'eed: "Why did you hit your brother's son?" He said: "I did not hit him, rather I hit the Shaitan. I heard the Messenger of Allah say: 'If one of you is praying and someone wants to pass in front of him, let him try to stop him as much as he can, and if he persists then let him fight him, for he is a devil.

Source: Sunan Nasai 4862 Grade: Sahih

It was narrated from An-Nu'man bin Bashir that:

a group of the Kala'iyin complaned to him about some people who had stolen some goods, so he detained them for several days, and then he let them go. They came and said: "You let them go without any pressure (to make them admit to their crime) or beating?" An-Nu'man said: "What do you want? If you wish, I will beat them, and if Allah brings back your goods thereby, all well and good. Otherwise I will take retaliation from your backs (by beating you) likewise." They said: "is this your ruling?" He said: "This is the ruling of Allah and His Messenger.

Source: Sunan Nasai 4874 Grade: Daif

It was narrated from Bahz bin Hakim, from his father, from his grandfather, that:

the Messenger of Allah detained a man who was under suspicion, and then he let him go.

Source: Suna Nasai 4876 Grade: Hasan

It was narrated that Safwan bin Umayyah said:

"I was sleeping in the Masjid on a Khmaishah of mine that was worth thirty dirhams, and a man came and stole it from me. The man was caught and taken to the Prophet, who ordered that his hand be cut off. I came to him and said: "Will you cut off his hand for the sake of only thirty Dirhams? I will sell it to him on credit." He said:" Why did you not say this before you brought him to me?"

Source: Sunan Nasai 4883 Grade Hasan

It was narrated that 'Aishah said:

"A woman borrowed some jewelry, saying that other people whose names were known but hers was not then she sold it and kept the money. She was brought to the Messenger of Allah, and her people went to Usamah bin Zaid, who spoke to the Messenger of Allah concerning her. The face of the Messenger of Allah changed color while he was speaking to him. Then the Messenger of Allah said to him: 'Are you interceding with me concerning one of the Hadd punishments decreed by Allah?' Usamah said: 'Pray for forgiveness for me, O Messenger of Allah! Then the Messenger of Allah stood up that evening, he praised and glorified Allah, the mighty and sublime, as he deserves, then he said: 'The people who came before you were destroyed because, whenever a noble person among them stole, they let him go. But if a low-class person stole, they would carry out the punishment on him. By the One in whose hand is the soul of Muhammad, if Fatimah bint Muhammad were to steal, I would cut off her hand.' Then he cut off that woman."*

Source: Sunan Nasai 4898 Grade: Sahih

It was narrated from 'Amr bin Shuaib, from his father, that his grandfather 'Abdullah bin 'Amr, that a man from Muzainah came to the Messenger of Allah and said:

'O Messenger of Allah, what do you think about a sheep stolen from the pasture?" He said: "(The thief must pay) double and be punished. There is no cutting off of the hand for (stealing) livestock, except what which has been put in the pen, if its value is equal to that of a shield, in which case the (thief's) hand is to be cut off. If its value is not equal to that of a shield, then he should pay a penalty of twice its value and be flogged as a

punishment." He said: "O Messenger of Allah! What do you think about fruit on the tree?" He said: "(The thief must pay) double and be punished. There is no cutting off of the hand for (stealing) fruit on the tree, except for that which has been stored properly if its value is equal to that of a shield, in which case the (thief's) hand is not equal to that of a shield, then he should pay a penalty of twice its value and be flogged as a punishment."

Source: Sunan Nasai 4959 Grade: Hasan

Nimran bin Jariyah narrated from his father that :

a man struck another man on the wrist with his sword and severed it, not at the joint. He appealed to the Prophet (ﷺ) who ordered that the Diyah be paid. The man said: "O Messenger of Allah (ﷺ), I want retaliation." He said: "Take the compensation and may Allah bless you therein." And he did not rule that he be allowed retaliation.

Source: Sunan Ibn Majah 2636 Grade: Daif

It was narrated from Mujalid that 'Amir said:

Sharahah had a husband who was absent in Syria. She became pregnant and her former master brought her to `Ali bin Abi Talib and said: This one has committed adultery, She admitted it, so he gave her one hundred lashes on Thursday and stoned her on Friday; he dug a hole for her to her navel, and I was present. Then he said: Stoning is a Sunnah established by the Messenger of Allah (ﷺ). If anyone saw her do it, the first one to throw a stone should be the one who witnessed it; he should give his testimony and follow his testimony with his stone. But she admitted it, so I will be the first one to stone her. He threw a stone at her, then the people stoned her and I was among them. By Allah, I was among those who killed her.

Source: Musnad Ahmed 978 Grade: Sahih

Saeed bin Jubair said:

"I walked with Ibn Umar and Ibn Abbas through one of the streets of Madinah and we saw some young boys who had taken a hen as a target and were shooting at it, and they (the owners of the hen) would have every arrow that missed it. He got angry and said: "Who has done this?" And they scattered. Ibn Umar said: The Messenger of Allah cursed the one who mutilates an animal."

Source: Musnad Ahmed 3133 Grade: Sahih

Alqama ibn Abi 'Alqama reported from his mother:

'A'isha heard that some people living in a room in her house had a backgammon game. She sent to them, saying, "If you do not remove it, I will evict you from my house." He censured them for playing that.

Source: Adab al Mufrad 1274

Kulthum ibn Jabir said:

"Ibn az-Zubayr addressed us and said, 'People of Makka, I have heard that there are men of Quraysh who play a game called backgammon. It is done with the left hand. Allah says, 'Wine and gambling.(5:90) I swear by Allah that if anyone who plays it is brought before me, I will punish him in his hair and skin, and I will give his booty to the one who brings him to me."

Source: Adab al Mufrad 1275

Narrated Mu'awiyah:

I heard the Messenger of Allah (ﷺ) say: If you search for the faults of the people, you will corrupt them, or will nearly corrupt them.

Source: Sunan abi Dawood 4889 Grade: Sahih

Narrated Abdullah ibn Mas'ud:

Zayd ibn Wahb said: A man was brought to Ibn Mas'ud. He was told: This is so and so, and wine was dropping from his beard. Abdullah thereupon said: We have been prohibited to seek out (faults). If anything becomes manifest to us, we shall seize it.

Source: Sunan abi Dawood 4890 Grade: Sahih

Abu Hurairah reported the Messenger of Allah saying:

Avoid suspicion for suspicion is the most lying form of talk. Do not be inquisitive about one another, or spy on one another.

Source: Sunan abi Dawood 4917 Grade: Sahih

It was narrated from Sahl bin Sa'd As-Saidi that:

a man looked through a hole in the door of the Prophet, who had with him a kind of comb with which he was scratching his head, When the Messenger of Allah saw him he said: "If I had known that you were watching me, I would have stabbed you in the eye with this. This rule of asking permission has been ordained so that one may not look unlawfully (into people's houses).

Source: Sunan Nasai 4859 Grade: Sahih

It was narrated from Ibn 'Umar that the Messenger of Allah (ﷺ) said:

"Whoever takes the wrongdoer's side in a dispute or supports wrongdoing, he will remain subject to the wrath of Allah until he gives it up."

Source: Sunan Ibn Majah 2320 Grade: Hasan

Narrated Abu Bakra:

Allah's Messenger said thrice, "Shall I not inform you of the biggest of the great sins?" We said, "Yes, O Allah's Messenger (ﷺ)" He said, "To join partners in worship with Allah: to be undutiful to one's parents." The Prophet (ﷺ) sat up after he had been reclining and added, "And I warn you against giving forged statement and a false witness; I warn you against giving a forged statement and a false witness." The Prophet kept on saying that warning till we thought that he would not stop.

Source: Sahih Bukhari 5976

Narrated Abu Sa`id Al-Khudri:

Allah's Messenger (ﷺ) said, "Noah will be called on the Day of Resurrection and he will say, 'Labbaik and Sa`daik(I respond to your call, I am obedient to your orders), O my Lord!' Allah will say, 'Did you convey the Message?' Noah will say, 'Yes.' His nation will then be asked, 'Did he convey the Message to you?' They will say, 'No Warner came to us.' Then Allah will say (to Noah), 'Who will bear witness in your favor?' He will say, 'Muhammad and his followers. So they (i.e. Muslims) will testify that he conveyed the Message. And the Apostle (Muhammad) will be a witness over yourselves, and that is what is meant by the Statement of Allah "Thus We have made *of you a just and the best nation that you may be witnesses over mankind and the Apostle (Muhammad) will be a witness over yourselves." (2:143)*

Source: Sahih Bukhari 4487

Abu Huraira reported the Prophet's Companions said:

Allah's Messenger, will we be able to see our Lord on the Day of Judgment? He said: Do you feel any difficulty in seeing the sun in the noon when there is no cloud over it? They said: No. He again said: Do you feel any difficulty in seeing the moon on the fourteenth night when there is no cloud over it? They said: No. Thereupon he said: By Allah Who is One in Whose Hand is my life. you will not face any difficulty in seeing your Lord but only so much as you feel in seeing one of them. Then Allah would sit in judgment upon the servant and would say: O, so and so, did I not honor you and make you the chief and provide you the spouse and subdue for you horses, camels, and afforded you an opportunity to rule over your subjects? He would say: Yes. And then it would be said: Did you not think that you would meet Us? And he would say: No. Thereupon He (Allah) would say: Well, We forget you as you forgot Us. Then the second person would be brought for judgment. (And Allah would) say: 0, so and so. did We not honor you and make you the chief and make you pair and subdue for you horses and camels and afford you an opportunity to rule over your subjects? He would say: Yes, my Lord. And He (the Lord) would say: Did you not think that you would be meeting Us? And he would say: No. And then He (Allah) would say: Well, I forget you today as you forgot Us. Then the third -one would be brought and He (Allah) would say to him as He said before.

And he (the third person) would say: O, my Lord, I affirmed my faith in Thee and in Thy Book and in Thy Messenger and I observed prayer and fasts and gave charity, and he would speak in good terms like this as he would be able to do. And He (Allah) would say: Well, We will bring our witnesses to you. And the man would think in his mind who would bear witness upon him and then his mouth would be sealed and it would be said to his thighs, to his flesh and to his bones to speak and his thighs. flesh and bones would bear witness to his deeds and it would be done so that he should not be able to make any excuse for himself and he would be a hypocrite and Allah would be annoyed with him.

Source: Sahih Muslim 2968

Anas bin Malik reported:

We were in the company of Allah's Messenger (ﷺ) when he smiled, and said: Do you know why I laughed? We said: Allah and His Messenger, know best. Thereupon he said: It was because (there came to my mind the) talk which the servant would have with his Lord (on the Day of judgment). He would say: My Lord, have you not guaranteed me protection against injustice? He would say: Yes. Then the servant would say: I do not deem valid any witness against me but my own self, and He would say: Well, enough would be the witness of your self against you and that of the two angels who had been appointed to record your deeds. Then the seal would be set upon his mouth and it would be said to his hands and feet to speak and they would speak of his deeds. Then the mouth would be made free to talk, he would say (to the hands and feet): Be away, let there be curse of Allah upon you. It was for your safety that I contended.

Source: Sahih Muslim 2969

www.ingramcontent.com/pod-product-compliance
Lightning Source LLC
Chambersburg PA
CBHW062115020426
42335CB00013B/974